Practical Data Science Cookbook

89 hands-on recipes to help you complete real-world data science projects in R and Python

Tony Ojeda

Sean Patrick Murphy

Benjamin Bengfort

Abhijit Dasgupta

BIRMINGHAM - MUMBAI

Practical Data Science Cookbook

First published: September 2014

Production reference: 1180914

Published by Packt Publishing Ltd.
Livery Place
35 Livery Street
Birmingham B3 2PB, UK.

ISBN 978-1-78398-024-6

www.packtpub.com

Cover image by Pratyush Mohanta (tysoncinematics@gmail.com)

Credits

Authors
Tony Ojeda
Sean Patrick Murphy
Benjamin Bengfort
Abhijit Dasgupta

Reviewers
Richard Heimann
Sarah Kelley
Liang Shi
Will Voorhees

Commissioning Editor
James Jones

Acquisition Editor
James Jones

Content Development Editor
Arvind Koul

Technical Editors
Pankaj Kadam
Sebastian Rodrigues

Copy Editors
Insiya Morbiwala
Sayanee Mukherjee
Stuti Srivastava

Project Coordinator
Priyanka Goel

Proofreaders
Simran Bhogal
Maria Gould
Ameesha Green
Paul Hindle
Kevin McGowan
Lucy Rowland

Indexers
Rekha Nair
Priya Sane

Graphics
Abhinash Sahu

Production Coordinator
Adonia Jones

Cover Work
Adonia Jones

About the Authors

Tony Ojeda is an accomplished data scientist and entrepreneur, with expertise in business process optimization and over a decade of experience creating and implementing innovative data products and solutions. He has a Master's degree in Finance from Florida International University and an MBA with concentrations in Strategy and Entrepreneurship from DePaul University. He is the founder of District Data Labs, a cofounder of Data Community DC, and is actively involved in promoting data science education through both organizations.

First and foremost, I'd like to thank my coauthors for the tireless work they put in to make this book something we can all be proud to say we wrote together. I hope to work on many more projects and achieve many great things with you in the future.

I'd like to thank our reviewers, specifically Will Voorhees and Sarah Kelley, for reading every single chapter of the book and providing excellent feedback on each one. This book owes much of its quality to their great advice and suggestions.

I'd also like to thank my family and friends for their support and encouragement in just about everything I do.

Last, but certainly not least, I'd like to thank my fiancée and partner in life, Nikki, for her patience, understanding, and willingness to stick with me throughout all my ambitious undertakings, this book being just one of them. I wouldn't dare take risks and experiment with nearly as many things professionally if my personal life was not the stable, loving, supportive environment she provides.

Sean Patrick Murphy spent 15 years as a senior scientist at The Johns Hopkins University Applied Physics Laboratory, where he focused on machine learning, modeling and simulation, signal processing, and high performance computing in the Cloud. Now, he acts as an advisor and data consultant for companies in SF, NY, and DC. He completed his graduation from The Johns Hopkins University and his MBA from the University of Oxford. He currently co-organizes the Data Innovation DC meetup and cofounded the Data Science MD meetup. He is also a board member and cofounder of Data Community DC.

Benjamin Bengfort is an experienced data scientist and Python developer who has worked in military, industry, and academia for the past 8 years. He is currently pursuing his PhD in Computer Science at the University of Maryland, College Park, doing research in Metacognition and Natural Language Processing. He holds a Master's degree in Computer Science from North Dakota State University, where he taught undergraduate Computer Science courses. He is also an adjunct faculty member at Georgetown University, where he teaches Data Science and Analytics. Benjamin has been involved in two data science start-ups in the DC region: leveraging large-scale machine learning and Big Data techniques across a variety of applications. He has a deep appreciation for the combination of models and data for entrepreneurial effect, and he is currently building one of these start-ups into a more mature organization.

I'd like to thank Will Voorhees for his tireless support in everything I've been doing, even agreeing to review my technical writing. He made my chapters understandable, and I'm thankful that he reads what I write. It's been essential to my career and sanity to have a classmate, a colleague, and a friend like him. I'd also like to thank my coauthors, Tony and Sean, for working their butts off to make this book happen; it was a spectacular effort on their part. I'd also like to thank Sarah Kelley for her input and fresh take on the material; so far, she's gone on many adventures with us, and I'm looking forward to the time when I get to review her books! Finally, I'd especially like to thank my wife, Jaci, who puts up with a lot, especially when I bite off more than I can chew and end up working late into the night. Without her, I wouldn't be writing anything at all. She is an inspiration, and one of the writers in my family, she is the one who students will be reading, even a hundred years from now.

Abhijit Dasgupta is a data consultant working in the greater DC-Maryland-Virginia area, with several years of experience in biomedical consulting, business analytics, bioinformatics, and bioengineering consulting. He has a PhD in Biostatistics from the University of Washington and over 40 collaborative peer-reviewed manuscripts, with strong interests in bridging the statistics/machine-learning divide. He is always on the lookout for interesting and challenging projects, and is an enthusiastic speaker and discussant on new and better ways to look at and analyze data. He is a member of Data Community DC and a founding member and co-organizer of Statistical Programming DC (formerly, R Users DC).

About the Reviewers

Richard Heimann is a technical fellow and Chief Data Scientist at L-3 National Security Solutions (NSS) (NYSE:LLL), and is also an EMC-certified data scientist with concentrations in spatial statistics, data mining, and Big Data. Richard also leads the data science team at the L-3 Data Tactics Business Unit. L-3 NSS and L-3 Data Tactics are both premier Big Data and analytics service providers based in Washington DC and serve customers globally.

Richard is an adjunct professor at the University of Maryland, Baltimore County, where he teaches Spatial Analysis and Statistical Reasoning. Additionally, he is an instructor at George Mason University, teaching Human Terrain Analysis; he is also a selection committee member for the 2014-2015 AAAS Big Data and Analytics Fellowship Program and member of the WashingtonExec Big Data Council.

Richard has recently published a book titled *Social Media Mining with R*, *Packt Publishing*. He recently supported DARPA, DHS, the US Army, and the Pentagon with analytical support.

Sarah Kelley is a junior Python developer and aspiring data scientist. She currently works at a start-up in Bethesda, Maryland, where she spends most of her time on data ingestion and wrangling. Sarah holds a Master's degree in Education from Seattle University. She is a self-taught programmer who became interested in the field through her desire to inspire her students to pursue careers in Mathematics, Science, and technology.

Liang Shi received his PhD in Computer Science and a Master's degree in Statistics from the University of Georgia in 2008 and 2006, respectively. His PhD study is on Machine Learning and AI, mainly solving surrogate model-assisted optimization problems. After graduation, he joined the Data Mining Research team at McAfee; his job was to detect network threats through machine-learning approaches based on Big Data and cloud computing platforms. He later joined Microsoft as a software engineer, and continued his security research and development leveraged by machine-learning algorithms, basically for online advertisement fraud detection on very large, real-time data scales. In 2012, he rejoined McAfee (Intel) as a senior researcher, conducting network threat research, again with the help of machine-learning and cloud computing techniques. Early this year, he joined Pivotal as a senior data scientist; his work is mainly on data scientist projects with clients of popular companies, mainly for IT and security data analytics. He is very familiar with statistical and machine-learning modeling and theories, and he is proficient with many programming languages and analytical tools. He has several journal- and conference-proceeding publications, and he also published a book chapter.

Will Voorhees is a software developer with experience in all sorts of interesting things from mobile app development and natural language processing to infrastructure security. After teaching English in Austria and bootstrapping an education technology start-up, he moved to the West Coast, joined a big tech company, and is now happily working on infrastructure security software used by thousands of developers.

In his free time, Will enjoys reviewing technical books, watching movies, and convincing his dog that she's a good girl, yes she is.

www.PacktPub.com

Support files, eBooks, discount offers, and more

You might want to visit www.PacktPub.com for support files and downloads related to your book.

Did you know that Packt offers eBook versions of every book published, with PDF and ePub files available? You can upgrade to the eBook version at www.PacktPub.com and as a print book customer, you are entitled to a discount on the eBook copy. Get in touch with us at service@packtpub.com for more details.

At www.PacktPub.com, you can also read a collection of free technical articles, sign up for a range of free newsletters and receive exclusive discounts and offers on Packt books and eBooks.

http://PacktLib.PacktPub.com

Do you need instant solutions to your IT questions? PacktLib is Packt's online digital book library. Here, you can access, read and search across Packt's entire library of books.

Why Subscribe?

- ▶ Fully searchable across every book published by Packt
- ▶ Copy and paste, print and bookmark content
- ▶ On demand and accessible via web browser

Free Access for Packt account holders

If you have an account with Packt at www.PacktPub.com, you can use this to access PacktLib today and view nine entirely free books. Simply use your login credentials for immediate access.

Table of Contents

Preface

We live in the age of data. As increasing amounts are generated each year, the need to analyze and create value from this asset is more important than ever. Companies that know what to do with their data and how to do it well will have a competitive advantage over companies that don't. Due to this, there will be increasing demand for people who possess both the analytical and technical abilities to extract valuable insights from data and the business acumen to create valuable and pragmatic solutions that put these insights to use.

This book provides multiple opportunities to learn how to create value from data through a variety of projects that run the spectrum of types of contemporary data science projects. Each chapter stands on its own, with step-by-step instructions that include screenshots, code snippets, more detailed explanations where necessary, and with a focus on process and practical application.

The goal of this book is to introduce you to the data science pipeline, show you how it applies to a variety of different data science projects, and get you comfortable enough to apply it in future to projects of your own. Along the way, you'll learn different analytical and programming lessons, and the fact that you are working through an actual project while learning will help cement these concepts and facilitate your understanding of them.

What this book covers

Chapter 1, Preparing Your Data Science Environment, introduces you to the data science pipeline and helps you get your data science environment properly set up with instructions for the Mac, Windows, and Linux operating systems.

Chapter 2, Driving Visual Analysis with Automobile Data (R), takes you through the process of analyzing and visualizing automobile data to identify trends and patterns in fuel efficiency over time.

Chapter 3, Simulating American Football Data (R), provides a fun and entertaining project where you will analyze the relative offensive and defensive strengths of football teams and simulate games, predicting which teams should win against other teams.

Chapter 4, Modeling Stock Market Data (R), shows you how to build your own stock screener and use moving averages to analyze historical stock prices.

Chapter 5, Visually Exploring Employment Data (R), shows you how to obtain employment and earnings data from the Bureau of Labor Statistics and conduct geospatial analysis at different levels with R.

Chapter 6, Creating Application-oriented Analyses Using Tax Data (Python), shows you how to use Python to transition your analyses from one-off, custom efforts to reproducible and production-ready code using income distribution data as the base for the project.

Chapter 7, Driving Visual Analyses with Automobile Data (Python), mirrors the automobile data analyses and visualizations in *Chapter 2, Driving Visual Analysis with Automobile Data (R)*, but does so using the powerful programming language, Python.

Chapter 8, Working with Social Graphs (Python), shows you how to build, visualize, and analyze a social network that consists of comic book character relationships.

Chapter 9, Recommending Movies at Scale (Python), walks you through building a movie recommender system with Python.

Chapter 10, Harvesting and Geolocating Twitter Data (Python), shows you how to connect to the Twitter API and plot the geographic information contained in profiles.

Chapter 11, Optimizing Numerical Code with NumPy and SciPy (Python), walks you through how to optimize numerically intensive Python code to save you time and money when dealing with large datasets.

What you need for this book

For this book, you will need a computer with access to the Internet and the ability to install the open source software needed for the projects. The primary software we will be using consists of the R and Python programming languages, with a myriad of freely available packages and libraries. Installation instructions are available in the first chapter.

Who this book is for

This book is intended for aspiring data scientists who want to learn data science and numerical programming concepts through hands-on, real-world projects. Whether you are brand new to data science or a seasoned expert, you will benefit from learning the structure of data science projects, the steps in the data science pipeline, and the programming examples presented in this book. Since the book is formatted to walk you through the projects with examples and explanations along the way, extensive prior programming experience is not required.

Conventions

In this book, you will find a number of styles of text that distinguish between different kinds of information. Here are some examples of these styles, and an explanation of their meaning.

Code words in text, database table names, folder names, filenames, file extensions, pathnames, dummy URLs, user input, and Twitter handles are shown as follows: "Next, you run the included `setup.py` script with the `install` flag."

A block of code is set as follows:

```
atvtype - type of alternative fuel or advanced technology
vehicle
barrels08 - annual petroleum consumption in barrels for
fuelType1 (1)
barrelsA08 - annual petroleum consumption in barrels for
fuelType2 (1)
charge120 - time to charge an electric vehicle in hours at
120 V
charge240 - time to charge an electric vehicle in hours at
240 V
```

Any command-line input or output is written as follows:

```
install.packages("lubridate")
install.packages("plyr")
install.packages("reshape2")
```

New terms and **important words** are shown in bold. Words that you see on the screen, in menus or dialog boxes for example, appear in the text like this: "Go to **Tools** in the menu bar and select **Install Packages ....**"

Warnings or important notes appear in a box like this.

Tips and tricks appear like this.

Reader feedback

Feedback from our readers is always welcome. Let us know what you think about this book—what you liked or may have disliked. Reader feedback is important for us to develop titles that you really get the most out of.

To send us general feedback, simply send an e-mail to feedback@packtpub.com, and mention the book title via the subject of your message.

If there is a topic that you have expertise in and you are interested in either writing or contributing to a book, see our author guide on www.packtpub.com/authors.

Customer support

Now that you are the proud owner of a Packt book, we have a number of things to help you to get the most from your purchase.

Downloading the example code

You can download the example code files for all Packt books you have purchased from your account at http://www.packtpub.com. If you purchased this book elsewhere, you can visit http://www.packtpub.com/support and register to have the files e-mailed directly to you.

Downloading the color images of this book

We also provide you a PDF file that has color images of the screenshots/diagrams used in this book. The color images will help you better understand the changes in the output. You can download this file from: http://www.packtpub.com/sites/default/files/downloads/02460S_ColorImages.pdf.

Errata

Although we have taken every care to ensure the accuracy of our content, mistakes do happen. If you find a mistake in one of our books—maybe a mistake in the text or the code—we would be grateful if you would report this to us. By doing so, you can save other readers from frustration and help us improve subsequent versions of this book. If you find any errata, please report them by visiting http://www.packtpub.com/submit-errata, selecting your book, clicking on the **errata submission form** link, and entering the details of your errata. Once your errata are verified, your submission will be accepted and the errata will be uploaded on our website, or added to any list of existing errata, under the Errata section of that title. Any existing errata can be viewed by selecting your title from http://www.packtpub.com/support.

Piracy

Piracy of copyright material on the Internet is an ongoing problem across all media. At Packt, we take the protection of our copyright and licenses very seriously. If you come across any illegal copies of our works, in any form, on the Internet, please provide us with the location address or website name immediately so that we can pursue a remedy.

Please contact us at copyright@packtpub.com with a link to the suspected pirated material.

We appreciate your help in protecting our authors, and our ability to bring you valuable content.

Questions

You can contact us at questions@packtpub.com if you are having a problem with any aspect of the book, and we will do our best to address it.

1
Preparing Your Data Science Environment

In this chapter, we will cover the following:

- ▶ Understanding the data science pipeline
- ▶ Installing R on Windows, Mac OS X, and Linux
- ▶ Installing libraries in R and RStudio
- ▶ Installing Python on Linux and Mac OS X
- ▶ Installing Python on Windows
- ▶ Installing the Python data stack on Mac OS X and Linux
- ▶ Installing extra Python packages
- ▶ Installing and using virtualenv

Introduction

A traditional cookbook contains culinary recipes of interest to the authors and helps readers expand their repertoire of foods to prepare. Many might believe that the end product of a recipe is the dish itself, and one can read this book much in the same way. Every chapter guides the reader through the application of the stages of the data science pipeline to different datasets with various goals. Also, just as in cooking, the final product can simply be the analysis applied to a particular set.

We hope that you will take a broader view, however. Data scientists learn by doing, ensuring that every iteration and hypothesis improves the practioner's knowledge base. By taking multiple datasets through the data science pipeline using two different programming languages (R and Python), we hope that you will start to abstract out the analysis patterns, see the bigger picture, and achieve a deeper understanding of this rather ambiguous field of data science.

We also want you to know that, unlike culinary recipes, data science recipes are ambiguous. When chefs begin a particular dish, they have a very clear picture in mind of what the finished product will look like. For data scientists, the situation is often different. One does not always know what the dataset in question will look like, and what might or might not be possible, given the amount of time and resources. Recipes are essentially a way to dig into the data and get started on the path towards asking the right questions to complete the best dish possible.

If you are from a statistical or mathematical background, the modeling techniques on display might not excite you per se. Pay attention to how many of the recipes overcome practical issues in the data science pipeline, such as loading large datasets and working with scalable tools to adapting known techniques to create data applications, interactive graphics, and web pages rather than reports and papers. We hope that these aspects will enhance your appreciation and understanding of data science and apply good data science to your domains.

Practicing data scientists require a great number and diversity of tools to get the job done. Data practitioners scrape, clean, visualize, model, and perform a million different tasks with a wide array of tools. If you ask most people working with data, you will learn that the foremost component in this toolset is the language used to perform the analysis and modeling of the data. Identifying the best programming language for a particular task is akin to asking which world religion is correct, just with slightly less bloodshed.

In this book, we split our attention between two highly regarded, yet very different, languages used for data analysis—R and Python—and leave it up to you to make your own decision as to which language you prefer. We will help you by dropping hints along the way as to the suitability of each language for various tasks, and we'll compare and contrast similar analyses done on the same dataset with each language.

When you learn new concepts and techniques, there is always the question of depth versus breadth. Given a fixed amount of time and effort, should you work towards achieving moderate proficiency in both R and Python, or should you go all in on a single language? From our professional experiences, we strongly recommend that you aim to master one language and have awareness of the other. Does that mean skipping chapters on a particular language? Absolutely not! However, as you go through this book, pick one language and dig deeper, looking not only to develop conversational ability, but also fluency.

To prepare for this chapter, ensure that you have sufficient bandwidth to download up to several gigabytes of software in a reasonable amount of time.

Understanding the data science pipeline

Before we start installing any software, we need to understand the repeatable set of steps that we will use for data analysis throughout the book.

How to do it...

The following five steps are key for data analysis:

1. **Acquisition**: The first step in the pipeline is to acquire the data from a variety of sources, including relational databases, NoSQL and document stores, web scraping, and distributed databases such as HDFS on a Hadoop platform, RESTful APIs, flat files, or, and hopefully this is not the case, PDFs.

2. **Exploration and understanding**: The second step is to come to an understanding of the data that you will use and how it was collected; this often requires significant exploration.

3. **Munging, wrangling, and manipulation**: This step is often the single most time-consuming and important step in the pipeline. Data is almost never in the needed form for the desired analysis.

4. **Analysis and modeling**: This is the fun part where the data scientist gets to explore the statistical relationships between the variables in the data and pulls out his or her bag of machine learning tricks to cluster, categorize, or classify the data and create predictive models to see into the future.

5. **Communicating and operationalizing**: At the end of the pipeline, we need to give the data back in a compelling form and structure, sometimes to ourselves to inform the next iteration, and sometimes to a completely different audience. The data products produced can be a simple one-off report or a scalable web product that will be used interactively by millions.

How it works...

Although the preceding list is a numbered list, don't assume that every project will strictly adhere to this exact linear sequence. In fact, agile data scientists know that this process is highly iterative. Often, data exploration informs how the data must be cleaned, which then enables more exploration and deeper understanding. Which of these steps comes first often depends on your initial familiarity with the data. If you work with the systems producing and capturing the data every day, the initial data exploration and understanding stage might be quite short, unless something is wrong with the production system. Conversely, if you are handed a dataset with no background details, the data exploration and understanding stage might require quite some time (and numerous non-programming steps, such as talking with the system developers).

The following diagram shows the data science pipeline:

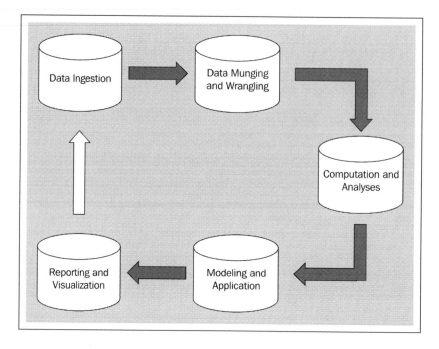

As you probably have heard or read by now, data munging or wrangling can often consume 80 percent or more of project time and resources. In a perfect world, we would always be given perfect data. Unfortunately, this is never the case, and the number of data problems that you will see is virtually infinite. Sometimes, a data dictionary might change or might be missing, so understanding the field values is simply not possible. Some data fields may contain garbage or values that have been switched with another field. An update to the web app that passed testing might cause a little bug that prevents data from being collected, causing a few hundred thousand rows to go missing. If it can go wrong, it probably did at some point; the data you analyze is the sum total of all of these mistakes.

The last step, communication and operationalization, is absolutely critical, but with intricacies that are not often fully appreciated. Note that the last step in the pipeline is not entitled data visualization and does not revolve around simply creating something pretty and/or compelling, which is a complex topic in itself. Instead, data visualizations will become a piece of a larger story that we will weave together from and with data. Some go even further and say that the end result is always an argument as there is no point in undertaking all of this effort unless you are trying to persuade someone or some group of a particular point.

Installing R on Windows, Mac OS X, and Linux

Straight from the R project, "R is a language and environment for statistical computing and graphics". And it has emerged as one of the de facto languages for statistical and data analysis. For us, it will be the default tool that we use in the first half of the book.

Getting ready

Make sure you have a good broadband connection to the Internet as you may have to download up to 200 MB of software.

How to do it...

Installing R is easy; use the following steps:

1. Go to **Comprehensive R Archive Network** (**CRAN**) and download the latest release of R for your particular operating system:

   □ For Windows, go to `http://cran.r-project.org/bin/windows/base/`

   □ For Linux, go to `http://cran.us.r-project.org/bin/linux/`

   □ For Mac OS X, go to `http://cran.us.r-project.org/bin/macosx/`

   As of February 2014, the latest release of R is Version 3.0.2 from September 2013.

2. Once downloaded, follow the excellent instructions provided by CRAN to install the software on your respective platform. For both Windows and Mac, just double-click on the downloaded install packages.

3. With R installed, go ahead and launch it. You should see a window similar to what is shown in the following screenshot:

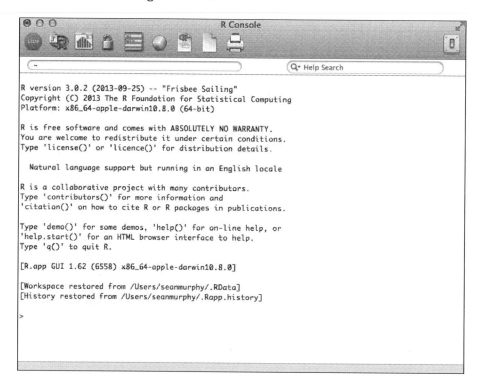

4. You can stop at just downloading R, but you will miss out on the excellent **Integrated Development Environment** (**IDE**) built for R, called RStudio. Visit `http://www.rstudio.com/ide/download/` to download RStudio, and follow the online installation instructions.

5. Once installed, go ahead and run RStudio. The following screenshot shows one of our author's customized RStudio configurations with the **Console** panel in the upper-left corner, the editor in the upper-right corner, the current variable list in the lower-left corner, and the current directory in the lower-right corner.

How it works...

R is an interpreted language that appeared in 1993 and is an implementation of the S statistical programming language that emerged from Bell Labs in the '70s (S-PLUS is a commercial implementation of S). R, sometimes referred to as GNU S due to its open source license, is a **domain-specific language** (**DSL**) focused on statistical analysis and visualization. While you can do many things with R, not seemingly related directly to statistical analysis (including web scraping), it is still a domain-specific language and not intended for general-purpose usage.

R is also supported by CRAN, the Comprehensive R Archive Network (http://cran.r-project.org/). CRAN contains an accessible archive of previous versions of R, allowing for analyses depending on older versions of the software to be reproduced. Further, CRAN contains hundreds of freely downloaded software packages greatly extending the capability of R. In fact, R has become the default development platform for multiple academic fields, including statistics, resulting in the latest and greatest statistical algorithms being implemented first in R.

RStudio (http://www.rstudio.com/) is available under the GNU Affero General Public License v3 and is open source and free to use. RStudio, Inc., the company, offers additional tools and services for R as well as commercial support.

See also

- ▸ Refer to the *Getting Started with R* article at `https://support.rstudio.com/hc/en-us/articles/201141096-Getting-Started-with-R`
- ▸ Visit the home page for RStudio at `http://www.rstudio.com/`
- ▸ Refer to the *Stages in the Evolution of S* article at `http://cm.bell-labs.com/cm/ms/departments/sia/S/history.html`
- ▸ Refer to the *A Brief History of S* PS file at `http://cm.bell-labs.com/stat/doc/94.11.ps`

Installing libraries in R and RStudio

R has an incredible number of libraries that add to its capabilities. In fact, R has become the default language for many college and university statistics departments across the country. Thus, R is often the language that will get the first implementation of newly developed statistical algorithms and techniques. Luckily, installing additional libraries is easy, as you will see in the following sections.

Getting ready

As long as you have R or RStudio installed, you should be ready to go.

How to do it...

R makes installing additional packages simple:

1. Launch the R interactive environment or, preferably, RStudio.
2. Let's install `ggplot2`. Type the following command, and then press the *Enter* key:

```
install.packages("ggplot2")
```

 Note that for the remainder of the book, it is assumed that when we specify entering a line of text, it is implicitly followed by hitting the *Return* or *Enter* key on the keyboard.

3. You should now see text similar to the following as you scroll down the screen:

```
trying URL 'http://cran.rstudio.com/bin/macosx/contrib/3.0/
ggplot2_0.9.3.1.tgz'

Content type 'application/x-gzip' length 2650041 bytes (2.5
Mb)

opened URL

=====================================================

downloaded 2.5 Mb


The downloaded binary packages are in

/var/folders/db/z54jmrxn4y9bjtv8zn_1zlb00000gn/T//Rtmpw0N1dA/
downloaded_packages
```

4. You might have noticed that you need to know the exact name, in this case, ggplot2, of the package you wish to install. Visit http://cran.us.r-project.org/web/packages/available_packages_by_name.html to make sure you have the correct name.

5. RStudio provides a simpler mechanism to install packages. Open up RStudio if you haven't already done so.

6. Go to **Tools** in the menu bar and select **Install Packages ...**. A new window will pop up, as shown in the following screenshot:

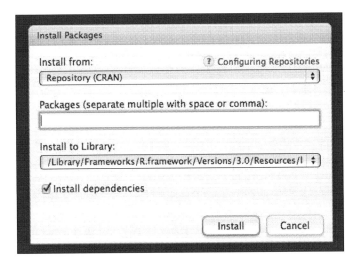

7. As soon as you start typing in the **Packages** field, RStudio will show you a list of possible packages. The autocomplete feature of this field simplifies the installation of libraries. Better yet, if there is a similarly named library that is related, or an earlier or newer version of the library with the same first few letters of the name, you will see it.

8. Let's install a few more packages that we highly recommend. At the R prompt, type the following commands:

```
install.packages("lubridate")
install.packages("plyr")
install.packages("reshape2")
```

Downloading the example code

You can download the example code files for all Packt books you have purchased from your account at `http://www.packtpub.com`. If you purchased this book elsewhere, you can visit `http://www.packtpub.com/support` and register to have the files e-mailed directly to you.

How it works...

Whether you use RStudio's graphical interface or the `install.packages` command, you do the same thing. You tell R to search for the appropriate library built for your particular version of R. When you issue the command, R reports back the URL of the location where it has found a match for the library in CRAN and the location of the binary packages after download.

There's more...

R's community is one of its strengths, and we would be remiss if we didn't briefly mention two things. R-bloggers is a website that aggregates R-related news and tutorials from over 450 different blogs. If you have a few questions on R, this is a great place to look for more information. The Stack Overflow site (`http://www.stackoverflow.com`) is a great place to ask questions and find answers on R using the tag **rstats**.

Finally, as your prowess with R grows, you might consider building an R package that others can use. Giving an in-depth tutorial on the library building process is beyond the scope of this book, but keep in mind that community submissions form the heart of the R movement.

See also

▶ Refer to the *10 R packages I wish I knew about earlier* article at `http://blog.yhathq.com/posts/10-R-packages-I-wish-I-knew-about-earlier.html`

▶ Visit the R-bloggers website at `http://www.r-bloggers.com/`

▶ Refer to the *Creating R Packages: A Tutorial* at `http://cran.r-project.org/doc/contrib/Leisch-CreatingPackages.pdf`

- ▸ Refer to the *Top 100 R packages for 2013 (Jan-May)!* article at `http://www.r-bloggers.com/top-100-r-packages-for-2013-jan-may/`
- ▸ Visit the Learning R blog website at `http://learnr.wordpress.com`

Installing Python on Linux and Mac OS X

Luckily for us, Python comes preinstalled on most versions of Mac OS X and many flavors of Linux (both the latest versions of Ubuntu and Fedora come with Python 2.7 or later versions out of the box). Thus, we really don't have a lot to do for this recipe, except check whether everything is installed.

For this book, we will work with Python 2.7.x and not Version 3. Thus, if Python 3 is your default installed Python, you will have to make sure to use Python 2.7.

Getting ready

Just make sure you have a good Internet connection, just in case we need to install anything.

How to do it...

Perform the following steps in the command prompt:

1. Open a new terminal window and type the following command:

   ```
   which python
   ```

2. If you have Python installed, you should see something like this:

   ```
   /usr/bin/python
   ```

3. Next, check which version you are running with the following command:

   ```
   python --version
   ```

   On my MacBook Air, I see the following:

   ```
   Python 2.7.5
   ```

How it works...

If you are planning on using OS X, you might want to set up a separate Python distribution on your machine for a few reasons. First, each time Apple upgrades your OS, it can and will obliterate your installed Python packages, forcing a reinstall of all previously installed packages. Secondly, new versions of Python will be released more frequently than Apple will update the Python distribution included with OS X. Thus, if you want to stay on the bleeding edge of Python releases, it is best to install your own distribution. Finally, Apple's Python release is slightly different from the official Python release and is located in a nonstandard location on the hard drive.

There are a number of tutorials available online to help walk you through the installation and setup of a separate Python distribution on your Mac. We recommend an excellent guide, available at `http://docs.python-guide.org/en/latest/starting/install/osx/`, to install a separate Python distribution on your Mac.

There's more...

One of the confusing aspects of Python is that the language is currently straddled between two versions. The Python 3.0 release is a fundamentally different version of the language that came out around Python Version 2.5. However, because Python is used in many operating systems (hence, it is installed by default on OS X and Linux), the Python Software Foundation decided to gradually upgrade the standard library to Version 3 to maintain backwards compatibility. Starting with Version 2.6, the Python 2.x versions have become increasingly like Version 3. The latest version is Python 3.4 and many expect a transition to happen in Python 3.5. Don't worry about learning the specific differences between Python 2.x and 3.x, although this book will focus primarily on the lastest 2.x version. Further, we have ensured that the code in this book is portable between Python 2.x and 3.x with some minor differences.

See also

- Refer to the *Python For Beginners* guide at `http://www.python.org/about/gettingstarted/`

- Refer to *The Hitchhiker's Guide to Python* at `http://docs.python-guide.org/en/latest/`

- Refer to the *Python Development Environment on Mac OS X Mavericks 10.9* article at `http://hackercodex.com/guide/python-development-environment-on-mac-osx/`

Installing Python on Windows

Installing Python on Windows systems is complicated, leaving you with three different options. First, you can choose to use the standard Windows release with executable installer from Python.org available at `http://www.python.org/download/releases/`. The potential problem with this route is that the directory structure, and therefore, the paths for configuration and settings will be different from the standard Python installation. As a result, each Python package that was installed (and there will be many) might have path problems. Further, most tutorials and answers online won't apply to a Windows environment, and you will be left to your own devices to figure out problems. We have witnessed countless tutorial-ending problems for students who install Python on Windows in this way. Unless you are an expert, we recommend that you do not choose this option.

The second option is to install a prebundled Python distribution that contains all scientific, numeric, and data-related packages in a single install. There are two suitable bundles, one from Enthought and another from Continuum Analytics. Enthought offers the Canopy distribution of Python 2.7.6 in both 32- and 64-bit versions for Windows. The free version of the software, Canopy Express, comes with more than 50 Python packages preconfigured so that they work straight out of the box, including pandas, NumPy, SciPy, IPython, and matplotlib, which should be sufficient for the purposes of this book. Canopy Express also comes with its own IDE reminiscent of MATLAB or RStudio.

Continuum Analytics offers Anaconda, a completely free (even for commercial work) distribution of Python 2.6, 2.7, and 3.3, which contains over 100 Python packages for science, math, engineering, and data analysis. Anaconda contains NumPy, SciPy, pandas, IPython, matplotlib, and much more, and it should be more than sufficient for the work that we will do in this book.

The third, and best option for purists, is to run a virtual Linux machine within Windows using the free VirtualBox (`https://www.virtualbox.org/wiki/Downloads`) from Oracle software. This will allow you to run Python in whatever version of Linux you prefer. The downsides to this approach are that virtual machines tend to run a bit slower than native software, and you will have to get used to navigating via the Linux command line, a skill that any practicing data scientist should have.

How to do it...

Perform the following steps to install Python using VirtualBox:

1. If you choose to run Python in a virtual Linux machine, visit `https://www.virtualbox.org/wiki/Downloads` to download VirtualBox from Oracle Software for free.

2. Follow the detailed install instructions for Windows at `https://www.virtualbox.org/manual/ch01.html#intro-installing`.

3. Continue with the instructions and walk through the sections entitled **1.6 Starting VirtualBox**, **1.7 Creating your first virtual machine**, and **1.8 Running your virtual machine**.

4. Once your virtual machine is running, head over to the *Installing Python on Linux and Mac OS X* recipe.

If you want to install Continuum Analytics' Anaconda distribution locally instead, follow these steps:

1. If you choose to install Continuum Analytics' Anaconda distribution, go to `http://continuum.io/downloads` and select either the 64- or 32-bit version of the software (the 64-bit version is preferable) under Windows installers.

2. Follow the detailed install instructions for Windows at `http://docs.continuum.io/anaconda/install.html`.

How it works...

For many readers, choosing between a prepackaged Python distribution and running a virtual machine might be easy based on their experience. If you are wrestling with this decision, keep reading. If you come from a Windows-only background and/or don't have much experience with a *nix command line, the virtual machine-based route will be challenging and will force you to expand your skill set greatly. This takes effort and a significant amount of tenacity, both useful for data science in general (trust us on this one). If you have the time and/or knowledge, running everything in a virtual machine will move you further down the path to becoming a data scientist and, most likely, make your code easier to deploy in production environments. If not, you can choose the backup plan and use the Anaconda distribution, as many people choose to do.

For the remainder of this book, we will always include Linux/Mac OS X-oriented Python package install instructions first and supplementary Anaconda install instructions second. Thus, for Windows users, we will assume you have either gone the route of the Linux virtual machine or used the Anaconda distribution. If you choose to go down another path, we applaud your sense of adventure and wish you the best of luck! Let Google be with you.

See also

- Refer to the Anaconda web page at `https://store.continuum.io/cshop/anaconda/`

- Visit the Enthought Canopy Express web page at `https://www.enthought.com/canopy-express/`

- Visit the VirtualBox website at `https://www.virtualbox.org/`

- Various installers of Python packages for Windows at `http://www.lfd.uci.edu/~gohlke/pythonlibs`

Installing the Python data stack on Mac OS X and Linux

While Python is often said to have "batteries included", there are a few key libraries that really take Python's ability to work with data to another level. In this recipe, we will install what is sometimes called the SciPy stack, which includes NumPy, SciPy, pandas, matplotlib, and IPython.

Getting ready

This recipe assumes that you have a standard Python installed.

 If, in the previous section, you decided to install the Anaconda distribution (or another distribution of Python with the needed libraries included), you can skip this recipe.

To check whether you have a particular Python package installed, start up your Python interpreter and try to import the package. If successful, the package is available on your machine. Also, you will probably need root access to your machine via the `sudo` command.

How to do it...

The following steps will allow you to install the Python data stack on Linux:

1. When installing this stack on Linux, you must know which distribution of Linux you are using. The flavor of Linux usually determines the package management system that you will be using, and the options include `apt-get`, `yum`, and `rpm`.

2. Open your browser and navigate to `http://www.scipy.org/install.html`, which contains detailed instructions for most platforms.

   These instructions may change and should supersede the instructions offered here, if different.

3. Open up a shell.

4. If you are using Ubuntu or Debian, type the following:

   ```
   sudo apt-get install build-essential python-dev python-
   setuptools python-numpy python-scipy python-matplotlib ipython
   ipython-notebook python-pandas python-sympy python-nose
   ```

5. If you are using Fedora, type the following:

```
sudo yum install numpy scipy python-matplotlib ipython python-
pandas sympy python-nose
```

You have several options to install the Python data stack on your Macintosh running OS X. These are:

▶ The first option is to download prebuilt installers (.dmg) for each tool, and install them as you would any other Mac application (this is recommended).

▶ The second option is if you have MacPorts, a command line-based system to install software, available on your system. You will also likely need XCode with the command-line tools already installed. If so, you can enter:

```
sudo port install py27-numpy py27-scipy py27-matplotlib py27-
ipython +notebook py27-pandas py27-sympy py27-nose
```

▶ As the third option, Chris Fonnesbeck provides a bundled way to install the stack on the Mac that is tested and covers all the packages we will use here. Refer to http://fonnesbeck.github.io/ScipySuperpack.

All the preceding options will take time as a large number of files will be installed on your system.

How it works...

Installing the SciPy stack has been challenging historically due to compilation dependencies, including the need for Fortran. Thus, we don't recommend that you compile and install from source code, unless you feel comfortable doing such things.

Now, the better question is, what did you just install? We installed the latest versions of NumPy, SciPy, matplotlib, IPython, IPython Notebook, pandas, SymPy, and nose. The following are their descriptions:

▶ **SciPy**: This is a Python-based ecosystem of open source software for mathematics, science, and engineering and includes a number of useful libraries for machine learning, scientific computing, and modeling.

▶ **NumPy**: This is the foundational Python package providing numerical computation in Python, which is C-like and incredibly fast, particularly when using multidimensional arrays and linear algebra operations. NumPy is the reason that Python can do efficient, large-scale numerical computation that other interpreted or scripting languages cannot do.

▶ **matplotlib**: This is a well-established and extensive 2D plotting library for Python that will be familiar to MATLAB users.

- ▶ **IPython**: This offers a rich and powerful interactive shell for Python. It is a replacement for the standard Python **Read-Eval-Print Loop** (**REPL**), among many other tools.

- ▶ **IPython Notebook**: This offers a browser-based tool to perform and record work done in Python with support for code, formatted text, markdown, graphs, images, sounds, movies, and mathematical expressions.

- ▶ **pandas**: This provides a robust data frame object and many additional tools to make traditional data and statistical analysis fast and easy.

- ▶ **nose**: This is a test harness that extends the unit testing framework in the Python standard library.

There's more...

We will discuss the various packages in greater detail in the chapter in which they are introduced. However, we would be remiss if we did not at least mention the Python IDEs. In general, we recommend using your favorite programming text editor in place of a full-blown Python IDE. This can include the open source Atom from GitHub, the excellent Sublime Text editor, or TextMate, a favorite of the Ruby crowd. Vim and Emacs are both excellent choices not only because of their incredible power but also because they can easily be used to edit files on a remote server, a common task for the data scientist. Each of these editors is highly configurable with plugins that can handle code completion, highlighting, linting, and more. If you must have an IDE, take a look at PyCharm (the community edition is free) from the IDE wizards at JetBrains, Spyder, and Ninja-IDE. You will find that most Python IDEs are better suited for web development as opposed to data work.

See also

- ▶ For more information on pandas, refer to the *Python Data Analysis Library* article at `http://pandas.pydata.org/`

- ▶ Visit the NumPy website at `http://www.numpy.org/`

- ▶ Visit the SciPy website at `http://www.scipy.org/`

- ▶ Visit the matplotlib website at `http://matplotlib.org/`

- ▶ Visit the IPython website at `http://ipython.org/`

- ▶ Refer the *History of SciPy* article at `http://wiki.scipy.org/History_of_SciPy`

- ▶ Visit the MacPorts home page at `http://www.macports.org/`

- ▶ Visit the XCode web page at `https://developer.apple.com/xcode/features/`

- ▶ Visit the XCode download page at `https://developer.apple.com/xcode/downloads/`

Installing extra Python packages

There are a few additional Python libraries that you will need throughout this book. Just as R provides a central repository for community-built packages, so does Python in the form of the **Python Package Index** (**PyPI**). As of August 28, 2014, there were 48,054 packages in PyPI.

Getting ready

A reasonable Internet connection is all that is needed for this recipe. Unless otherwise specified, these directions assume that you are using the default Python distribution that came with your system, and not Anaconda.

How to do it...

The following steps will show you how to download a Python package and install it from the command line:

1. Download the source code for the package in the place you like to keep your downloads.

2. Unzip the package.

3. Open a terminal window.

4. Navigate to the base directory of the source code.

5. Type in the following command:

   ```
   python setup.py install
   ```

6. If you need root access, type in the following command:

   ```
   sudo python setup.py install
   ```

To use pip, the contemporary and easiest way to install Python packages, follow these steps:

1. First, let's check whether you have pip already installed by opening a terminal and launching the Python interpreter. At the interpreter, type:

   ```
   >>>import pip
   ```

2. If you don't get an error, you have pip installed and can move on to step 5. If you see an error, let's quickly install pip.

3. Download the `get-pip.py` file from `https://raw.github.com/pypa/pip/master/contrib/get-pip.py` onto your machine.

4. Open a terminal window, navigate to the downloaded file, and type:

```
python get-pip.py
```

Alternatively, you can type in the following command:

```
sudo python get-pip.py
```

5. Once pip is installed, make sure you are at the system command prompt.
6. If you are using the default system distribution of Python, type in the following:

```
pip install networkx
```

Alternatively, you can type in the following command:

```
sudo pip install networkx
```

7. If you are using the Anaconda distribution, type in the following command:

```
conda install networkx
```

8. Now, let's try to install another package, ggplot. Regardless of your distribution, type in the following command:

```
pip install ggplot
```

Alternatively, you can type in the following command:

```
sudo pip install ggplot
```

How it works...

You have at least two options to install Python packages. In the preceding "old fashioned" way, you download the source code and unpack it on your local computer. Next, you run the included setup.py script with the install flag. If you want, you can open the setup.py script in a text editor and take a more detailed look at exactly what the script is doing. You might need the sudo command, depending on the current user's system privileges.

As the second option, we leverage the pip installer, which automatically grabs the package from the remote repository and installs it to your local machine for use by the system-level Python installation. This is the preferred method, when available.

There's more...

pip is capable, so we suggest taking a look at the user guide online. Pay special attention to the very useful pip freeze > requirements.txt functionality so that you can communicate about external dependencies with your colleagues.

Finally, `conda` is the package manager and pip replacement for the Anaconda Python distribution or, in the words of its home page, "a cross-platform, Python-agnostic binary package manager". Conda has some very lofty aspirations that transcend the Python language. If you are using Anaconda, we encourage you to read further on what `conda` can do and use it, and not pip, as your default package manager.

See also

▶ Refer to the pip *User Guide* at `http://www.pip-installer.org/en/latest/user_guide.html`

▶ Visit the Conda home page at `http://conda.pydata.org`

▶ Refer to the Conda blog posts from *Continuum Blog* at `http://www.continuum.io/blog/conda`

Installing and using virtualenv

virtualenv is a transformative Python tool. Once you start using it, you will never look back. virtualenv creates a local environment with its own Python distribution installed. Once this environment is activated from the shell, you can easily install packages using `pip install` into the new local Python.

At first, this might sound strange. Why would anyone want to do this? Not only does this help you handle the issue of package dependencies and versions in Python but also allows you to experiment rapidly without breaking anything important. Imagine that you build a web application that requires Version 0.8 of the `awesome_template` library, but then your new data product needs the `awesome_template` library Version 1.2. What do you do? With virtualenv, you can have both.

As another use case, what happens if you don't have admin privileges on a particular machine? You can't install the packages using `sudo pip install` required for your analysis so what do you do? If you use virtualenv, it doesn't matter.

Virtual environments are development tools that software developers use to collaborate effectively. Environments ensure that the software runs on different computers (for example, from production to development servers) with varying dependencies. The environment also alerts other developers to the needs of the software under development. Python's virtualenv ensures that the software created is in its own holistic environment, can be tested independently, and built collaboratively.

Getting ready

Assuming you have completed the previous recipe, you are ready to go for this one.

How to do it...

Install and test the virtual environment using the following steps:

1. Open a command-line shell and type in the following command:

   ```
   pip install virtualenv
   ```

   Alternatively, you can type in the following command:

   ```
   sudo pip install virtualenv
   ```

2. Once installed, type virtualenv in the command window, and you should be greeted with the information shown in the following screenshot:

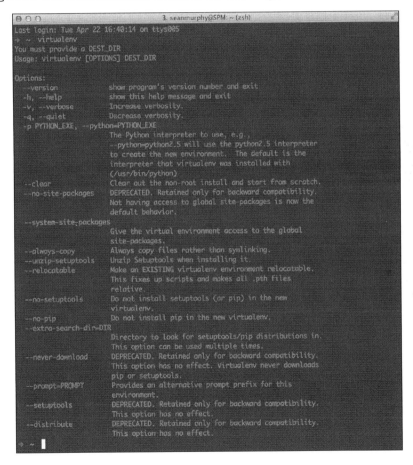

3. Create a temporary directory and change location to this directory using the following commands:

   ```
   mkdir temp
   cd temp
   ```

4. From within the directory, create the first virtual environment named `venv`:

```
virtualenv venv
```

5. You should see text similar to the following:

```
New python executable in venv/bin/python
Installing setuptools, pip...done.
```

6. The new local Python distribution is now available. To use it, we need to activate `venv` using the following command:

```
source ./venv/bin/activate
```

7. The activated script is not executable and must be activated using the `source` command. Also, note that your shell's command prompt has probably changed and is prefixed with `venv` to indicate that you are now working in your new virtual environment.

8. To check this fact, use `which` to see the location of Python, as follows:

```
which python
```

You should see the following output:

```
/path/to/your/temp/venv/bin/python
```

So, when you type `python` once your virtual environment is activated, you will run the local Python.

9. Next, install something by typing the following:

```
pip install flask
```

Flask is a micro-web framework written in Python; the preceding command will install a number of packages that Flask uses.

10. Finally, we demonstrate the versioning power that virtual environment and pip offer, as follows:

```
pip freeze > requirements.txt
cat requirements.txt
```

This should produce the following output:

```
Flask==0.10.1
Jinja2==2.7.2
MarkupSafe==0.19
Werkzeug==0.9.4
itsdangerous==0.23
wsgiref==0.1.2
```

11. Note that not only the name of each package is captured, but also the exact version number. The beauty of this `requirements.txt` file is that if we have a new virtual environment, we can simply issue the following command to install each of the specified versions of the listed Python packages:

```
pip install -r requirements.txt
```

12. To deactivate your virtual environment, simply type the following at the shell prompt:

```
deactivate
```

How it works...

virtualenv creates its own virtual environment with its own installation directories that operate independently from the default system environment. This allows you to try out new libraries without polluting your system-level Python distribution. Further, if you have an application that just works and want to leave it alone, you can do so by making sure the application has its own virtualenv.

There's more...

virtualenv is a fantastic tool, one that will prove invaluable to any Python programmer. However, we wish to offer a note of caution. Python provides many tools that connect to C-shared objects in order to improve performance. Therefore, installing certain Python packages, such as NumPy and SciPy, into your virtual environment may require external dependencies to be compiled and installed, which are system specific. Even when successful, these compilations can be tedious, which is one of the reasons for maintaining a virtual environment. Worse, missing dependencies will cause compilations to fail, producing errors that require you to troubleshoot alien error messages, dated make files, and complex dependency chains. This can be daunting to even the most veteran data scientist.

A quick solution is to use a package manager to install complex libraries into the system environment (aptitude or Yum for Linux, Homebrew or MacPorts for OS X, and Windows will generally already have compiled installers). These tools use precompiled forms of the third-party packages. Once you have these Python packages installed in your system environment, you can use the `--system-site-packages` flag when initializing a virtualenv. This flag tells the virtualenv tool to use the system site packages already installed and circumvents the need for an additional installation that will require compilation. In order to nominate packages particular to your environment that might already be in the system (for example, when you wish to use a newer version of a package), use `pip install -I` to install dependencies into virtualenv and ignore the global packages. This technique works best when you only install large-scale packages on your system, but use virtualenv for other types of development.

For the rest of the book, we will assume that you are using a virtualenv and have the tools mentioned in this chapter ready to go. Therefore, we won't enforce or discuss the use of virtual environments in much detail. Just consider the virtual environment as a safety net that will allow you to perform the recipes listed in this book in isolation.

See also

- ▶ Read an introduction to virtualenv at `http://www.virtualenv.org/en/latest/virtualenv.html`
- ▶ Explore virtualenvwrapper at `http://virtualenvwrapper.readthedocs.org/en/latest/`
- ▶ Explore virtualenv at `https://pypi.python.org/pypi/virtualenv`

2
Driving Visual Analysis with Automobile Data (R)

In this chapter, we will cover the following:

- ▶ Acquiring automobile fuel efficiency data
- ▶ Preparing R for your first project
- ▶ Importing automobile fuel efficiency data into R
- ▶ Exploring and describing fuel efficiency data
- ▶ Analyzing automobile fuel efficiency over time
- ▶ Investigating the makes and models of automobiles

Introduction

The first project we will introduce in this book is an analysis of automobile fuel economy data. The primary tool that we will use to analyze this dataset is the R statistical programming language. R is often referred to as the lingua franca of data science, as it is currently the most popular language for statistics and data analysis. As you'll see from the examples in the first half of this book, R is an excellent tool for data manipulation, analysis, modeling, visualization, and creating useful scripts to get analytical tasks done.

The recipes in this chapter will roughly follow these five steps in the data science pipeline:

- ▸ Acquisition
- ▸ Exploration and understanding
- ▸ Munging, wrangling, and manipulation
- ▸ Analysis and modeling
- ▸ Communication and operationalization

Process-wise, the backbone of data science is the data science pipeline, and in order to get good at data science, you need to gain experience going through this process while swapping various tools and methods along the way so that you always use the ones that are appropriate for the dataset you are analyzing.

The goal of this chapter is to guide you through an analysis project on automobile fuel efficiencies via step-by-step examples that you can learn from and apply to other datasets and analysis projects in the future. Think of this chapter as a warm-up for the longer and more challenging chapters to come.

Acquiring automobile fuel efficiency data

Every data science project starts with data and this chapter is no different. For this recipe, we will dive into a dataset that contains fuel efficiency performance metrics, measured in **miles per gallon** (**MPG**) over time, for most makes and models of automobiles available in the U.S. since 1984. This data is courtesy of the U.S. Department of Energy and the US Environmental Protection Agency. In addition to fuel efficiency data, the dataset also contains several features and attributes of the automobiles listed, thereby providing the opportunity to summarize and group data to determine which groups tend to have better fuel efficiency historically and how this has changed over the years. The latest version of the dataset is available at `http://www.fueleconomy.gov/feg/epadata/vehicles.csv.zip`, and information about the variables in the dataset can be found at `http://www.fueleconomy.gov/feg/ws/index.shtml#vehicle`. The data was last updated on December 4, 2013 and was downloaded on December 8, 2013.

We recommend that you use the copy of the data set provided with the code for this book to ensure that the results described in this chapter match what your efforts produce.

Getting ready

To complete this recipe, you will need a computer with access to the Internet and a text editor of your choice.

How to do it...

Perform the following simple steps to acquire the data needed for the rest of the chapter:

1. Download the dataset from `http://www.fueleconomy.gov/feg/epadata/vehicles.csv.zip`.

2. Unzip `vehicles.csv` with the decompression tool of your choice and move it to your working code directory.

3. Take a moment and open the unzipped `vehicles.csv` file with Microsoft Excel, Google Spreadsheet, or a simple text editor. **Comma-separated value** (**csv**) files are very convenient to work with as they can be edited and viewed with very basic, freely available tools. With the file open, scroll through some of the data and get a sense of what you will be working with.

4. Navigate to `http://www.fueleconomy.gov/feg/ws/index.shtml#vehicle`.

5. Select and copy all the text below the **vehicle** heading under **Data Description**, and paste it into a text file. Do not include the **emissions** heading. Save this file in your working directory as `varlabels.txt`. The first five lines of the file are as follows:

```
atvtype - type of alternative fuel or advanced technology
vehicle
barrels08 - annual petroleum consumption in barrels for
fuelType1 (1)
barrelsA08 - annual petroleum consumption in barrels for
fuelType2 (1)
charge120 - time to charge an electric vehicle in hours at
120 V
charge240 - time to charge an electric vehicle in hours at
240 V
```

 Note that this file is provided for your convenience in the repository containing the chapter's code.

How it works...

There isn't much to explain in this first simple recipe, but note that we are starting off relatively easily here. In many data science projects, you will not be able to access and view the data so easily.

Preparing R for your first project

For the following recipes, you will need the R statistical programming language installed on your computer (either the base R or RStudio, but the authors strongly recommend using the excellent and free RStudio) and the automobile fuel efficiency dataset. This quick recipe will help you ensure that you have everything you will need to complete this analysis project.

Getting ready

You will need an Internet connection to complete this recipe, and we assume that you have installed RStudio for your particular platform, based on the instructions in the previous chapter.

How to do it...

If you are using RStudio, the following three steps will get you ready to roll:

1. Launch RStudio on your computer.
2. At the R console prompt, install the two R packages needed for this project:

    ```
    install.packages("plyr")
    install.packages("ggplot2")
    install.packages("reshape2")
    ```

3. Load the R packages, as follows:

    ```
    library(plyr)
    library(ggplot2)
    library(reshape2)
    ```

How it works...

R's strength comes from the community that has developed around the language and the packages that have been created and made available by the ones in the community. There are currently over 4,000 packages and libraries that you can import and utilize to make your data analysis tasks much easier.

Dr. Hadley Wickham is a notable member of the R community and has produced a large number of highly regarded and often-used R packages. In this chapter, you will primarily use two of his biggest hits, `plyr` and `ggplot2` and a third package called `reshape2`. `Plyr` will be used to apply the split-apply-combine data analysis pattern, explained later in this chapter, to our dataset and `ggplot2` will make complex data visualizations significantly easier.

See also

> ▶ *The R Project for Statistical Computing* web page at `http://www.r-project.org/`

> ▶ Visit the RStudio home page at `http://www.rstudio.com/`

> ▶ Refer to the *R Tutorial* at `http://www.cyclismo.org/tutorial/R/`

> ▶ A comprehensive guide to R at `http://www.statmethods.net/about/sitemap.html`

> ▶ Refer to the *plyr* reference manual at `http://cran.r-project.org/web/packages/plyr/plyr.pdf`

> ▶ Refer to the *ggplot2* reference manual at `http://cran.r-project.org/web/packages/ggplot2/ggplot2.pdf`

> ▶ Visit Dr. Wickham's home page (`http://had.co.nz/`)

Importing automobile fuel efficiency data into R

Once you have downloaded and installed everything in the previous recipe, you can import the dataset into R to start doing some preliminary analysis and get a sense of what the data looks like.

Getting ready

Much of the analysis in this chapter is cumulative, and the efforts of the previous recipes will be used for subsequent recipes. Thus, if you completed the previous recipe, you should have everything you need to continue.

How to do it...

The following steps will walk you through the initial import of the data into the R environment:

1. First, set the working directory to the location where we saved the `vehicles.csv.zip` file:

```
setwd("path")
```

 Substitute the path for the actual directory.

2. We can load the data directly from compressed (ZIP) files, as long as you know the filename of the file inside the ZIP archive that you want to load:

```
vehicles <- read.csv(unz("vehicles.csv.zip", "vehicles.csv"),
stringsAsFactors = F)
```

3. To see whether this worked, let's display the first few rows of data using the head command:

```
head(vehicles)
```

You should see the first few rows of the dataset printed on your screen.

 Note that we could have used the tail command, which would have displayed the last few rows of the data frame instead of the first few rows.

4. The labels command gives the variable labels for the vehicles.csv file. Note that we use labels, since labels is a function in R. A quick look at the file shows that the variable names and their explanations are separated by -. So, we will try to read the file using - as the separator:

```
labels <- read.table("varlabels.txt", sep = "-", header =
FALSE)
## Error: line 11 did not have 2 elements
```

5. This doesn't work! A closer look at the error shows that in line 11 of the data file, there are two - symbols, and it thus gets broken into three parts rather than two, unlike the other rows. We need to change our file-reading approach to ignore hyphenated words:

```
labels <- do.call(rbind, strsplit(readLines("varlabels.txt"),
" - "))
```

6. To check whether it works, we use the head function again:

```
head(labels)
```

```
          [,1]            [,2]
[1,] "atvtype"     "type of alternative fuel or advanced
technology vehicle"
[2,] "barrels08"   "annual petroleum consumption in barrels for
fuelType1 (1)"
[3,] "barrelsA08"  "annual petroleum consumption in barrels for
fuelType2 (1)"
[4,] "charge120"   "time to charge an electric vehicle in hours
at 120 V"
[5,] "charge240"   "time to charge an electric vehicle in hours
at 240 V"
```

How it works...

Let's break down the last complex statement in step 5, piece-by-piece, starting from the innermost portion and working outward.

First, let's read the file line by line:

```
x <- readLines("varlabels.txt")
```

Each line needs to be split at the string -. The spaces are important, so we don't split hyphenated words (such as in line 11). This results in each line split into two parts as a vector of strings, and the vectors stored in a single list:

```
y <- strsplit(x, " - ")
```

Now, we stack these vectors together to make a matrix of strings, where the first column is the variable name and the second column is the description of the variable:

```
labels <- do.call(rbind, y)
```

There's more...

Astute readers might have noticed that the `read.csv` function call included `stringsAsFactors = F` as its final parameter. By default, R converts strings to a datatype, known as factors in many cases. Factors are the names for R's categorical datatype, which can be thought of as a label or tag applied to the data. Internally, R stores factors as integers with a mapping to the appropriate label. This technique allows older versions of R to store factors in much less memory than the corresponding character.

Categorical variables do not have a sense of order (where one value is considered greater than another). In the following snippet, we create a quick toy example converting four values of the `character` class to factor and do a comparison:

```
colors <- c('green', 'red', 'yellow', 'blue')
colors_factors <- factor(colors)
colors_factors
[1] green   red     yellow blue
Levels: blue green red yellow
colors_factors[1] > colors_factors[2]
[1] NA
Warning message:
In Ops.factor(colors_factors[1], colors_factors[2]) :
>not meaningful for factors
```

However, there is an ordered categorical variable, also known in the statistical world as ordinal data. Ordinal data is just like categorical data, with one exception. There is a sense of scale or value to the data. It can be said that one value is larger than another, but the magnitude of the difference cannot be measured.

Further, when importing data into R, we often run into the situation where a column of numeric data might contain an entry that is non-numeric. In this case, R might import the column of data as factors, which is often not what was intended by the data scientist. Converting from factor to character is relatively routine, but converting from factor to numeric can be a bit tricky.

There's more...

R is capable of importing data from a wide range of formats. In this recipe, we handled a CSV file, but we could have used a Microsoft Excel file as well. CSV files are preferred as they are universally supported across operating systems and far more portable. Additionally, R can import data from numerous popular statistical programs, including SPSS, Stata, and SAS.

See also

- ▶ Refer to the *R Data Import/Export* guide at `http://cran.r-project.org/doc/manuals/r-release/R-data.html`
- ▶ Explore the datatypes in R at `http://www.statmethods.net/input/datatypes.html`

Exploring and describing fuel efficiency data

Now that we have imported the automobile fuel efficiency dataset into R and learned a little about the nuances of importing, the next step is to do some preliminary analysis of the dataset. The purpose of this analysis is to explore what the data looks like and get your feet wet with some of R's most basic commands.

Getting ready

If you completed the previous recipe, you should have everything you need to continue.

How to do it...

The following steps will lead you through the initial exploration of our dataset, where we compute some basic parameters about the dataset:

1. First, let's find out how many observations (rows) are in our data:

   ```
   nrow(vehicles)
   ## 34287
   ```

2. Next, let's find out how many variables (columns) are in our data:

   ```
   ncol(vehicles)
   ## 74
   ```

3. Now, let's get a sense of which columns of data are present in the data frame using the `name` function:

   ```
   > names(vehicles)
   ```

   The preceding command will give you the following output:

   ```
   > names(vehicles)
     [1] "barrels08"       "barrelsA08"      "charge120"       "charge240"       "city08"          "city08U"
     [7] "cityA08"         "cityA08U"        "cityCD"          "cityE"           "cityUF"          "co2"
    [13] "co2A"            "co2TailpipeAGpm" "co2TailpipeGpm"  "comb08"          "comb08U"         "combA08"
    [19] "combA08U"        "combE"           "combinedCD"      "combinedUF"      "cylinders"       "displ"
    [25] "drive"           "engId"           "eng_dscr"        "feScore"         "fuelCost08"      "fuelCostA08"
    [31] "fuelType"        "fuelType1"       "ghgScore"        "ghgScoreA"       "highway08"       "highway08U"
    [37] "highwayA08"      "highwayA08U"     "highwayCD"       "highwayE"        "highwayUF"       "hlv"
    [43] "hpv"             "id"              "lv2"             "lv4"             "make"            "model"
    [49] "mpgData"         "phevBlended"     "pv2"             "pv4"             "range"           "rangeCity"
    [55] "rangeCityA"      "rangeHwy"        "rangeHwyA"       "trany"           "UCity"           "UCityA"
    [61] "UHighway"        "UHighwayA"       "VClass"          "year"            "youSaveSpend"    "guzzler"
    [67] "trans_dscr"      "tCharger"        "sCharger"        "atvType"         "fuelType2"       "rangeA"
    [73] "evMotor"         "mfrCode"         "trany2"
   >
   ```

   Luckily, a lot of these column or variable names are pretty descriptive and give us an idea of what they might contain. Remember, a more detailed description of the variables is available at http://www.fueleconomy.gov/feg/ws/index.shtml#vehicle.

4. Let's find out how many unique years of data are included in this dataset by computing a vector of the unique values in the `year` column, and then computing the length of the vector:

   ```
   length(unique(vehicles[, "year"]))
   ## 31
   ```

5. Now, we determine the first and last years present in the dataset using the `min` and `max` functions:

```
first_year <- min(vehicles[, "year"])
## 1984
last_year <- max(vehicles[, "year"])
## 2014
```

 Note that depending on when you downloaded the dataset, the value of `last_year` maybe greater than 2014.

6. Also, since we might use the `year` variable a lot, let's make sure that we have each year covered. The list of years from 1984 to 2014 should contain 31 unique values. To test this, use the following command:

```
> length(unique(vehicles$year))
[1] 31
```

7. Next, let's find out what types of fuel are used as the automobiles' primary fuel types:

```
table(vehicles$fuelType1)
##              Diesel    Electricity Midgrade Gasoline
Natural Gas
##                1025            56                  41
57
##  Premium Gasoline  Regular Gasoline
##              8521            24587
```

From this, we can see that most cars in the dataset use regular gasoline, and the second most common fuel type is premium gasoline.

8. Let's explore the types of transmissions used by these automobiles. We first need to take care of all missing data by setting it to `NA`:

```
vehicles$trany[vehicles$trany == ""] <- NA
```

9. Now, the `trany` column is text, and we only care whether the car's transmission is automatic or manual. Thus, we use the `substr` function to extract the first four characters of each `trany` column value and determine whether it is equal to `Auto`. If so, we set a new variable, `trany2`, equal to `Auto`; otherwise, the value is set to `Manual`:

```
vehicles$trany2 <- ifelse(substr(vehicles$trany, 1, 4) ==
"Auto", "Auto", "Manual")
```

10. Finally, we convert the new variable to a factor and then use the table function to see the distribution of values:

```
vehicles$trany <- as.factor(vehicles$trany)

table(vehicles$trany2)

##   Auto Manual

##  22451  11825
```

We can see that there are roughly twice as many automobile models with automatic transmission as there are models with manual transmission.

How it works...

The data frame is an incredibly powerful datatype used by R, and we will leverage it heavily throughout this recipe. The data frame allows us to group variables of different datatypes (numeric, strings, logical, factors, and so on) into rows of related information. One example will be a data frame of customer information. Each row in the data frame can contain the name of the person (a string), along with an age (numeric), a gender (a factor), and a flag to indicate whether they are a current customer (Boolean). If you are familiar with relational databases, this is much like a table in a database.

Further, in this recipe, we looked at several ways of getting a quick read on a dataset imported into R. Most notably, we used the powerful `table` function to create a count of the occurrence of values for the `fuelType1` variable. This function is capable of much more, including cross tabulations, as follows:

```
with(vehicles, table(sCharger, year))
```

The preceding command will give you the following output:

```
> with(vehicles, table(sCharger, year))
        year
sCharger 1984 1985 1986 1987 1988 1989 1990 1991 1992 1993 1994 1995 1996 1997 1998 1999 2000 2001 2002 2003 2004 2005
         1964 1701 1210 1247 1130 1149 1074 1130 1116 1088  979  962  767  757  800  840  826  891  949 1015 1089 1136
       S    0    0    0    0    0    4    4    2    5    5    3    5    6    5   12   12   14   20   26   29   33   30
        year
sCharger 2006 2007 2008 2009 2010 2011 2012 2013 2014
         1067 1098 1152 1166 1091 1077 1125 1141 1051
       S   37   28   35   19   18   20   28   42   57
>
```

Here, we looked at the number of automobile models by year, with and without a super charger (and we saw that super chargers have seemingly become more popular more recently than they were in the past).

Also, note that we use the `with` command. This command tells R to use vehicles as the default data when performing the subsequent command, in this case, table. Thus, we can omit prefacing the `sCharger` and `year` column names with the name of the data frame and vehicles, followed by the dollar sign.

There's more...

To provide a cautionary tale about data import, let's look at the `sCharger` and `tCharger` columns more closely. Note that these columns indicate whether the car contains a super charger or a turbo charger, respectively.

Starting with `sCharger`, we look at the class of the variable and the unique values present in the data frame:

```
> class(vehicles$sCharger)
[1] "character"
> unique(vehicles$sCharger)
[1] ""  "S"
```

We next look at `tCharger`, expecting things to be the same:

```
> class(vehicles$tCharger)
[1] "logical"
> unique(vehicles$tCharger)
[1]    NA TRUE
```

However, what we find is that these two seemingly similar variables are different datatypes completely. While the `tCharger` variable is a logical variable, also known as a Boolean variable in other languages, and is used to represent the binary values of `true` and `false`, the `sCharger` variable appears to be the more general character datatype. Something seems wrong. In this case, because we can, let's check the original data. Luckily, the data is in a `.csv` file, and we can use a simple text editor to open and read the file. (Notepad on Windows and vi on Unix systems are recommended for the task, but feel free to use your favorite, basic text editor.) When we open the file, we can see that `sCharger` and `tCharger` data columns either are blank or contains an `S` or `T`, respectively.

Thus, R has read in the `T` character in the `tCharger` column as a Boolean `TRUE` variable, as opposed to the character `T`. This isn't a fatal flaw and might not impact an analysis. However, undetected bugs such as this can cause problems far down the analytical pipeline and necessitate significant repeated work.

Analyzing automobile fuel efficiency over time

We have now successfully imported the data and looked at some important high-level statistics that provided us with a basic understanding of what values are in the dataset and how frequently some features appear. With this recipe, we continue the exploration by looking at some of the fuel efficiency metrics over time and in relation to other data points.

Getting ready

If you completed the previous recipe, you should have everything you need to continue.

How to do it...

The following steps will use both `plyr` and the graphing library, `ggplot2`, to explore the dataset:

1. Let's start by looking at whether there is an overall trend of how MPG changes over time on an average. To do this, we use the `ddply` function from the `plyr` package to take the `vehicles` data frame, aggregate rows by year, and then, for each group, we compute the mean highway, city, and combine fuel efficiency. The result is then assigned to a new data frame, `mpgByYr`. Note that this is our first example of split-apply-combine. We split the data frame into groups by year, we apply the mean function to specific variables, and then we combine the results into a new data frame:

    ```
    mpgByYr <- ddply(vehicles, ~year, summarise, avgMPG =
    mean(comb08), avgHghy = mean(highway08), avgCity =
    mean(city08))
    ```

2. To gain a better understanding of this new data frame, we pass it to the `ggplot` function, telling it to plot the `avgMPG` variable against the `year` variable, using points. In addition, we specify that we want axis labels, a title, and even a smoothed conditional mean (`geom_smooth()`) represented as a shaded region of the plot:

    ```
    ggplot(mpgByYr, aes(year, avgMPG)) + geom_point() +
    geom_smooth() + xlab("Year") + ylab("Average MPG") +
    ggtitle("All cars")

    ## geom_smooth: method="auto" and size of largest group is
    <1000, so using

    ## loess. Use 'method = x' to change the smoothing method.
    ```

The preceding commands will give you the following plot:

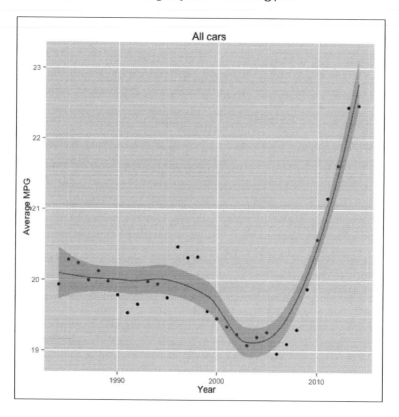

3. Based on this visualization, one might conclude that there has been a tremendous increase in the fuel economy of cars sold in the last few years. However, this can be a little misleading as there have been more hybrid and non-gasoline vehicles in the later years, which is shown as follows:

```
table(vehicles$fuelType1)
```

```
##            Diesel      Electricity Midgrade Gasoline
Natural Gas
##              1025              56                  41
57

## Premium Gasoline  Regular Gasoline
##              8521            24587
```

4. Let's look at just gasoline cars, even though there are not many non-gasoline powered cars, and redraw the preceding plot. To do this, we use the subset function to create a new data frame, `gasCars`, which only contains the rows of vehicles in which the `fuelType1` variable is one among a subset of values:

```
gasCars <- subset(vehicles, fuelType1 %in% c("Regular
Gasoline", "Premium Gasoline", "Midgrade Gasoline") &
fuelType2 == "" & atvType != "Hybrid")
```

```
mpgByYr_Gas <- ddply(gasCars, ~year, summarise, avgMPG =
mean(comb08))
```

```
ggplot(mpgByYr_Gas, aes(year, avgMPG)) + geom_point() +
geom_smooth() + xlab("Year") + ylab("Average MPG") +
ggtitle("Gasoline cars")
```

```
## geom_smooth: method="auto" and size of largest group is
<1000, so using
```

```
## loess. Use 'method = x' to change the smoothing method.
```

The preceding commands will give you the following plot:

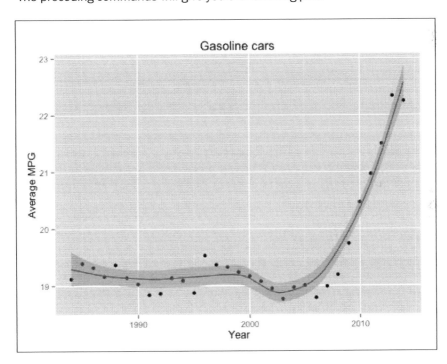

5. Have fewer large engine cars been made recently? If so, this can explain the increase. First, let's verify whether cars with larger engines have worse fuel efficiency. We note that the `displ` variable, which represents the displacement of the engine in liters, is currently a string variable that we need to convert to a numeric variable:

```
typeof(gasCars$displ)
```
```
##   "character"
```
```
gasCars$displ <- as.numeric(gasCars$displ)
```
```
ggplot(gasCars, aes(displ, comb08)) + geom_point() +
geom_smooth()
```

```
## geom_smooth: method="auto" and size of largest group is
>=1000, so using
## gam with formula: y ~ s(x, bs = "cs"). Use 'method = x' to
change the
## smoothing method.
## Warning: Removed 2 rows containing missing values
(stat_smooth).
## Warning: Removed 2 rows containing missing values
(geom_point).
```

The preceding commands will give you the following plot:

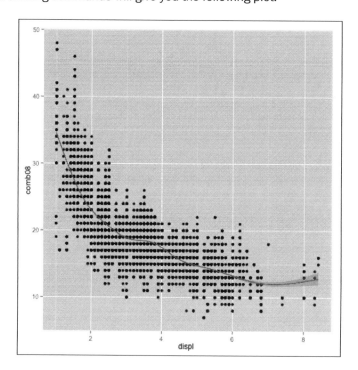

This scatter plot of the data offers the convincing evidence that there is a negative, or even inverse correlation, between engine displacement and fuel efficiency; thus, smaller cars tend to be more fuel-efficient.

6. Now, let's see whether more small cars were made in later years, which can explain the drastic increase in fuel efficiency:

```
avgCarSize <- ddply(gasCars, ~year, summarise, avgDispl =
mean(displ))
```

```
ggplot(avgCarSize, aes(year, avgDispl)) + geom_point() +
geom_smooth() + xlab("Year") + ylab("Average engine
displacement (l)")
```

```
## geom_smooth: method="auto" and size of largest group is
<1000, so using
```

```
## loess. Use 'method = x' to change the smoothing method.
```

```
## Warning: Removed 1 rows containing missing values
(stat_smooth).
```

```
## Warning: Removed 1 rows containing missing values
(geom_point).
```

The preceding commands will give you the following plot:

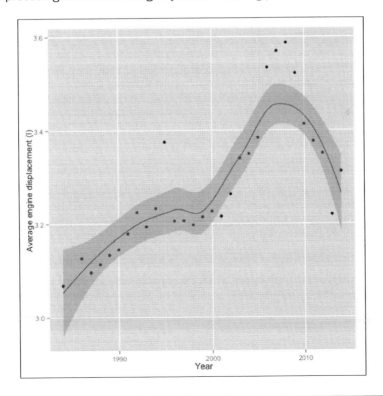

7. From the preceding figure, the average engine displacement has decreased substantially since 2008. To get a better sense of the impact this might have had on fuel efficiency, we can put both MPG and displacement by year on the same graph. Using ddply, we create a new data frame, byYear, which contains both the average fuel efficiency and the average engine displacement by year:

```
byYear <- ddply(gasCars, ~year, summarise, avgMPG =
mean(comb08), avgDispl = mean(displ))

> head(byYear)

  year    avgMPG avgDispl
1 1984 19.12162 3.068449
2 1985 19.39469       NA
3 1986 19.32046 3.126514
4 1987 19.16457 3.096474
5 1988 19.36761 3.113558
6 1989 19.14196 3.133393
```

8. The head function shows us that the resulting data frame has three columns: year, avgMPG, and avgDispl. To use the faceting capability of ggplot2 to display Average MPG and Avg engine displacement by year on separate but aligned plots, we must melt the data frame, converting it from what is known as a wide format to a long format:

```
byYear2 = melt(byYear, id = "year")
levels(byYear2$variable) <- c("Average MPG", "Avg engine
displacement")


head(byYear2)

  year    variable    value
1 1984 Average MPG 19.12162
2 1985 Average MPG 19.39469
3 1986 Average MPG 19.32046
4 1987 Average MPG 19.16457
5 1988 Average MPG 19.36761
6 1989 Average MPG 19.14196
```

If we use the `nrow` function, we can see that the `byYear2` data frame has 62 rows and the `byYear` data frame has only 31. The two separate columns from `byYear` (`avgMPG` and `avgDispl`) have now been melted into one new column (`value`) in the `byYear2` data frame. Note that the variable column in the `byYear2` data frame serves to identify the column that the value represents:

```
ggplot(byYear2, aes(year, value)) + geom_point() +
geom_smooth() + facet_wrap(~variable, ncol = 1, scales =
"free_y") + xlab("Year") + ylab("")
```

```
## geom_smooth: method="auto" and size of largest group is
<1000, so using
```

```
## loess. Use 'method = x' to change the smoothing method.
## geom_smooth: method="auto" and size of largest group is
<1000, so using
```

```
## loess. Use 'method = x' to change the smoothing method.
```

```
## Warning: Removed 1 rows containing missing values
(stat_smooth).
```

```
## Warning: Removed 1 rows containing missing values
(geom_point).
```

The preceding commands will give you the following plot:

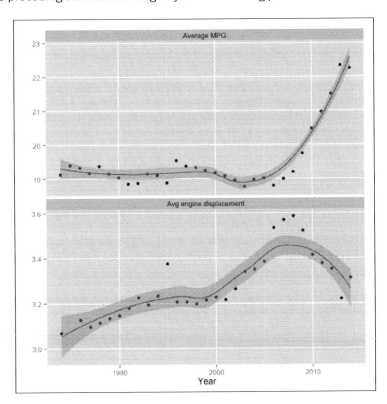

From this plot, we can see the following:

- ❑ Engine sizes have generally increased until 2008, with a sudden increase in large cars between 2006 and 2008.

- ❑ Since 2009, there has been a decrease in the average car size, which partially explains the increase in fuel efficiency.

- ❑ Until 2005, there was an increase in the average car size, but the fuel efficiency remained roughly constant. This seems to indicate that engine efficiency has increased over the years.

- ❑ The years 2006–2008 are interesting. Though the average engine size increased quite suddenly, the MPG remained roughly the same as in previous years. This seeming discrepancy might require more investigation.

9. Given the trend toward smaller displacement engines, let's see whether automatic or manual transmissions are more efficient for four cylinder engines, and how the efficiencies have changed over time:

```
gasCars4 <- subset(gasCars, cylinders == "4")
```

```
ggplot(gasCars4, aes(factor(year), comb08)) + geom_boxplot()
+ facet_wrap(~trany2, ncol = 1) + theme(axis.text.x = element_
text(angle = 45)) + labs(x = "Year", y = "MPG")
```

The preceding command will give you the following plot:

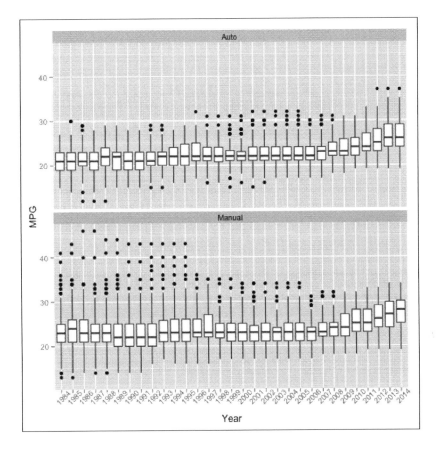

This time, `ggplot2` was used to create box plots that help visualize the distribution of values (and not just a single value, such as a mean) for each year.

10. Next, let's look at the change in proportion of manual cars available each year:

```
ggplot(gasCars4, aes(factor(year), fill = factor(trany2))) +
geom_bar(position = "fill") + labs(x = "Year", y = "Proportion
of cars", fill = "Transmission") + theme(axis.text.x =
element_text(angle = 45)) + geom_hline(yintercept = 0.5,
linetype = 2)
```

The preceding command will give you the following plot:

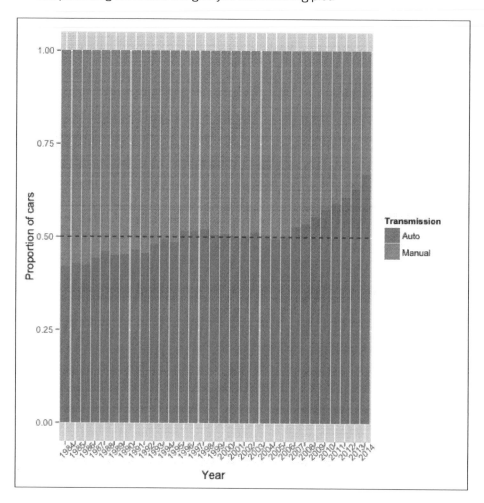

In step 9, it appears that manual transmissions are more efficient than automatic transmissions, and they both exhibit the same increase, on an average, since 2008. However, there is something odd here. There appear to be many very efficient cars (less than 40 MPG) with automatic transmissions in later years, and almost no manual transmission cars with similar efficiencies in the same time frame. The pattern is reversed in earlier years. Is there a change in the proportion of manual cars available each year? Yes. What are these very efficient cars? In the next section, we look at the makes and models of the cars in the database.

How it works...

With this recipe, we threw you into the deep end of data analysis with R, using two very important R packages, `plyr` and `ggplot2`. Just as traditional software development has design patterns for common constructs, a few such patterns are emerging in the field of data science. One of the most notable is the split-apply-combine pattern highlighted by Dr. Hadley Wickham. In this strategy, one breaks up the problem into smaller, more manageable pieces by some variable. Once aggregated, you perform an operation on the new grouped data, and then combine the results into a new data structure. As you can see in this recipe, we used this strategy of split-apply-combine repeatedly, examining the data from many different perspectives, as a result.

Beyond `plyr`, this recipe heavily leveraged the `ggplot2` library, which deserves additional exposition. We will refrain from providing an extensive `ggplot2` tutorial as there are a number of excellent tutorials available online. What is important is that you understand the important idea of how `ggplot2` allows you to construct such complex statistical visualizations in such a terse fashion.

The `ggplot2` library is an open source implementation of the foundational grammar of graphics by Wilkinson, Anand, and Grossman for R. *The Grammar of Graphics* attempts to decompose statistical data visualizations into component parts to better understand how such graphics are created. With `ggplot2`, Hadley Wickham, takes these ideas and implements a layered approach, allowing the user to assemble complex visualizations from individual pieces very quickly. Take, for example, the first graph for this recipe, which shows the average fuel efficiency of all models of cars in a particular year over time:

```
ggplot(mpgByYr, aes(year, avgMPG)) + geom_point() + geom_smooth() +
xlab("Year") + ylab("Average MPG") + ggtitle("All cars")
```

To construct this plot, we first tell `ggplot` the data frame that will serve as the data for the plot (`mpgByYr`), and then the aesthetic mappings that will tell `ggplot2` which variables will be mapped into visual characteristics of the plot. In this case, `aes(year, avgMPG)` implicitly specifies that the year will be mapped to the x axis and `avgMPG` will be mapped to the y axis. `Geom_point()` tells the library to plot the specified data as points and a second geom, `geom_smooth()`, adds a shaded region showing the smoothed mean (with a confidence interval set to 0.95, by default) for the same data. Finally, the `xlab()`, `ylab()`, and `ggtitle()` functions are used to add labels to the plot. Thus, we can generate a complex, publication quality graph in a single line of code; `ggplot2` is capable of doing far more complex plots.

Also, it is important to note that `ggplot2`, and the grammar of graphics in general, does not tell you how best to visualize your data, but gives you the tools to do so rapidly. If you want more advice on this topic, we strongly recommend looking into the works of Edward Tufte, who has numerous books on the matter, including the classic *The Visual Display of Quantitative Information, Graphics Press USA*. Further, `ggplot2` does not allow for dynamic data visualizations.

See also

▸ Refer to *The Split-Apply-Combine Strategy for Data Analysis* paper at `http://www.jstatsoft.org/v40/i01/paper`

▸ Refer to *The Grammar of Graphics, Leland Wilkinson, Springer Science & Business Media*

▸ Refer to the *Package 'ggplot2'* article from CRAN at `http://cran.r-project.org/web/packages/ggplot2/ggplot2.pdf`

▸ Refer to the *A Layered Grammar of Graphics* article at `http://vita.had.co.nz/papers/layered-grammar.pdf`

Investigating the makes and models of automobiles

With the first set of questions asked and answered about this dataset, let's move on to additional analyses.

Getting ready

If you completed the previous recipe, you should have everything you need to continue.

How to do it...

This recipe will investigate the makes and models of automobiles and how they have changed over time:

1. Let's look at how the makes and models of cars inform fuel efficiency over time. First, let's look at the frequency of the makes and models of cars available in the US over this time and concentrate on four-cylinder cars:

```
carsMake <- ddply(gasCars4, ~year, summarise, numberOfMakes =
length(unique(make)))
```

```
ggplot(carsMake, aes(year, numberOfMakes)) + geom_point() +
labs(x = "Year", y = "Number of available makes") + ggtitle("Four
cylinder cars")
```

We see in the following graph that there has been a decline in the number of makes available over this period, though there has been a small uptick in recent times:

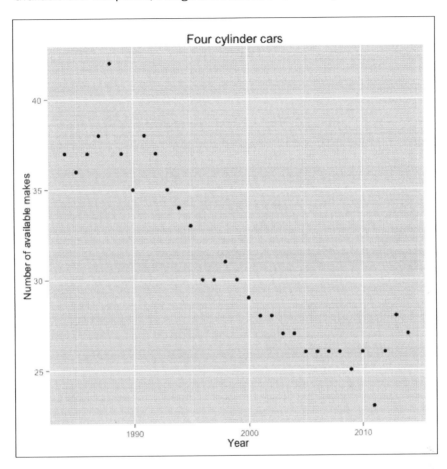

2. Can we look at the makes that have been available for every year of this study? We find there are only 12 manufactures that made four-cylinder cars every year during this period:

```
uniqMakes <- dlply(gasCars4, ~year, function(x)
unique(x$make))

commonMakes <- Reduce(intersect, uniqMakes)

commonMakes

##  [1] "Ford"       "Honda"      "Toyota"     "Volkswagen"
"Chevrolet"

##  [6] "Chrysler"   "Nissan"     "Dodge"      "Mazda"
"Mitsubishi"

## [11] "Subaru"     "Jeep"
```

3. How have these manufacturers done over time with respect to fuel efficiency? We find that most manufacturers have shown improvement over this time, though several manufacturers have demonstrated quite sharp fuel efficiency increases in the last 5 years:

```
carsCommonMakes4 <- subset(gasCars4, make %in% commonMakes)

avgMPG_commonMakes <- ddply(carsCommonMakes4, ~year + make,
summarise, avgMPG = mean(comb08))

ggplot(avgMPG_commonMakes, aes(year, avgMPG)) + geom_line() +
facet_wrap(~make, nrow = 3)
```

The preceding commands will give you the following plot:

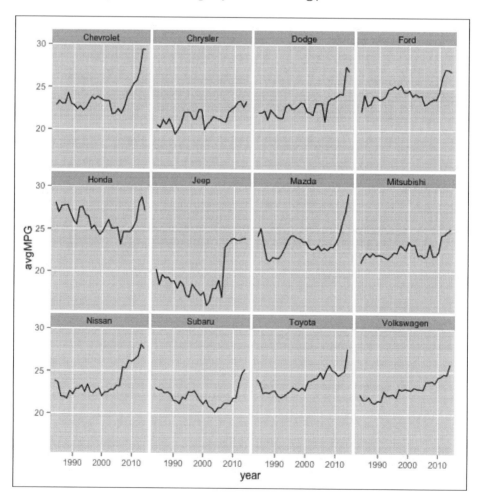

How it works...

In step 2, there is definitely some interesting magic at work, with a lot being done in only a few lines of code. This is both a beautiful and a problematic aspect of R. It is beautiful because it allows the concise expression of programmatically complex ideas, but it is problematic because R code can be quite inscrutable if you are not familiar with the particular library.

In the first line, we use `dlply` (not `ddply`) to take the `gasCars4` data frame, split it by year, and then apply the unique function to the `make` variable. For each year, a list of the unique available automobile makes is computed, and then `dlply` returns a list of these lists (one element each year). Note `dlply`, and not `ddply`, because it takes a data frame (d) as input and returns a list (l) as output, whereas `ddply` takes a data frame (d) as input and outputs a data frame (d):

```
uniqMakes <- dlply(gasCars4, ~year, function(x) unique(x$make))

commonMakes <- Reduce(intersect, uniqMakes)

commonMakes
```

The next line is even more interesting. It uses the `Reduce` higher order function, and this is the same `Reduce` function and idea in the map reduce programming paradigm introduced by Google that underlies Hadoop. R is, in some ways, a functional programming language and offers several higher order functions as part of its core. A higher order function accepts another function as input. In this line, we pass the `intersect` function to `Reduce`, which will apply the `intersect` function pairwise to each element in the list of unique makes per year that was created previously. Ultimately, this results in a single list of automobile makes that is present every year.

The two lines of code express a very simple concept (determining all automobile makes present every year) that took two paragraphs to describe.

There's more...

The final graph in this recipe is an excellent example of the faceted graphics capabilities of `ggplot2`. Adding `+ facet_wrap(~make, nrow = 3)` tells `ggplot2` that we want a separate set of axes for each make of automobile and distribute these subplots between three different rows. This is an incredibly powerful data visualization technique as it allows us to clearly see patterns that might only manifest for a particular value of a variable.

We kept things simple in this first data science project. The dataset itself was small—only 12 megabytes uncompressed, easily stored, and handled on a basic laptop. We used R to import the dataset, check the integrity of some (but not all) of the data fields, and summarize the data. We then moved on to exploring the data by asking a number of questions and using two key libraries, `plyr` and `ggplot2`, to manipulate the data and visualize the results. In this data science pipeline, our final stage was simply the text that we wrote to summarize our conclusions and the visualizations produced by `ggplot2`.

See also

- ▸ Read a great post titled *Higher Order Functions in R* by John Myles White at
  `http://www.johnmyleswhite.com/notebook/2010/09/23/higher-order-functions-in-r/`

3

Simulating American Football Data (R)

In this chapter, we will cover:

- ▶ Acquiring and cleaning football data
- ▶ Analyzing and understanding football data
- ▶ Constructing indexes to measure offensive and defensive strength
- ▶ Simulating a single game with the outcome decided by calculations
- ▶ Simulating multiple games with the outcomes decided by calculations

Introduction

American football is the most popular sport in the United States and is the ninth most popular sport worldwide. Every year, football fans look forward to the start of a new season in September, the 17 weeks of play that follow, the playoffs that start in January, and the championship game known as the Super Bowl in late January or early February.

In this chapter, we will obtain some football statistics, analyze them to get a sense of what the data looks like, determine a way to calculate which team should win when two teams play each other, and then use this to simulate games to produce a *virtual* winning team and losing team. There are many different ways in which you can construct such a simulation. For example, if you want to construct your simulation at the level of individual plays, you can get the statistics for every single player on a team and every play that a team runs, and use these to simulate a game in a play-by-play fashion. This approach would be great if we were football video game makers, as we would need a very detailed output and a play-by-play simulation in order to make the experience of playing the game as realistic as possible. However, the approach we will take will be much simpler. Using aggregated team-level data instead of a more detailed player and play statistics, we will be able to efficiently determine which team should win each game.

The goal of this chapter will be to learn how to complete a data science project that involves obtaining data from a web page, coming up with our own formulas and calculations, applying the calculations to several scenarios, and setting up a simulation where we can determine how many times we want the process to run. This project will use the **R** statistical programming language and some of its packages for data acquisition, manipulation, and visualization. This chapter will also showcase R's flexibility to act as a programming language in addition to showcasing its statistical modeling features.

The recipes in this chapter will roughly follow the data science pipeline. We will adapt the pipeline to the type of data we are working with and the types of tasks we would like to perform using this data.

Requirements

For this chapter, you need a computer with access to the Internet. You also need to have R installed and have the following packages installed and loaded:

```
install.packages("XML")
install.packages("RSQLite")
install.packages("stringr")
install.packages("ggplot2")

library(XML)
library(RSQLite)
library(stringr)
library(ggplot2)
```

The XML package will help us with reading the HTML data we pull from the Web, RSQLite and stringr will help us with data manipulation, and ggplot2 will be used to create graphs and visualizations.

Additionally, if you are not familiar with American football, you can find a brief explanation of the basics at `http://www.nfl.com/rulebook/beginnersguidetofootball`.

Acquiring and cleaning football data

There are many places on the Internet to obtain football data, including various websites that track schedules, scores, and statistics. When looking for datasets, the main things we take into consideration are the usefulness, quality, and format of the data. For this project, we will pull data from `http://sports.yahoo.com/` as it is a well-established source and has the necessary stats in a relatively well-organized format, which will only require some light cleaning.

Getting ready

If you've installed and loaded the packages listed in the *Introduction* section of this chapter and set your working directory to the location where you want to save your files, you should have everything you need to continue.

How to do it...

Perform the following steps to acquire and clean the data:

1. The first thing we will do is acquire offensive data for each team for a season. Since the last complete season, at the time of writing this book, is the 2013 season, it is the one we will use. So, we will set the `year` variable to `2013`:

    ```
    year <- 2013
    ```

2. Next, we will embed the year into the URL where the data is located and assign the entire URL string to the `url` variable:

    ```
    url <-
    paste("http://sports.yahoo.com/nfl/stats/byteam?group=Offense&
    cat=Total&conference=NFL&year=season_",year,"&sort=530&old_cat
    egory=Total&old_group=Offense")
    ```

3. Now that we have the complete URL, we can pull the data from it:

    ```
    offense <- readHTMLTable(url, encoding = "UTF-8",
    colClasses="character")[[7]]
    ```

This will create a data frame named `offense` that will contain the offensive stats for all 32 teams, as shown in the following screenshot:

	Team	G	Pts/G	Yds/G	PassYds/G	RushYds/G	1stD/G	3rdM	3rdD⁵
1	Denver Broncos	16	37.9	457.3	340.3	117.1	27.2	95	46.3
2	Chicago Bears	16	27.8	381.8	267.6	114.3	21.5	83	42.1
3	New England Patriots	16	27.8	384.5	255.4	129.1	23.6	83	37.6
4	Philadelphia Eagles	16	27.6	417.3	256.9	160.4	22.2	83	39.0
5	Dallas Cowboys	16	27.4	341.1	247.1	94.0	20.3	63	35.0
6	Kansas City Chiefs	16	26.9	337.3	208.8	128.5	20.2	74	34.7
7	Cincinnati Bengals	16	26.9	368.2	258.5	109.7	20.6	92	40.9
8	Seattle Seahawks	16	26.1	339.0	202.3	136.8	19.2	76	37.3
9	Green Bay Packers	16	26.1	400.3	266.8	133.5	21.9	89	41.2
10	New Orleans Saints	16	25.9	399.4	307.4	92.1	22.4	97	43.9
11	San Francisco 49ers	16	25.4	323.8	186.2	137.6	17.9	77	36.5
12	San Diego Chargers	16	24.8	393.3	270.5	122.8	23.3	101	49.0
13	Detroit Lions	16	24.7	392.1	280.1	112.0	21.9	95	43.0
14	Minnesota Vikings	16	24.4	344.3	214.2	130.1	19.3	78	36.4

4. The first thing we notice when we take a look at the data that we've just pulled is that it needs a little bit of cleaning up. There are a lot of blank columns, and we want to make sure that the fields we've pulled are formatted correctly. So, let's get rid of the blank columns and then assign data types to each of the remaining columns, using the following command:

```
offense <- offense[,-c(2,4,6,8,10,12,14,16,18,20,22,24,26,28)]

offense[,1] <- as.character(offense[,1])

offense[,2:13] <- apply(offense[,2:13],2,as.numeric)

offense[,14] <- as.numeric(substr(offense[,14], 1, 2))*60 +
as.numeric(substr(offense[,14], 4, 6))
```

The last column, labeled **TOP**, is the time of possession, or the average amount of time the team was on offense per game. It was previously formatted as minutes:seconds, so we just changed it so that it reflects the total number of seconds per game during which the team's offense has possession of the ball.

Now, our offense data is clean and formatted properly, as shown in the following screenshot:

	Team	G	Pts/G	Yds/G	PassYds/G	RushYds/G	1stD/G	3rdM	3rdD%	4thM	4thD%	Pen	PYds
1	Denver Broncos	16	37.9	457.3	340.3	117.1	27.2	95	46.3	8	88.9	117	1000
2	Chicago Bears	16	27.8	381.8	267.6	114.3	21.5	83	42.1	8	61.5	85	708
3	New England Patriots	16	27.8	384.5	255.4	129.1	23.6	83	37.6	7	46.7	69	625
4	Philadelphia Eagles	16	27.6	417.3	256.9	160.4	22.2	83	39.0	7	50.0	95	846
5	Dallas Cowboys	16	27.4	341.1	247.1	94.0	20.3	63	35.0	4	66.7	102	867
6	Kansas City Chiefs	16	26.9	337.3	208.8	128.5	20.2	74	34.7	4	36.4	101	774
7	Cincinnati Bengals	16	26.9	368.2	258.5	109.7	20.6	92	40.9	12	57.1	102	1000
8	Seattle Seahawks	16	26.1	339.0	202.3	136.8	19.2	76	37.3	6	54.5	128	1183
9	Green Bay Packers	16	26.1	400.3	266.8	133.5	21.9	89	41.2	9	69.2	86	801
10	New Orleans Saints	16	25.9	399.4	307.4	92.1	22.4	97	43.9	9	47.4	95	817
11	San Francisco 49ers	16	25.4	323.8	186.2	137.6	17.9	77	36.5	9	63.6	103	845
12	San Diego Chargers	16	24.8	393.3	270.5	122.8	23.3	101	49.0	5	83.3	95	765
13	Detroit Lions	16	24.7	392.1	280.1	112.0	21.9	95	43.0	5	35.7	110	925
14	Minnesota Vikings	16	24.4	344.3	214.2	130.1	19.3	78	36.4	10	52.6	70	695

5. Next, let's do the same thing with the data for defense. As with offense, we will start by embedding the year into the URL where we can obtain the defense data:

```
url <-
paste("http://sports.yahoo.com/nfl/stats/byteam?group=Defense&
cat=Total&conference=NFL&year=season_",year,"&sort=530&old_cat
egory=Total&old_group=Defense")
```

6. Next, we will pass this URL string into the readHTMLTable function to pull the data:

```
defense <- readHTMLTable(url, encoding = "UTF-8",
colClasses="character")[[7]]
```

When scraping data from a web page using the readHTMLTable function, it will initially read the entire page. We add [[7]] at the end because the table we want to pull data from is the seventh element in the page. For fun, try changing this number to see what the other page elements look like when they are read by the function.

The following screenshot shows the data:

	Team	G	Pts/G	Yds/G	RushYds/G	PassYds/G	Int	IntTD	FFum
1	Arizona Cardinals	16	20.3	317.4	84.4	233.0	20	4	11
2	Pittsburgh Steelers	16	23.1	337.2	115.6	221.6	10	3	14
3	San Diego Chargers	16	21.8	366.5	107.8	258.7	11	1	9
4	Philadelphia Eagles	16	23.9	394.0	104.3	289.8	19	1	11
5	New York Jets	16	24.2	334.9	88.3	246.7	13	1	9
6	New Orleans Saints	16	19.0	305.7	111.6	194.1	12	0	10
7	New York Giants	16	23.9	332.3	108.9	223.3	17	2	13
8	San Francisco 49ers	16	17.0	316.9	95.9	221.0	18	2	11
9	Seattle Seahawks	16	14.4	273.6	101.6	172.0	28	3	15
10	Baltimore Ravens	16	22.0	335.5	105.4	230.1	16	1	14
11	Houston Texans	16	26.8	317.6	122.4	195.2	7	1	9
12	Jacksonville Jaguars	16	28.1	379.4	131.8	247.6	11	1	14
13	Carolina Panthers	16	15.1	301.3	86.9	214.3	20	4	11

7. Just as our offense data needed to be cleaned, so does the defense data. We will use the exact same commands to do this, just substituting the name `offense` for `defense`. Also, note that since the time of possession does not apply to defense, it is not included in the defense data:

```
defense <- defense[,-c(2,4,6,8,10,12,14,16,18,20,22,24,26)]
defense[,1] <- as.character(defense[,1])
defense[,2:13] <- apply(defense[,2:13],2,as.numeric)
```

Now, our defense data is also clean and formatted, as shown in the following screenshot:

	Team	G	Pts/G	Yds/G	RushYds/G	PassYds/G	Int	IntTD	FFum	DefTD	Tack	PD	Sack
1	Arizona Cardinals	16	20.3	317.4	84.4	233.0	20	4	11	5	686	103	47
2	Pittsburgh Steelers	16	23.1	337.2	115.6	221.6	10	3	14	3	637	72	34
3	San Diego Chargers	16	21.8	366.5	107.8	258.7	11	1	9	1	678	70	35
4	Philadelphia Eagles	16	23.9	394.0	104.3	289.8	19	1	11	2	739	101	37
5	New York Jets	16	24.2	334.9	88.3	246.7	13	1	9	1	599	64	41
6	New Orleans Saints	16	19.0	305.7	111.6	194.1	12	0	10	0	564	69	49
7	New York Giants	16	23.9	332.3	108.9	223.3	17	2	13	2	742	83	34
8	San Francisco 49ers	16	17.0	316.9	95.9	221.0	18	2	11	5	681	87	38
9	Seattle Seahawks	16	14.4	273.6	101.6	172.0	28	3	15	4	575	90	44
10	Baltimore Ravens	16	22.0	335.5	105.4	230.1	16	1	14	1	585	101	40
11	Houston Texans	16	26.8	317.6	122.4	195.2	7	1	9	1	640	71	32
12	Jacksonville Jaguars	16	28.1	379.4	131.8	247.6	11	1	14	2	703	72	31
13	Carolina Panthers	16	15.1	301.3	86.9	214.3	20	4	11	4	615	67	60
14	Tampa Bay Buccaneers	16	24.3	348.0	110.1	237.9	21	3	13	3	676	75	35

How it works...

The `paste()` function in R is used to concatenate two strings together. For those that are new to manipulating data, concatenation means joining two things together. We used this function because we wanted to embed the year that we want to pull into the URL for the web page. This lets us change from year to year by simply changing the value of the `year` variable. Try changing the value to `2012` or `2011` and then rerunning the steps in this recipe. It will automatically pull the stats for the year that you chose, assuming that the data is available.

Another useful R function used in this section is `apply()`. We use it to format several columns as numeric with a single line of code. The `apply()` function can do this with many mathematical operations as well, and not just for changing field types. For example, if we wanted to take the mean for columns 2 through 13 in the defense data frame after converting them to numeric types, we would use the following command:

```
means <- apply(defense[,2:13],2,mean)
```

See also

▶ The `paste()` function available at `https://stat.ethz.ch/R-manual/R-devel/library/base/html/paste.html`

▶ The `apply()` function available at `https://stat.ethz.ch/R-manual/R-devel/library/base/html/apply.html`

▶ The `XML` package available at `http://cran.r-project.org/web/packages/XML/XML.pdf`

Analyzing and understanding football data

Now that we have obtained and cleaned the data, let's take some time to explore it, gain an understanding of what the different fields mean, and learn how we can use them to create something useful.

Getting ready

If you completed the previous recipe, you should have cleaned and formatted offense and defense datasets in preparation for this recipe.

How to do it...

In order to analyze the data, complete the following steps:

1. The first thing we will do is combine the `offense` and `defense` data frames into a data frame called `combined`. This will get all of our data in one place and make it easier for us to do some exploration:

```
combined <- merge(offense, defense, by.x="Team", by.y="Team")
```

Since some of the offense and defense columns have the same name, we will rename them to avoid confusion later. We'll also get rid of the column from the `defense` data frame that shows the number of games because it is redundant now that we have combined data:

```
colnames(combined)[2] <- "Games"
colnames(combined)[3] <- "OffPPG"
colnames(combined)[4] <- "OffYPG"
colnames(combined)[5] <- "OffPassYPG"
colnames(combined)[6] <- "OffRushYPG"
combined$G.y <- NULL
colnames(combined)[15] <- "DefPPG"
```

```
colnames(combined)[16] <- "DefYPG"
colnames(combined)[17] <- "DefRushYPG"
colnames(combined)[18] <- "DefPassYPG"
```

2. Now, we're ready to start exploring our data! One of the best places to start when exploring data is histograms. Histograms visually show how every column of the data frame is distributed so that you can get a sense of which values are normal, which values are low, and which values are high. First, let's create a histogram of offensive points per game by each team:

```
hist(combined$OffPPG, breaks=10, main="Offensive Points Per
Game", xlab="Offensive PPG",ylab="Number of Teams")
```

The histogram will look like the following diagram:

According to the histogram, most teams score an average of 18 to 28 points per game. There is one team that averages significantly more, and one team that averages significantly less.

The average offensive points scored per game is 23.4, and the standard deviation is 4.36. The highest scoring team averaged 37.9 points per game or 3.32 standard deviations above the mean. The lowest scoring team averaged 15.4 points per game or 1.83 standard deviations below the mean. This is shown through the following commands:

```
mean(combined$OffPP G)
[1] 23.41875
sd(combined$OffPPG)
[1] 4.361373
```

```
max(combined$OffPPG
[1] 37.9
min(combined$OffPPG)
[1] 15.4
```

3. Next, let's see how points allowed per game, a defensive statistic, are distributed:

   ```
   hist(combined$DefPPG, breaks=10, main="Defensive Points Per
   Game", xlab="Defensive PPG",ylab="Number of Teams")
   ```

   This produces the following diagram:

   There is a little less variability here, as most teams allow between 20 and 30 points per game. There are only a few teams with very good defenses that limit the offenses that they face to fewer than 20 points per game on average.

4. Let's do one more histogram on the number of first downs per game, an offensive statistic:

   ```
   hist(combined$"1stD/G", breaks=10, main="Offensive 1st Downs
   Per Game", xlab="1st Downs/Game",ylab="Number of Teams")
   ```

The diagram produced should look like the following:

From this, we can tell that most teams gain between 17 and 20 first downs per game. Again, as in the points per game histogram, there is one team that gets an exceedingly high number of first downs per game. In both cases, offensive points per game and first downs per game, the outlier is the Denver Broncos team.

You can create histograms for any column in your dataset by simply swapping the name of the column from any of the lines of code we just used. Try a few more and see what other insights you find!

5. The next type of chart we will use is the bar chart. These sometimes look similar to the histogram, but we will use bar charts to see how figures for the different teams compare to each other, whereas we binned the values and counted the frequency (number of teams) that fell into each bin in the case of our histograms. Let's start off by creating a bar chart for offensive points per game:

```
ppg <- transform(combined,Team=reorder(Team,combined$OffPPG))

ggplot(ppg,aes(x=Team, y=OffPPG)) +

  geom_bar(stat='identity',color="black",fill="blue") +
coord_flip() + labs(x="Team",y="Avg Points per Game") +

  ggtitle("Avg Points per Game") + theme(plot.title =
element_text(size=18, face="bold"))
```

This produces the following diagram:

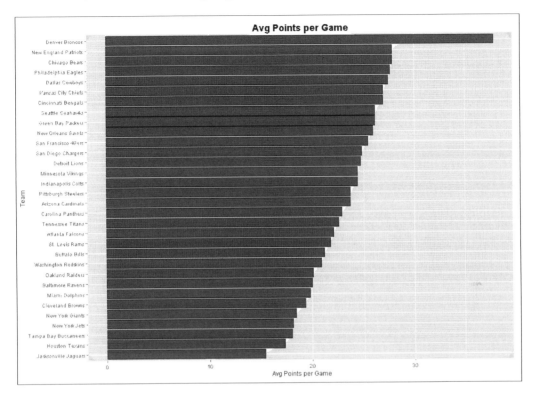

Here, you can see the individual point per game figures visually and in descending order.

6. Next, let's try another bar graph for defense yards allowed per game:

```
ypg <- transform(combined,Team=reorder(Team,-combined$DefYPG))
ggplot(ypg,aes(x=Team, y=DefYPG)) +
  geom_bar(stat='identity',color="black",fill="blue") +
coord_flip() + labs(x="Team",y="Avg Yards Allowed per Game") +
  ggtitle("Avg Yards Allowed per Game") + theme(plot.title =
element_text(size=18, face="bold"))
```

You can refer to the following diagram:

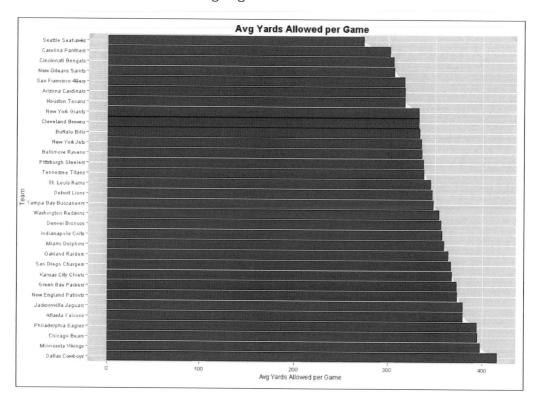

From these charts, we can get a visual sense of what fans saw throughout the season, specifically the incredible offense of the Denver Broncos team and the unstoppable defense of the Seattle Seahawks team, which ultimately led them to a Super Bowl victory against the Broncos.

Try creating bar charts for a few more fields and see what other insights about the teams you can draw.

7. The final type of graph we will use in this section is the scatter plot. These graphs are good at showing relationships and correlations between two different variables visually. For example, let's see how offensive yards and offensive points per game are related:

```
ggplot(combined, aes(x=combined$OffYPG, y=combined$OffPPG)) +
  geom_point(shape=5, size=2) + geom_smooth() +
  labs(x="Yards per Game",y="Points per Game") +
ggtitle("Offense Yards vs. Points per Game") +
  theme(plot.title = element_text(size=18, face="bold"))
```

This produces the following diagram:

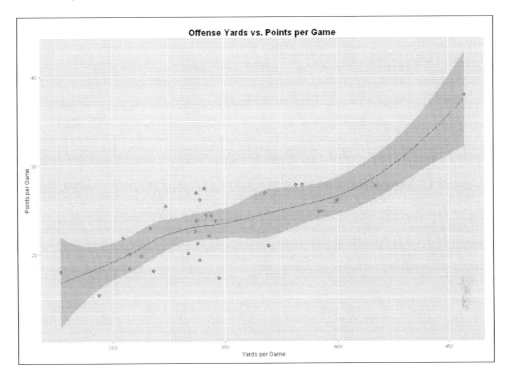

As you can see, these two variables are positively correlated—as yards per game increases, points per game also usually increases. We can calculate the correlation coefficient with the following code:

```
cor(combined$OffYPG,combined$OffPPG) [1] 0.7756408
```

8. Let's look at whether the same is true for defense for yards allowed and points allowed per game. Theoretically, if a defense is able to limit the number of yards an offense gains, it should correlate strongly with the number of points (or lack of points) the offense is able to score:

```
ggplot(combined, aes(x=combined$DefYPG, y=combined$DefPPG)) +
  geom_point(shape=5, size=2) + geom_smooth() +
  labs(x="Yards Allowed per Game",y="Points Alloed per Game")
+ ggtitle("Defense Yards vs. Points per Game") +
  theme(plot.title = element_text(size=18, face="bold"))
```

This produces the following graph:

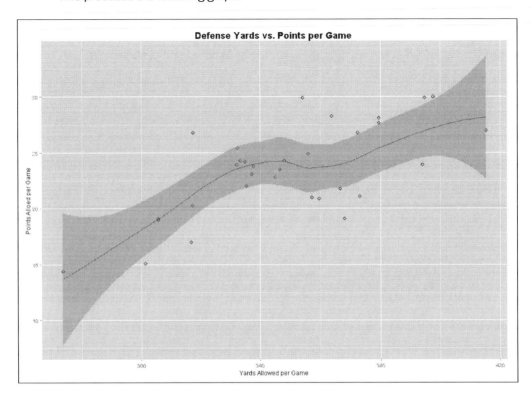

Looking at the scatter plot, there does seem to be some positive correlation here too, although not quite as strong as the previous offense relationship. Let's calculate the correlation for these two variables as well:

```
cor(combined$DefYPG,combined$DefPPG)
```

```
[1] 0.6823588
```

9. Let's try one more correlation. One can postulate that the longer a team is on offense, the more points per game they are likely to score. To test whether this is true, we can scatter plot time of possession and offensive points per game:

```
ggplot(combined, aes(x=combined$TOP, y=combined$OffPPG)) +
    geom_point(shape=5, size=2) + geom_smooth() +
    labs(x="Time of Possession (Seconds)",y="Points per Game") +
ggtitle("Time of Possession vs. Points per Game") +
    theme(plot.title = element_text(size=18, face="bold"))
```

This produces the following graph:

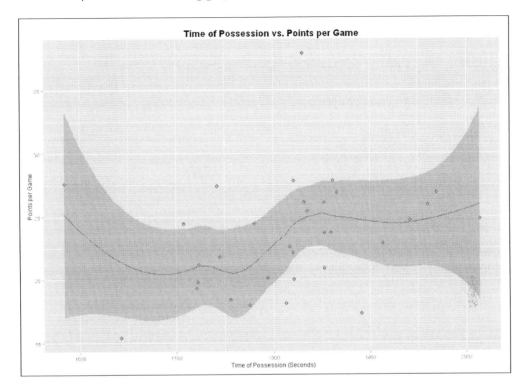

Oddly enough, the correlation between these two variables is not as strong as we might have guessed. Apparently, there are teams at different levels of efficiency, some scoring lots of points in very little time, and others scoring relatively few points over longer periods of time. When we calculate the correlation coefficient for these, we find that the value is much lower:

```
cor(combined$TOP,combined$OffPPG)
```

```
[1] 0.2530245
```

How it works...

When creating histograms in R, an important thing to consider is the number of breaks (columns) you want the histogram to have. Having more breaks gives you a finer level of detail, but having too many defeats the purpose of the histogram, which is to bin values that are close together to compare how often observations occur in a given range of values versus other ranges. In our experience, using 10 bins is usually a good starting point, and then you can adjust it higher or lower as you see fit.

We created the bar charts using the `ggplot2` package. We first arranged the data into the desired order using the `transform` function and then graphed the resulting data frame. With `ggplot2`, you can change just about any feature of the charts that you create, including the outline and fill colors of the bars, how the axes and chart titles look, and much more!

The same is true of the scatter plots we created in this section with `ggplot2`. For example, we changed the plots to be hollow diamonds (`shape=5`), though we could have chosen from a number of different shapes and sizes for our plots.

There's more...

Hadley Wickham, the creator of the `ggplot2` package, has a great reference website that you can use to figure out how to make your charts and plots look exactly like you want them to look. The site can be found at `http://docs.ggplot2.org/current/`.

See also

- ▶ The `ggplot2` package available at `http://docs.ggplot2.org/current/`
- ▶ American football rules available at `http://en.wikipedia.org/wiki/American_football_rules`

Constructing indexes to measure offensive and defensive strength

At this point, we have clean datasets and a decent understanding of our data fields. Now it's time to put the data and knowledge to use! In this section, we will build offensive and defensive indexes out of several of the statistics just analyzed.

Indexes are descriptive statistics that combine information from multiple data fields to give an observer a sense of what is going on without the observer needing to drill down into the components of the index. Sticking with the professional football theme, a quarterback is assigned a passer rating that is designed to communicate his passing ability (relative to other quarterbacks), without someone having to drill down into his completion percentage, yards per completion, touchdowns, and so on.

In this section, we will use the underlying team level statistics to construct indexes for the offensive and defensive strengths of each team. The offense strength index will depend on the teams' passing and rushing strength, and the defense strength index will depend on the ability of the teams to defend against the pass and the rush. This will allow us compare the different aspects of each team's game to other teams and will let us arrive at a winner and a loser in our simulated games later on.

Getting ready

The recipes in this chapter are cumulative. If you completed the previous recipes, you should have everything you need to continue.

How to do it...

Perform the following steps to construct the offensive and defensive strength indexes:

1. The first thing that we will do in this section is calculate an offensive passing strength score. The most useful field we have to inform us about passing strength is the `PassYds/G` (average passing yards per game) field. The higher this number, the stronger the team's passing game:

    ```
    offense$OPassStrength <- max(offense[,5])-offense[,5]

    offense$OPassStrength <- (1-
    (offense$OPassStrength/max(offense$OPassStrength)))*100
    ```

    First, we calculated the difference between each team and the team with the most passing yards per game. Then, we divided the difference by the maximum number to normalize it, subtracted it from one (since higher the difference from the max, the worse the team's passing game will be), and then multiplied it by 100 so that we end up with values between 0 and 100.

     Due to the way we normalized this, the team with the strongest statistic will always get a 100, the team with the weakest statistic will always get a 0. Had we simply divided the team's value by the maximum value, our index would not have this characteristic.

2. Next, we will do the exact same thing for offensive rushing strength. The field we will use to calculate this is `RushYds/G` (average rushing yards per game):

    ```
    offense$ORushStrength <- max(offense[,6])-offense[,6]

    offense$ORushStrength <- (1-
    (offense$ORushStrength/max(offense$ORushStrength)))*100
    ```

3. Let's calculate index values for a couple more fields before aggregating them into a single offensive strength value. For example, let's choose points and yards per game:

    ```
    offense$OPPGStrength <- max(offense[,3])-offense[,3]

    offense$OPPGStrength <- (1-
    (offense$OPPGStrength/max(offense$OPPGStrength)))*100


    offense$OYPGStrength <- max(offense[,4])-offense[,4]
    ```

```
offense$OYPGStrength <- (1-
(offense$OYPGStrength/max(offense$OYPGStrength)))*100
```

```
offense$OffStrength <-
(offense$OPassStrength+offense$ORushStrength+offense$OPPGStren
gth+offense$OYPGStrength)/4
```

In this last line of code, we simply took the average of each of the index values we calculated previously to come up with the offensive strength index.

4. We will now follow the exact same steps for our defense dataset, starting with calculating a passing defense strength index from the number of passing yards allowed per game figures:

    ```
    defense$DPassStrength <- max(defense[,6])-defense[,6]
    ```

    ```
    defense$DPassStrength <-
    defense$DPassStrength/max(defense$DPassStrength)*100
    ```

5. Next, we'll do the same thing with rushing defense strength:

    ```
    defense$DRushStrength <- max(defense[,5])-defense[,5]
    ```

    ```
    defense$DRushStrength <-
    defense$DRushStrength/max(defense$DRushStrength)*100
    ```

6. As with offense, we will calculate indexes using points allowed per game and total yards allowed per game before averaging all four to arrive at an overall defensive strength index:

    ```
    defense$DPPGStrength <- max(defense[,3])-defense[,3]
    ```

    ```
    defense$DPPGStrength <-
    defense$DPPGStrength/max(defense$DPPGStrength)*100
    ```

    ```
    defense$DYPGStrength <- max(defense[,4])-defense[,4]
    ```

    ```
    defense$DYPGStrength <-
    defense$DYPGStrength/max(defense$DYPGStrength)*100
    ```

    ```
    defense$DefStrength <-
    (defense$DPassStrength+defense$DRushStrength+defense$DPPGStren
    gth+defense$DYPGStrength)/4
    ```

One difference to note between the offense and defense calculations is that we are not subtracting from 1 in the second step of each set of formulas. This is because for defense, lower numbers indicate more strength, whereas for offense, it is indicated by higher numbers.

How it works...

As mentioned previously, the purpose of indexes is to simplify and standardize the underlying statistics so that they can easily be interpreted and compared, and this is essentially what we did in this recipe. We boiled down several of the offensive and defensive statistics to a single value for each team.

We kept the examples relatively simple for illustrative purposes, but you can incorporate many more figures into the index values. We also kept the way to aggregate the individual indexes as simple as possible, choosing to just take the average of the four that we calculated. As a more complicated way, you can potentially weigh each of the indexes according to how important you consider them to be. For example, if you wanted to weigh the offensive ability to score the highest, followed by the passing strength, the ability to gain yards, and the rushing strength, respectively, instead of simply dividing by 4, you could assign the weights as follows:

```
offense$OffStrength <- (offense$OPPGStrength * 0.4) +
(offense$OPassStrength * 0.25) + (offense$OYPGStrength * 0.2) +
(offense$ORushStrength * 0.15)
```

This way, the values that you believe to be more important will contribute more toward the overall offensive or defensive index than other values that are relatively not as important, but important enough to be taken into consideration in your calculations.

See also

▶ The index number statistic available at `http://mathworld.wolfram.com/IndexNumber.html`

▶ The passer rating statistic available at `http://en.wikipedia.org/wiki/Passer_rating`

Simulating a single game with outcomes decided by calculations

Now that we have calculated offensive and defensive strength indexes for each team in the league, we can start having teams *play* each other and, using our strength calculations, determine which team *should* win each game. The team that wins will be the stronger team overall, as measured by our recently created indices. We are going to do this by comparing the offensive strength of one team to the defensive strength of another team and vice versa. The general idea is that the team with the largest offense-to-defense difference should be the stronger of the two.

Getting ready

If you successfully calculated the offensive and defensive strengths for each team, you should have everything you need to continue.

How to do it...

Use the following steps to create a single game simulation:

1. Let's start by simulating a single game between two teams. The first thing we will do is designate which two teams will play. We will call one team the home team, and the other, the away team:

   ```
   home_team <- "Chicago Bears"

   away_team <- "New Orleans Saints"
   ```

   You can choose any two teams you want, just make sure you have typed out the full name of each team.

2. Next, we will bring together the offensive and defensive strengths we calculated for these teams earlier in the chapter:

   ```
   off_game <- subset(offense,Team==home_team |
   Team==away_team)[,c(1,15,16,19)]
   ```

   ```
   def_game <- subset(defense,Team==home_team |
   Team==away_team)[,c(1,14,15,18)]
   ```

   ```
   game <- merge(off_game,def_game,by.x="Team",by.y="Team")
   ```

   The first command here selects only the records for the two teams indicated from the `offense` data frame. The second command performs the same task, but for the `defense` data frame. The third command merges the results of the previous two together so that you can look at all their strength scores in one place.

   Here is what the `game` data frame looks like so far:

	Team	OPassStrength	ORushStrength	OffStrength	DPassStrength	DRushStrength	DefStrength
1	Chicago Bears	55.67073	44.12121	53.25710	48.13243	0.00000	15.84545
2	New Orleans Saints	79.93902	17.21212	52.92617	81.23939	64.67532	73.44351

   Notice that the **DRushStrength** value for the **Chicago Bears** team is zero. This means that they had the worst defense against the rush out of all teams in the league.

3. Now that we have the strength figures in one place, let's perform some calculations that will help us determine which team is the stronger of the two and, thus, should win this game. The first thing we will calculate is the difference between the offensive pass strength of the team and the defensive pass strength of the opposing team. This will give us a sense of how effective each team's passing game should be:

```
game$Net_Pass[game$Team==home_team] <-
game$OPassStrength[game$Team==home_team] -
game$DPassStrength[game$Team==away_team]

game$Net_Pass[game$Team==away_team] <-
game$OPassStrength[game$Team==away_team] -
game$DPassStrength[game$Team==home_team]
```

The game data frame should now look like the following screenshot:

	Team	OPassStrength	ORushStrength	OffStrength	DPassStrength	DRushStrength	DefStrength	Net_Pass
1	Chicago Bears	55.67073	44.12121	53.25710	48.13243	0.00000	15.84545	-25.56866
2	New Orleans Saints	79.93902	17.21212	52.92617	81.23939	64.67532	73.44351	31.80660

As you can see from the screenshot, in the **Net_Pass** column, the effectiveness of the **Chicago Bears** team's passing game should be very low due to the **New Orleans Saints** team's ability to defend against the passing game; New Orleans can be expected to pass the ball somewhat effectively against the Bears.

4. Next, we will perform the exact same calculations for the rushing strength of each team and for their total strength:

```
game$Net_Rush[game$Team==home_team] <-
game$ORushStrength[game$Team==home_team] -
game$DRushStrength[game$Team==away_team]

game$Net_Rush[game$Team==away_team] <-
game$ORushStrength[game$Team==away_team] -
game$DRushStrength[game$Team==home_team]

game$Net_Total[game$Team==home_team] <-
game$OffStrength[game$Team==home_team] -
game$DefStrength[game$Team==away_team]

game$Net_Total[game$Team==away_team] <-
game$OffStrength[game$Team==away_team] -
game$DefStrength[game$Team==home_team]
```

The game data frame should now look like the following screenshot:

	Team	OPassStrength	ORushStrength	OffStrength	DPassStrength	DRushStrength	DefStrength	Net_Pass	Net_Rush	Net_Total
1	Chicago Bears	55.67073	44.12121	53.25710	48.13243	0.00000	15.84545	-25.56866	-20.55411	-20.18641
2	New Orleans Saints	79.93902	17.21212	52.92617	81.23939	64.67532	73.44351	31.80660	17.21212	37.08072

The new columns show us that in addition to the **Chicago Bears** team having a disadvantage in passing strength, they also have a disadvantage in rushing strength, and thus a disadvantage overall. So, now it is becoming clear that we should expect the **New Orleans Saints** team to win this game.

5. Since the passing, rushing, and overall strengths were originally calculated from different figures, let's overwrite the values in the Net_Total column with the sum of the three differences. Then, we will write a conditional statement to evaluate the new Net_Total figures and have the program output the results of this virtual game:

```
game$Net_Total <- game$Net_Pass + game$Net_Rush +
game$Net_Total


if(game$Net_Total[game$Team==home_team] >=
game$Net_Total[game$Team==away_team]){
  winner <- home_team
  loser <- away_team
}else{
  winner <- away_team
  loser <- home_team
}


print(paste(winner, "beat", loser))
[1] "New Orleans Saints beat Chicago Bears"
```

How it works...

In this recipe, we used a few more of R's features.

The subset function lets us filter a dataset by defining the values that we want for specific fields. This works very much like a query in the database world, where you specify what data you want to see and what criteria the data should meet. We use this to select only the calculated strengths for the teams we explicitly designated in the off_game and def_game data frames.

Another concept we used in this recipe was the conditional assignment. This let us change values only when certain criteria were met. We were able to do this by embedding the condition in square brackets ([]) after the field we wanted to assign the conditions to. In R, conditional assignments look like this:

```
data_frame$changing_field[condition] <- value_replacing_it
```

The last concept we covered in this recipe was conditional (`if` and `else`) statements. Conditional statements in R work similar to conditional statements in other programming languages, databases, and spreadsheet programs. In R, conditional statements are always structured like this:

```
if(some condition){
    what you want to happen if condition is true
}else{
    what you want to happen if condition is false
}
```

Simulating multiple games with outcomes decided by calculations

It turns out that once we build a way to calculate the outcome of a single game, simulating multiple games doesn't require much more work. In fact, you just need a way to determine a schedule of games in advance, put the code we used in the last section into a loop, and then create a way to keep track of how many games each team has won or lost. This is exactly what we will do in this section.

Getting ready

If you completed the previous recipe, you should already have approximately a third of the code you will need for this section.

How to do it...

Perform the following steps to simulate multiple games using the same logic as in the previous recipe:

1. As mentioned previously, the first thing we will need to do is create a schedule of games to know which teams are going to play each other. There are a few ways to do this, one of which is importing the actual season schedule. For illustrative purposes, we will generate our own schedule, which will be randomly generated and can be as many weeks as we want. For players' health reasons, we are glad that the NFL does not have a 50-game season. We will use the following command:

   ```
   games_per_team <- 50

   for(week in 1:games_per_team){
       home_index <- sample(1:32, 16, replace=F)
       home_teams <- data.frame(HomeTeam=offense[home_index, 1])
   ```

```
      away_teams <- data.frame(AwayTeam=offense[-home_index, 1])



    if(week==1){
       schedule <-
    cbind(Week=week,HomeTeam=home_teams,AwayTeam=away_teams)
      }else{
       temp <-
    cbind(Week=week,HomeTeam=home_teams,AwayTeam=away_teams)
       schedule <- rbind(schedule,temp)
     }
  }
```

This should create a data frame that looks something like the following screenshot. Your games might be different due to the randomness of the sampling.

	Week	HomeTeam	AwayTeam
1	1	San Diego Chargers	Denver Broncos
2	1	Indianapolis Colts	Chicago Bears
3	1	San Francisco 49ers	Philadelphia Eagles
4	1	Tennessee Titans	Dallas Cowboys
5	1	Baltimore Ravens	Cincinnati Bengals
6	1	Detroit Lions	Seattle Seahawks
7	1	New England Patriots	Green Bay Packers
8	1	Minnesota Vikings	Pittsburgh Steelers
9	1	Washington Redskins	Carolina Panthers
10	1	Atlanta Falcons	St. Louis Rams
11	1	Tampa Bay Buccaneers	Buffalo Bills
12	1	New Orleans Saints	Oakland Raiders
13	1	Kansas City Chiefs	Miami Dolphins
14	1	Arizona Cardinals	New York Giants

2. Next, we will create a team record tracker that will track the number of wins and losses for each team:

```
records <- data.frame(Team=offense$Team)

records$Wins <- 0

records$Losses <- 0
```

This will create a data frame that looks like the following:

	Team	Wins	Losses
1	Denver Broncos	0	0
2	Chicago Bears	0	0
3	New England Patriots	0	0
4	Philadelphia Eagles	0	0
5	Dallas Cowboys	0	0
6	Kansas City Chiefs	0	0
7	Cincinnati Bengals	0	0
8	Seattle Seahawks	0	0
9	Green Bay Packers	0	0
10	New Orleans Saints	0	0
11	San Francisco 49ers	0	0
12	San Diego Chargers	0	0
13	Detroit Lions	0	0
14	Minnesota Vikings	0	0

3. Now, we need to have our program play out each of the games in the schedule, and then update the **Wins** and **Losses** columns for the winning and losing teams, respectively. We will accomplish this by taking the code we used in the last section and embedding it into a `for` loop. To help you understand what each piece is doing, we will break the loop up into a few parts:

```
for(i in 1:nrow(schedule)){

    home_team <- schedule[i,2]
    away_team <- schedule[i,3]
    week <- schedule[i,1]
```

This snippet of code begins the `for` loop and tells it to run for as many rows as we have in the `schedule` data frame (that is, the number of games we have scheduled).

Then, it automatically assigns the home team and the away team based on the schedule, and also records the week number.

4. The next part of the loop is where our previous code goes. As we saw earlier in the chapter, this calculates the differences in the pass, rush, and total strengths of a team when compared with their opponent, and then uses these calculations to determine which team wins the game and which team loses:

```
off_game <- subset(offense,Team==home_team |
Team==away_team)[,c(1,15,16,19)]

def_game <- subset(defense,Team==home_team |
Team==away_team)[,c(1,14,15,18)]

game <- merge(off_game,def_game,by.x="Team",by.y="Team")


game$Net_Pass[game$Team==home_team] <-
game$OPassStrength[game$Team==home_team] -
game$DPassStrength[game$Team==away_team]

game$Net_Pass[game$Team==away_team] <-
game$OPassStrength[game$Team==away_team] -
game$DPassStrength[game$Team==home_team]


game$Net_Rush[game$Team==home_team] <-
game$ORushStrength[game$Team==home_team] -
game$DRushStrength[game$Team==away_team]

game$Net_Rush[game$Team==away_team] <-
game$ORushStrength[game$Team==away_team] -
game$DRushStrength[game$Team==home_team]


game$Net_Total[game$Team==home_team] <-
game$OffStrength[game$Team==home_team] -
game$DefStrength[game$Team==away_team]

game$Net_Total[game$Team==away_team] <-
game$OffStrength[game$Team==away_team] -
game$DefStrength[game$Team==home_team]

game$Net_Total <- game$Net_Pass + game$Net_Rush +
game$Net_Total


if(game$Net_Total[game$Team==home_team] >=
game$Net_Total[game$Team==away_team]){
    winner <- home_team
    loser <- away_team
}else{
    winner <- away_team
    loser <- home_team
}
```

5. The next bit of code records the results of every game, and then updates the win/loss records and prints out the results of each game, before finally closing our `for` loop:

```
if(i==1){
    winnerdf <- data.frame(Winner=winner)
    loserdf <- data.frame(Loser=loser)
    results <- cbind(winnerdf,loserdf)
}else{
    winnerdf <- data.frame(Winner=winner)
    loserdf <- data.frame(Loser=loser)
    temp <- cbind(winnerdf,loserdf)
    results <- rbind(results,temp)
}


records$Wins[records$Team==winner] <-
as.numeric(records$Wins[records$Team==winner]) + 1
    records$Losses[records$Team==loser] <-
as.numeric(records$Losses[records$Team==loser]) + 1


    print(paste("Week", week,":", winner, "beat", loser))
}
[1] "Week 1 : Denver Broncos beat San Diego Chargers"
[1] "Week 1 : Indianapolis Colts beat Chicago Bears"
[1] "Week 1 : San Francisco 49ers beat Philadelphia Eagles"
[1] "Week 1 : Tennessee Titans beat Dallas Cowboys"
[1] "Week 1 : Cincinnati Bengals beat Baltimore Ravens"
[1] "Week 1 : Seattle Seahawks beat Detroit Lions"
[1] "Week 1 : Green Bay Packers beat New England Patriots"
[1] "Week 1 : Pittsburgh Steelers beat Minnesota Vikings"
```

The results data frame this generates should look something like this:

	Winner	Loser
1	Denver Broncos	San Diego Chargers
2	Indianapolis Colts	Chicago Bears
3	San Francisco 49ers	Philadelphia Eagles
4	Tennessee Titans	Dallas Cowboys
5	Cincinnati Bengals	Baltimore Ravens
6	Seattle Seahawks	Detroit Lions
7	Green Bay Packers	New England Patriots
8	Pittsburgh Steelers	Minnesota Vikings
9	Carolina Panthers	Washington Redskins
10	St. Louis Rams	Atlanta Falcons
11	Buffalo Bills	Tampa Bay Buccaneers
12	New Orleans Saints	Oakland Raiders
13	Kansas City Chiefs	Miami Dolphins

6. Finally, we will sort our records by the number of wins a team has so that we can easily see which teams had the best records:

```
records <- records[order(-records$Wins),]
```

Here is what the sorted data frame looks like:

	row.names	Team	Wins	Losses
1	8	Seattle Seahawks	50	0
2	1	Denver Broncos	49	1
3	10	New Orleans Saints	47	3
4	13	Detroit Lions	45	5
5	7	Cincinnati Bengals	44	6
6	4	Philadelphia Eagles	43	7
7	18	Carolina Panthers	43	7
8	11	San Francisco 49ers	42	8
9	16	Arizona Cardinals	35	15
10	12	San Diego Chargers	33	17
11	22	Buffalo Bills	32	18
12	9	Green Bay Packers	31	19
13	31	Houston Texans	31	19

Let's briefly compare this with the results from the actual 2013 season to see how we performed. Here are the top 10 teams based on their actual win/loss records:

Team	Wins	Losses
Denver Broncos	13	3
Seattle Seahawks	13	3
New England Patriots	12	4
Carolina Panthers	12	4
San Francisco 49ers	12	4
Cincinnati Bengals	11	5
Indianapolis Colts	11	5
Kansas City Chiefs	11	5
New Orleans Saints	11	5
Philadelphia Eagles	10	6

We can see that 7 out of 10 teams in our top 10 list were also in the actual top 10. This tells us that we did a reasonable job with our simulation, but there is always room for improvement!

How it works...

In this recipe, we used the `sample` function of R to generate a randomized schedule for the number of weeks we wanted to play out in our simulation, as follows:

```
home_index <- sample(1:32, 16, replace=F)
```

The preceding command basically takes a random sample of 16 from a range of 32 numbers, without replacement. We then simply make the team numbers select the home teams for the week, and the teams left over become the away teams for the week. We repeat this for as many weeks as we designate, and this is how we generated the schedule.

We also use a `for` loop to play out each game in our schedule, determining a winner and a loser for each along the way. In R, the basic format for a `for` loop is as follows:

```
for (i in times-you-want-to-loop){
    do what you want to repeat
}
```

As you saw, you can embed anything else you want inside the `for` loop, and it will repeat it the number of times you tell it to. In this recipe, we did this with conditional statements several times.

There's more...

Throughout this chapter, we used R's flexibility as a calculator, chart generator, and programming language to complete a project, where we ended up with a simulation engine that can acquire football statistics for any season from the last decade or so, calculate the strengths of each team for the season, play teams against each other, and determine the relative statistical strengths and weaknesses of each team.

So, where do we go from here? Well, now that you have the basics down, you can pursue a few different avenues on your own, each of which will continue to sharpen the skills we used in this chapter.

One of these avenues is trying to improve upon the strength index calculations. You can try including different fields in the calculation, try to add a weighting scheme to the different inputs, or try a different formula altogether. A key part of data science is experimentation and iteration, so trying several approaches and recording the quality of the results will get you a good process to continue down this particular avenue.

Another avenue you can pursue is trying to make the simulation closer to real life. Instead of randomly generating a schedule, you can use the actual schedules that were used in each season. You can also try introducing an element of chance into the simulation, for example, when the strengths indicate that it would have been a close game. Again, experimentation and iteration will be great for this avenue as well.

If you want to get more granular with the model, you can try incorporating player statistics, which can help you predict the future performance of teams, and even factor player injuries and the impact they can have on the team into your model.

Yet another fun avenue would be to pull in teams from different seasons and seeing how they stack up against each other. How will the current Super Bowl champion Seattle Seahawks fare against the former Super Bowl champions New England Patriots or New York Giants? You can generate your own answer to what was truly the best football team of the last decade!

4

Modeling Stock Market Data (R)

In this chapter, we will cover:

- ▸ Acquiring stock market data
- ▸ Summarizing the data
- ▸ Cleaning and exploring the data
- ▸ Generating relative valuations
- ▸ Screening stocks and analyzing historical prices

Introduction

This chapter will walk you through a financial analysis project where you will analyze stock market data, determine whether stocks are over- or under-valued, use this information to identify a list of target stocks that may make good investments, and visually analyze the price histories of the target stocks.

We must caution that the goal of this chapter is not to make you an expert in stock market analysis or to make you rich. Quants on Wall Street study engineering models that perform significantly more sophisticated operations than those we will touch upon here. Entire books have been written on stock market models and financial engineering, but we only have a single chapter to dedicate to this topic. So, given the time and format constraints, the goals of this chapter will be:

- ▸ To get a basic understanding of the data that we will work with
- ▸ To find useful and interesting ways to analyze and model this data

▶ To learn how to leverage data science tools and techniques to perform the types of analytical tasks we need to perform on the data

The data we will use for this chapter consists of current data for stocks tracked by the website `finviz.com` and daily histories of stock prices obtained from Yahoo! Finance.

As in previous chapters, the tool we will rely on most heavily for this project will be the R statistical programming language. As you've probably noticed by now, R has strong packages available that can assist us in the needed analytical tasks; we will be leveraging some of these packages in this chapter. Additionally, the recipes in this chapter will roughly follow the data science pipeline, which we will adapt to the type of data we are working with and the types of analysis we would like to conduct on the data.

Requirements

For this chapter, you will need a computer with access to the Internet. You will also need to have R installed and the following packages installed and loaded:

```
install.packages("XML")
install.packages("ggplot2")
install.packages("plyr")
install.packages("reshape2")
install.packages("zoo")


library(XML)
library(ggplot2)
library(plyr)
library(reshape2)
library(zoo)
```

The XML package will assist us with acquiring data from the Internet, ggplot2 will let us create beautiful graphs and visualizations from our data, plyr will help us with summarizing our data, and the zoo package will allow us to calculate moving averages.

You will also want to set a working directory where some of the charts that we generate will be saved:

```
setwd("path/where/you/want/to save/charts")
```

Acquiring stock market data

If you look on the Internet for stock market data, you will quickly find yourself inundated with sources providing stock quotes and financial data. An important but often overlooked factor when acquiring data is the efficiency of getting the data. All else being equal, you don't want to spend hours piecing together a dataset that you could have acquired in far less time. Taking this into consideration, we will try to obtain the largest amount of data from the least number of sources. This not only helps to keep the data as consistent as possible, but it also improves the repeatability of the analysis and the reproducibility of the results.

How to do it...

The first piece of data we want to obtain is a snapshot of the stocks we want to analyze. One of the best ways to do this is to download data from one of the many stock screener applications that exist. Our favorite screener to download stock data from belongs to http://finviz.com.

Let's acquire the stock market data we will use for this chapter with the help of the following steps:

1. First, let's pull up FINVIZ.com's stock screener available at http://finviz.com/screener.ashx:

As you can see, the site has multiple fields that can be filtered. If you click on the **All** tab, you can see all of fields that can be displayed.

2. For this project, we want to export all the fields for all the companies in the screener. You can either customize the screener by checking 69 checkboxes, as of the time of writing, or you can use the following URL to make all the fields show up automatically:

```
http://finviz.com/screener.ashx?v=152&c=
0,1,2,3,4,5,6,7,8,9,10,11,12,13,14,15,16,17,18,19,20,21,22,23,2
4,25,26,27,28,29,30,31,32,33,34,35,36,37,38,39,40,41,42,43,44,4
5,46,47,48,49,50,51,52,53,54,55,56,57,58,59,60,61,62,63,64,65,
66,67,68
```

You should now see the screener with all the available fields.

3. If you scroll all the way to the bottom right of the screen, there should be an **export** link. Click on this link and save the CSV file as `finviz.csv`.

4. Finally, we will launch RStudio, read the `finviz.csv` file from the path where we saved it, and assign it to a data frame, as follows:

```
finviz <- read.csv("path/finviz.csv")
```

 In data analysis, it is always better for each step that is performed to be in code instead of as a series of point-and-click actions that require human intervention. This way, it is much easier and faster to reproduce your results.

5. After going through steps 1 to 4 for the first time (and some clever reading of URLs from our browser), we can replace the previous lines of code with the following two commands:

```
url_to_open <-
'http://finviz.com/export.ashx?v=152&c=0,1,2,3,4,5,6,7,8,9,10,
11,12,13,14,15,16,17,18,19,20,21,22,23,24,25,26,27,28,29,30,31
,32,33,34,35,36,37,38,39,40,41,42,43,44,45,46,47,48,49,50,51,5
2,53,54,55,56,57,58,59,60,61,62,63,64,65,66,67,68'

finviz <- read.csv(url(url_to_open))
```

 Note the structure of the URL in step 2; it contains a comma-separated list of the checkboxes we wish to select. You can programmatically generate this URL to easily select whichever combination of companies' data you want to download.

If you want to avoid typing the numbers 0 through 68, you can use a combination of the `sprintf` and `paste` commands to accomplish the same thing:

```
url_to_open <-
sprintf("http://finviz.com/export.ashx?v=152&c=%s",
paste(0:68, collapse = ","))
```

Summarizing the data

Now that we have acquired our stock data, let's use a couple of commands to find out what fields our data contains and get some useful information about the values contained in these fields.

Getting ready

You will need the data downloaded from the previous recipe to begin the summary.

How to do it...

The following steps will walk you through a quick summarization of the data:

1. Take a look at the fields you imported using the following command:

    ```
    > head(finviz)
    ```

    This command will show you the first six rows of your data, as shown in the following snippet, so that you can see what fields are in your data and also examples of possible values for the fields. In this example, we can also see that there is some missing data, identified by NA:

    ```
      No. Ticker                               Company
    Sector
    1   1     A              Agilent Technologies Inc.
    Healthcare
    2   2    AA                            Alcoa, Inc. Basic
    Materials
    3   3   AADR    WCM/BNY Mellon Focused Growth ADR ETF
    Financial
    4   4   AAIT    iShares MSCI AC Asia Information Tech
    Financial
    5   5    AAL              American Airlines Group Inc.
    Services
    6   6   AAMC Altisource Asset Management Corporation
    Financial
                              Industry Country Market.Cap     P.E
    Forward.P.E  PEG   P.S
    1 Medical Laboratories & Research       USA    19505.83 28.06
    16.52 2.92 2.88
    2                          Aluminum     USA    10817.70 40.44
    24.72 1.91 0.46
    3              Exchange Traded Fund     USA          NA     NA
    NA    NA    NA
    ```

```
4                 Exchange Traded Fund    USA        NA      NA
NA    NA    NA

5                     Major Airlines      USA     9861.60 25.97
8.55    NA 0.39

6                 Asset Management       USA      2406.40    NA
NA    NA    NA

...
```

2. The next command will return a summary of each field. For numeric fields, it will tell you what the min, max, mean, median, and quartiles are, and for character fields, it will tell you which appear most often:

```
> summary(finviz)
No.              Ticker                     Company
 Min.    :    1   A        :    1   Banco Bradesco S.A.      :    2
 1st Qu.:1677     AA       :    1   Banco Santander-Chile    :    2
 Median :3354     AADR     :    1   Berkshire Hathaway Inc.  :    2
 Mean   :3354     AAIT     :    1   Embotelladora Andina S.A.:    2
 3rd Qu.:5030     AAL      :    1   First Bancorp            :    2
 Max.   :6706     AAMC     :    1   Gray Television Inc.     :    2
                  (Other) :6700    (Other)                  :6694

            Sector                    Industry
Country
 Financial      :2915   Exchange Traded Fund   :1382   USA
:5863
 Technology     : 867   Closed-End Fund - Debt : 306   Canada
: 175
 Services       : 864   Biotechnology          : 217   China
: 174
 Basic Materials: 608   Independent Oil & Gas  : 112   Israel
:  68
 Healthcare     : 578   Application Software   : 109   United
Kingdom:  44
 Consumer Goods : 375   Closed-End Fund - Equity: 109
Bermuda         :  42
 (Other)        : 499   (Other)                :4471
(Other)         : 340

....
```

How it works...

Now that we've taken an initial glance at the data, it's important to take some time out to identify the fields that will be most important to us, and understand what these fields mean.

The first few fields contain identifying information about the company.

The ticker (sometimes also called the symbol) is the identifier for the stock of a company. No two companies will have the exact same ticker symbol. So AA is always Alcoa, AAPL is always Apple, and so on.

Next, we have the company name, sector, industry, and home country of the company. The sector and industry details serve as ways to classify stocks to inform us of each company's primary line of business; sector is more general (higher level), and industry is more specific (lower level). For example, Apple Inc. (AAPL) is in the Consumer Goods sector and primarily produces consumer goods in the Electronic Equipment industry.

There's more...

Once we get past these fields, most of the other fields in our dataset are numeric. Let's define some of the most important ones:

- ▶ **Price**: This indicates the ongoing dollar value to purchase one share of a company's stock.

- ▶ **Volume**: This indicates the most recent number of shares of the stock transacted in a day.

- ▶ **Shares Outstanding**: This is the total number of stock shares the company has issued.

- ▶ **P/E**: The Price to Earnings ratio is the price of the company's stock divided by the company's earnings per share outstanding.

- ▶ **PEG**: The P/E Growth ratio is the company's P/E ratio divided by its annual growth rate, and it gives you a sense of the valuation of the company's earnings relative to its growth.

- ▶ **EPS growth next year**: This is the expected rate at which the company's earnings per share will grow in the next year.

- ▶ **Total Debt/Equity**: The total debt to equity is used as a measure of financial health calculated by dividing the dollar value of the company's total debt with the equity in the company. This gives you a sense of how the company has been financing its growth and operations. Debt is more risky than equity, so a high ratio will be cause for concern.

▶ **Beta**: This is a measure of the stock's volatility (swings in its price) relative to the overall stock market. A beta of 1 means the stock is as volatile as the market. A beta more than 1 means it's more volatile, while a beta less than 1 means it's less volatile.

▶ **RSI**: The Relative Strength Index is a metric based on stock price activity, which uses the number of days a stock has closed higher than its opening price and the number of days a stock has closed lower than its opening price within the last two weeks to determine a score between 0 and 100. A higher index value indicates that the stock might be overvalued, and therefore, the price might drop soon; a lower value indicates that the stock might be undervalued, so the price might rise soon.

If you want to know the definitions of some of the other fields, `http://investopedia.com` is a great place to find definitions of financial and investment terms.

Cleaning and exploring the data

Now that we've acquired the data and learned a little about what the fields mean, the next step is to clean up the data and conduct some exploratory analysis.

Getting ready

Make sure you have the packages mentioned at the beginning of the chapter installed and you have successfully imported the FINVIZ data into R using the steps in the previous sections.

How to do it...

To clean and explore the data, closely follow the ensuing instructions:

1. Imported numeric data often contains special characters such as percentage signs, dollar signs, commas, and so on. This causes R to think that the field is a character field instead of a numeric field. For example, our FINVIZ dataset contains numerous values with percentage signs that must be removed. To do this, we will create a `clean_numeric` function that will strip away any unwanted characters using the `gsub` command. We will create this function once and then use it multiple times throughout the chapter:

```
clean_numeric <- function(s){
  s <- gsub("%|\\$|,|\\)|\\(", "", s)
  s <- as.numeric(s)
}
```

2. Next, we will apply this function to the numeric fields in our `finviz` data frame:

```
finviz <- cbind(finviz[,1:6],apply(finviz[,7:68], 2,
clean_numeric))
```

3. If you look at the data again, all the pesky percentage signs will be gone, and the fields will all be numeric.

 In this command, and throughout the rest of this chapter, there will be many instances where we reference columns by their column number. If the number of columns changes for some reason, the numbers referenced will need to be adjusted accordingly.

4. Now we are ready to really start exploring our data! The first thing to do is take a look at how the prices are distributed in order to get a visual sense of what is a high stock price, what is a low stock price, and where the prices of most stocks fall:

```
hist(finviz$Price, breaks=100, main="Price Distribution",
xlab="Price")
```

You will get the following graph as output:

Here, we encounter our first problem. Outlier stocks with very high prices cause R to scale the x axis of the histogram in such a way as to make the graph useless. We simply cannot see what the distribution for the more normally priced stocks looks like. This is a very common issue when first histogramming data.

5. Let's put a cap on the x axis of $150 and see what that produces for us:

    ```
    hist(finviz$Price[finviz$Price<150], breaks=100, main="Price
    Distribution", xlab="Price")
    ```

    You will get the following graph as output:

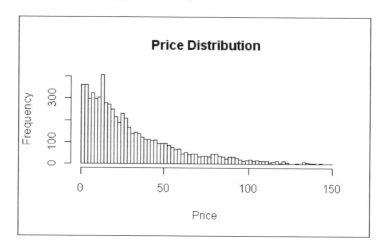

    This is much better! It shows that the majority of stocks in our dataset are priced under $50. So, in absolute terms, a stock that was priced at $100 would be considered expensive.

6. But of course, things aren't so simple. Perhaps different sectors and industries have different price levels. So, theoretically, a $100 stock might be cheap if all the other stocks in its industry are priced in the $120 to $150 range. Let's get the average prices by sector and see how they compare. Note that we are not excluding any stocks:

    ```
    sector_avg_prices <-
    aggregate(Price~Sector,data=finviz,FUN="mean")

    colnames(sector_avg_prices)[2] <- "Sector_Avg_Price"


    ggplot(sector_avg_prices, aes(x=Sector, y=Sector_Avg_Price,
    fill=Sector)) +
      geom_bar(stat="identity") + ggtitle("Sector Avg Prices") +
      theme(axis.text.x = element_text(angle = 90, hjust = 1))
    ```

You will get the following graph as output:

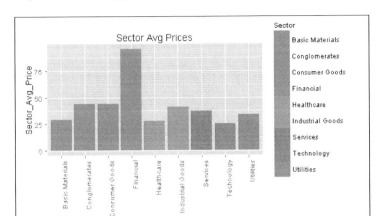

This is interesting. Stocks in the financial sector seem to have a significantly higher average price than stocks in other sectors. I'm willing to bet that this is due to some of the outliers that messed up our distribution earlier.

7. Let's get to the bottom of this! Let's find out which industries and companies are responsible for making the average price of the financial sector so much higher than all the others.

First, we create a summary of the average prices by industry:

```
industry_avg_prices <-
aggregate(Price~Sector+Industry,data=finviz,FUN="mean")
```

```
industry_avg_prices <-
industry_avg_prices[order(industry_avg_prices$Sector,industry_
avg_prices$Industry),]
```

```
colnames(industry_avg_prices)[3] <- "Industry_Avg_Price"
```

Then, we isolate the industries in the financial sector:

```
industry_chart <-
subset(industry_avg_prices,Sector=="Financial")
```

Finally, we create a chart showing the average price of each industry in the financial sector:

```
ggplot(industry_chart, aes(x=Industry, y=Industry_Avg_Price,
fill=Industry)) +
  geom_bar(stat="identity") + theme(legend.position="none") +
ggtitle("Industry Avg Prices") +
  theme(axis.text.x = element_text(angle = 90, hjust = 1))
```

You will get the following graph as output:

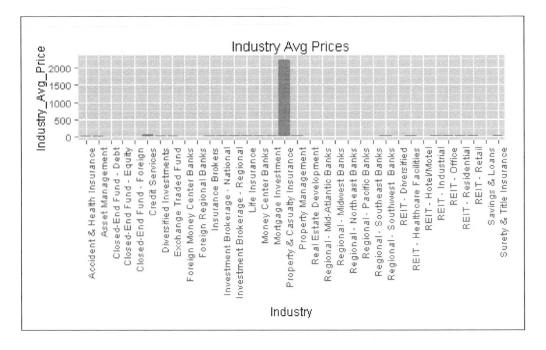

From this graph, it looks like the **Property & Casualty Insurance** industry is the main culprit that is driving the average prices up.

8. Next, we will drill down further into the **Property & Casualty Insurance** industry to identify which companies are the outliers:

```
company_chart <- subset(finviz,Industry=="Property & Casualty
Insurance")
```

```
ggplot(company_chart, aes(x=Company, y=Price, fill=Company)) +
  geom_bar(stat="identity") + theme(legend.position="none") +
  ggtitle("Company Avg Prices") +
  theme(axis.text.x = element_text(angle = 90, hjust = 1))
```

You will get the following graph as output:

It's hard to see because there are so many companies, but if you zoom in on the graph, it is clear that the outlier company is Berkshire Hathaway, where the stock price is currently over $172,000 per share.

9. Since their stock price is so extreme, let's remove them from our dataset and then re-average the sectors so that we have a more realistic average price for the financial sector:

```
finviz <- subset(finviz, Ticker!="BRK-A")

sector_avg_prices <-
aggregate(Price~Sector,data=finviz,FUN="mean")

colnames(sector_avg_prices)[2] <- "Sector_Avg_Price"


ggplot(sector_avg_prices, aes(x=Sector, y=Sector_Avg_Price,
fill=Sector)) +

  geom_bar(stat="identity") + ggtitle("Sector Avg Prices") +

  theme(axis.text.x = element_text(angle = 90, hjust = 1))
```

You will get the following graph as output:

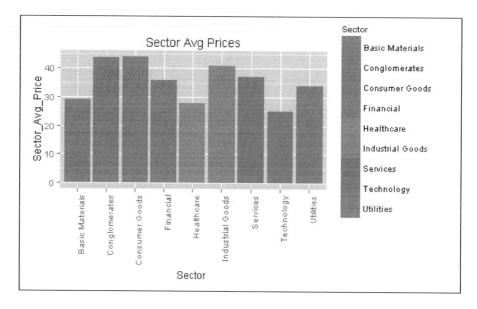

Now, our averages look much better and we have a decent basis to compare stock prices to their industry and sector averages.

How it works...

In this section, we used the `aggregate` command to summarize our data. Here's a reminder of the code we used:

```
sector_avg_prices <- aggregate(Price~Sector,data=finviz,FUN="mean")
```

An alternative way to do this is with the `ddply` command that is part of the `plyr` package:

```
sector_avg_prices <- ddply(finviz, "Sector", summarise,
Price=mean(Price, na.rm=TRUE))
```

Wherever you see the `aggregate` command used in this chapter, feel free to challenge yourself by also trying to summarize the data, using `ddply`.

See also

▶ The `gsub` command at `http://stat.ethz.ch/R-manual/R-devel/library/base/html/grep.html`

▶ The `cbind` command at `http://stat.ethz.ch/R-manual/R-devel/library/base/html/cbind.html`

▶ The plyr documentation at `http://cran.r-project.org/web/packages/plyr/plyr.pdf`

▶ The `aggregate` command at `http://stat.ethz.ch/R-manual/R-devel/library/stats/html/aggregate.html`

Generating relative valuations

One of the most interesting things that you can do with stock market data is come up with a valuation model. The ultimate goal is to arrive at a decision about whether the stock might be overvalued or undervalued. There are two main ways to do this. Intrinsic valuation is generally more time consuming because it involves digging into the financial statements of a company to arrive at a valuation decision. The alternative method is relative valuation, which will quickly provide a sense of how the stock is valued but does not take into account a comprehensive set of factors. The basic idea is that it compares a stock's price and valuation ratios to similar stocks to arrive at a conclusion. In this section, we will value stocks using the simpler relative valuation method.

Getting ready

This recipe requires the data downloaded and cleaned in the previous recipes.

How to do it...

We will essentially do three major things in this section. First, we calculate sector averages for fields that we can use in our relative valuation efforts. Then, we do the same at the industry level. Finally, we compare the stocks' statistics to the averages to arrive at an index value for each stock that indicates whether it might be undervalued. The following steps will guide you:

1. In order to calculate averages in multiple columns in R, we first need to melt the data. This will make every column after **Sector** a row and then display its value, essentially making the data long instead of wide. Take a look at the following screenshots for the different steps in this recipe to better understand how the data changes shape. It goes from being wide to long, and then back to wide again, but in summary form.

Sector	Industry	Country	Market.Cap	P.E	Forward.P.E	PEG	P.S	P.B	P.Cash
Healthcare	Medical Laboratories & Research	USA	19823.59	28.52	16.78	2.97	2.92	3.75	7.41
Basic Materials	Aluminum	USA	12062.38	NA	19.33	NA	0.52	1.15	8.39
Financial	Exchange Traded Fund	USA	NA	NA	NA	NA	NA	NA	NA
Financial	Exchange Traded Fund	USA	NA	NA	NA	NA	NA	NA	NA
Services	Major Airlines	USA	11645.76	30.67	6.61	0.87	0.46	NA	1.72
Financial	Asset Management	USA	2348.00	NA	NA	NA	78.27	671.14	23.00
Financial	Life Insurance	USA	83.71	8.73	NA	NA	0.52	0.86	2.24
Services	Rental & Leasing Services	USA	2297.49	17.15	15.81	2.34	1.02	1.85	7.43
Technology	Semiconductor - Integrated Circuits	USA	159.82	NA	13.24	NA	2.17	NA	21.89
Industrial Goods	General Building Materials	USA	1035.39	31.31	24.94	3.13	3.18	6.39	47.28
Services	Auto Parts Stores	USA	9090.47	22.56	15.17	1.46	1.42	6.19	16.02
Consumer Goods	Electronic Equipment	USA	400222.89	13.29	11.60	0.68	2.76	3.70	11.80
Financial	REIT - Office	USA	1296.44	651.20	95.76	132.90	5.11	1.99	19.73
Basic Materials	Gold	Canada	99.68	NA	NA	NA	332.28	2.27	6.83
Basic Materials	Oil & Gas Drilling & Exploration	Canada	520.70	NA	NA	NA	2.19	0.53	NA
Services	Air Services, Other	USA	789.65	7.06	8.05	3.07	0.48	8.62	2.70
Financial	Exchange Traded Fund	USA	NA	NA	NA	NA	NA	NA	NA
Financial	Asset Management	USA	2176.37	17.35	13.70	2.17	14.53	1.53	NA
Healthcare	Diagnostic Substances	USA	857.43	50.66	41.31	2.89	4.77	4.59	8.41
Industrial Goods	Industrial Equipment & Components	Switzerland	58963.99	20.54	15.88	1.77	1.42	3.35	12.61
Healthcare	Drug Manufacturers - Major	USA	81300.48	19.67	14.29	1.47	4.33	22.77	8.47
Services	Drugs Wholesale	USA	15598.96	43.42	15.76	3.13	0.16	6.94	44.89
Financial	Regional - Mid-Atlantic Banks	USA	480.18	26.65	10.99	3.33	3.80	1.66	1.69
Services	Education & Training Services	USA	91.80	NA	NA	NA	0.61	NA	1.71
Services	Business Services	USA	2150.47	93.64	41.22	5.70	4.41	6.95	27.61
Services	Trucking	USA	828.76	54.47	12.45	5.45	0.36	1.59	5.87
Services	Auto Dealerships	USA	1469.79	14.83	10.95	0.95	0.28	3.12	1130.61

We will use the following command to perform this action:

```
sector_avg <- melt(finviz, id="Sector")
```

2. Next, we need to filter so that the data frame contains only the fields we want
    to average:

```
sector_avg <-
subset(sector_avg,variable%in%c("Price","P.E","PEG","P.S","P.B"))
```

Now your `sector_avg` data frame should look like this:

Sector	variable	value
Healthcare	P.E	28.52
Services	P.E	30.67
Financial	P.E	8.73
Services	P.E	17.15
Industrial Goods	P.E	31.31
Services	P.E	22.56
Consumer Goods	P.E	13.29
Financial	P.E	651.2
Services	P.E	7.06
Financial	P.E	17.35
Healthcare	P.E	50.66
Industrial Goods	P.E	20.54
Healthcare	P.E	19.67
Services	P.E	43.42
Financial	P.E	26.65

Each column heading (variable) is now listed vertically alongside its value. This allows
us to do some grouping later to get the averages for each variable.

3. Not all stocks in our original dataset had all of these values; where the values were
    null, we wanted to remove the records. We also wanted to make sure all of our values
    are numeric:

```
sector_avg <- (na.omit(sector_avg))
```

```
sector_avg$value <- as.numeric(sector_avg$value)
```

4. The next step is to cast the data to make it wide again. This will produce a column for each of the fields we filtered, and will now contain the average by sector. We will also rename the columns so that we know they are sector averages:

```
sector_avg <- dcast(sector_avg, Sector~variable, mean)

colnames(sector_avg)[2:6] <-
c("SAvgPE","SAvgPEG","SAvgPS","SAvgPB","SAvgPrice")
```

You will get the following plot as output:

	Sector	SAvgPE	SAvgPEG	SAvgPS	SAvgPB	SAvgPrice
1	Basic Materials	42.87945	5.390194	35.677311	10.203838	29.22257
2	Conglomerates	20.79571	1.045000	1.532000	58.426316	40.11000
3	Consumer Goods	30.29197	3.446652	1.380000	4.712809	42.40154
4	Financial	32.88929	5.403305	12.335628	4.465120	35.38289
5	Healthcare	38.44733	12.175091	184.600614	9.349106	27.94912
6	Industrial Goods	32.73892	3.314206	1.856246	3.765014	40.78930
7	Services	44.43990	3.927596	1.992289	33.536609	36.45865
8	Technology	59.85766	4.749591	9.386424	4.697576	24.87183
9	Utilities	27.20184	97.133068	7.979917	2.030339	34.01273

5. We will now do the exact same thing, but at the industry level:

```
industry_avg <- melt(finviz, id=c("Sector","Industry"))

industry_avg <- subset(industry_avg,variable %in%
c("Price","P.E","PEG","P.S","P.B"))

industry_avg <- (na.omit(industry_avg))

industry_avg$value <- as.numeric(industry_avg$value)

industry_avg <- dcast(industry_avg, Sector+Industry~variable,
mean)

industry_avg <- (na.omit(industry_avg))

colnames(industry_avg)[3:7] <-
c("IAvgPE","IAvgPEG","IAvgPS","IAvgPB","IAvgPrice")
```

6. We will now add the sector and industry average columns to our original `finviz` dataset:

```
finviz <- merge(finviz, sector_avg, by.x="Sector",
by.y="Sector")

finviz <- merge(finviz, industry_avg,
by.x=c("Sector","Industry"), by.y=c("Sector","Industry"))
```

You might have noticed that the number of records in the `finviz` data frame decreased when we executed the last line of code. It removed all stock that didn't have an industry average from the dataset. This is fine since the overall goal is to narrow down the list of stocks, and we wouldn't have had sufficient information to generate a valuation for these stocks anyway.

7. Now, it's time to put these new fields to use. First, we will add 10 placeholder fields that contain all 0s. These will be used to track whether a stock is undervalued, based on being lower than the sector or industry average:

```
finviz$SPEUnder <- 0
finviz$SPEGUnder <- 0
finviz$SPSUnder <- 0
finviz$SPBUnder <- 0
finviz$SPriceUnder <- 0
finviz$IPEUnder <- 0
finviz$IPEGUnder <- 0
finviz$IPSUnder <- 0
finviz$IPBUnder <- 0
finviz$IPriceUnder <- 0
```

8. Next, we will replace the 0s with 1s wherever the respective value for the stock is less than the average to indicate that these stocks might be undervalued based on that metric:

```
finviz$SPEUnder[finviz$P.E<finviz$SAvgPE] <- 1
finviz$SPEGUnder[finviz$PEG<finviz$SAvgPEG] <- 1
finviz$SPSUnder[finviz$P.S<finviz$SAvgPS] <- 1
finviz$SPBUnder[finviz$P.B<finviz$SAvgPB] <- 1
finviz$SPriceUnder[finviz$Price<finviz$SAvgPrice] <- 1
finviz$IPEUnder[finviz$P.E<finviz$IAvgPE] <- 1
finviz$IPEGUnder[finviz$PEG<finviz$IAvgPEG] <- 1
finviz$IPSUnder[finviz$P.S<finviz$IAvgPS] <- 1
finviz$IPBUnder[finviz$P.B<finviz$IAvgPB] <- 1
finviz$IPriceUnder[finviz$Price<finviz$IAvgPrice] <- 1
```

9. Finally, we will sum these 10 columns to create a new column with the index value telling you, on a scale of 1 to 10, how undervalued the stock is based on the different dimensions that were considered:

```
finviz$RelValIndex <- apply(finviz[79:88],1,sum)
```

How it works...

Relative valuation involves comparing a stock's statistics with that of similar stocks in order to determine whether the stock is overvalued or undervalued. In an overly simplified example, a stock with a lower P/E ratio relative to the industry average P/E ratio for their industry (all else being equal) can be considered undervalued and might make a decent investment if the company has good financial health. Once we have this, we can filter for the stocks that look most promising, such as ones that have a `RelValIndex` of 8 or higher:

```
potentially_undervalued <- subset(finviz,RelValIndex>=8)
```

The `potentially_undervalued` data frame we just created should look like this:

	row.names	Ticker	Company	RelValIndex
1	1	CGA	China Green Agriculture, Inc.	10
2	4	UAN	CVR Partners, LP	8
3	7	YONG	Yongye International, Inc.	8
4	8	AVD	American Vanguard Corp.	9
5	16	MOS	The Mosaic Company	8
6	27	ARSD	Arabian American Development Company	8
7	32	CE	Celanese Corporation	8
8	33	LNDC	Landec Corp.	10
9	36	ASH	Ashland Inc.	8
10	38	ACET	Aceto Corp.	10
11	40	DOW	The Dow Chemical Company	8
12	42	SQM	Chemical & Mining Co. of Chile Inc.	8
13	43	FF	FutureFuel Corp.	10

We admit that this is an overly simplistic approach. However, it provides a framework to expand into more complex calculations. For example, once comfortable with this process, you can:

-   Add in customized criteria to assign a 1 to indicate that the stock is undervalued
-   Weigh the values differently
-   Add or remove criteria
-   Create more precise index values than just 1s and 0s, and so on

The sky is the limit here, but the process is the same.

Screening stocks and analyzing historical prices

When we are looking for stocks to invest in, we need to have a way to narrow the list down. In other words, we need to eliminate stocks that we don't think will be good investments. The definition of a good investment varies from person to person, but in this section, we will use some basic criteria to reduce our master list of stocks to just a few that we think might make good prospects. Once comfortable with the process, we encourage you to modify the criteria based on your own opinion of what defines a stock worth investing in. Once we have our prospects, we will analyze their historical prices and see what conclusions we can draw from them.

Getting ready

We will start with the `finviz` dataset as it was at the end of the previous section, along with the sector and industry averages columns, the binary undervalued columns, and the index values that summed up the values in the binary columns.

In addition to the packages we have used so far in this chapter, we will also need the `zoo` package for this section. This will help us calculate moving averages for the historical stock prices that we will pull.

How to do it...

The steps that you are about to embark upon will allow you to screen stocks:

1. First, choose some stock screening criteria, that is, a way to select the stocks within the `finviz` dataset that we feel have the potential to be good investments. Here are some sample criteria to start with:

   - Only US companies
   - Price per share between $20 and $100
   - Volume greater than 10,000
   - Positive earnings per share currently and projected for the future
   - Total debt to equity ratio less than 1
   - Beta less than 1.5
   - Institutional ownership less than 30 percent
   - Relative valuation index value greater than 8

2. As mentioned, these are just examples. Feel free to remove criteria, add criteria, or make changes based on what you think will give you the best output. The goal is to narrow the list down to less than 10 stocks.

3. Next, we apply our criteria to subset the `finviz` data frame into a new data frame called `target_stocks`:

```
target_stocks <- subset(finviz, Price>20 & Price<100 &
Volume>10000 &
                                 Country=="USA" &
                                 EPS..ttm.>0 &
                                 EPS.growth.next.year>0 &
                                 EPS.growth.next.5.years>0 &
                                 Total.Debt.Equity<1 & Beta<1.5 &
                                 Institutional.Ownership<30 &
                                 RelValIndex>8)
```

At the time of writing this book, this produces a target list of six stocks, as shown in the following screenshot. You might get a different number or different stocks altogether if you pull updated data from the Web.

Sector	Industry	No.	Ticker	Company	Country
Basic Materials	Specialty Chemicals	6538	WPZ	Williams Partners L.P.	USA
Financial	Credit Services	5786	TCAP	Triangle Capital Corporation	USA
Financial	Diversified Investments	3694	MAIN	Main Street Capital Corporation	USA
Services	Medical Equipment Wholesale	4434	OMI	Owens & Minor Inc.	USA
Services	Rental & Leasing Services	8	AAN	Aaron's, Inc.	USA
Services	Research Services	4257	NRCIB	National Research Corp.	USA

4. Now, let's go out and get historical prices for our target list of stocks so that we can see how their prices have looked over time. We will use a `for` loop to iterate through the list of symbols and pull prices for each one, but we will break up the loop across several steps and explain what each chunk is doing:

```
counter <- 0


for (symbol in target_stocks$Ticker){
```

The preceding command initializes a counter to keep track of where we are in our list of target stocks. Immediately after, we begin the `for` loop by telling every symbol in our target list to do the following:

```
url <-
paste0("http://ichart.finance.yahoo.com/table.csv?s=",symbol,"&a=0
8&b=7&c=1984&d=01&e=23&f=2014&g=d&ignore=.csv")
```

```
stock <- read.csv(url)
stock <- na.omit(stock)
colnames(stock)[7] <- "AdjClose"
stock[,1] <- as.Date(stock[,1])
stock <- cbind(Symbol=symbol,stock)
```

This code assigns a URL to the `url` variable that has the current stock symbol embedded into it. Then, we read the data located at this URL and assign it to a data frame called `stock`. We then do some clean up and formatting by removing all null values from the data frame, renaming the last column, making sure the `Date` column is formatted as a date that R can recognize, and adding the stock's symbol to the first row of the data frame.

5. The next few lines of our `for` loop will calculate some moving averages so that we can compare them with the daily stock prices. For this step, make sure you have the `zoo` package mentioned at the beginning of this section installed and loaded.

    The first part will calculate both a 50-day moving average and a 200-day moving average:

```
maxrow <- nrow(stock)-49
ma50 <-
cbind(stock[1:maxrow,1:2],rollmean(stock$AdjClose,50,align="ri
ght"))
maxrow <- nrow(stock)-199
ma200 <-
cbind(stock[1:maxrow,1:2],rollmean(stock$AdjClose,200,align="r
ight"))
```

The second part will combine the moving average data frames with the data frame containing the historical stock prices so that everything is part of the same dataset:

```
stock <-
merge(stock,ma50,by.x=c("Symbol","Date"),by.y=c("Symbol",
"Date"),all.x=TRUE)

colnames(stock)[9] <- "MovAvg50"

stock <-
merge(stock,ma200,by.x=c("Symbol","Date"),by.y=c("Symbol",
"Date"),all.x=TRUE)

colnames(stock)[10] <- "MovAvg200"
```

6. Next, we will plot a historical chart for each stock that our `for` loop iterates through, and then save that plot:

```
price_chart <-
melt(stock[,c(1,2,8,9,10)],id=c("Symbol","Date"))


qplot(Date, value, data=price_chart, geom="line",
color=variable,

        main=paste(symbol,"Daily Stock Prices"),ylab="Price")
    ggsave(filename=paste0("stock_price_",counter,".png"))
```

The charts that get generated and saved should look like the following two charts:

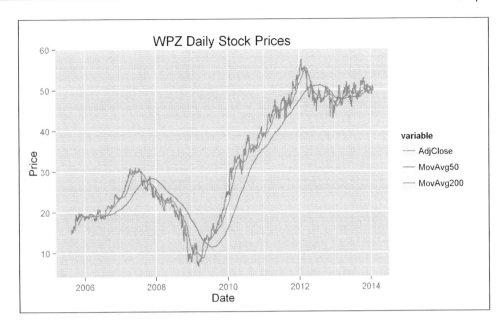

The next part of our loop summarizes the opening, high, low, and closing prices of the current stock:

```
price_summary <- ddply(stock, "Symbol", summarise,
open=Open[nrow(stock)],
                            high=max(High),
low=min(Low),close=AdjClose[1])
```

Then, it accumulates the summarized opening, high, low, and closing prices in a data frame called `stocks` so that the different stocks can be compared later. Also, it separately accumulates all the daily historical prices for the stocks in a data frame called `price summaries` so that they can be compared as well:

```
if(counter==0){
  stocks <- rbind(stock)
  price_summaries <- rbind(price_summary)
}else{
  stocks <- rbind(stocks, stock)
  price_summaries <- rbind(price_summaries, price_summary)
}
```

At the end of the loop, we increment our counter by one, and then close our `for` loop with a curly bracket:

```
counter <- counter+1
   }
```

 We broke our loop into pieces in order to explain what each part of the loop does. If you want to see what the entire `for` loop should look like, check the accompanying code file for this chapter.

7. Once we have iterated through all the stock symbols, we are left with a data frame named `stocks` that contains the historical prices for all the symbols in our target list and a data frame named `price_summaries` that holds the summaries for all our stocks. Let's graph them and see what they look like.

    First, we will graph the historical prices for all our stocks:

    ```
    qplot(Date, AdjClose, data=stocks, geom="line", color=Symbol,
          main="Daily Stock Prices")
    ggsave(filename=("stock_price_combined.png"))
    ```

    The preceding commands will produce the following graph:

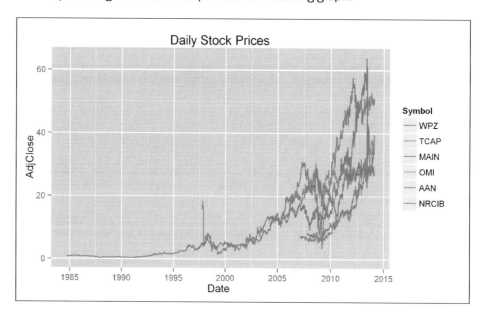

8. Then, let's graph the price summaries:

```
summary <- melt(price_summaries,id="Symbol")

ggplot(summary, aes(x=variable, y=value, fill=Symbol)) +
  geom_bar(stat="identity") + facet_wrap(~Symbol)
ggsave(filename=("stock_price_summaries.png"))
```

The resulting graph should look similar to this:

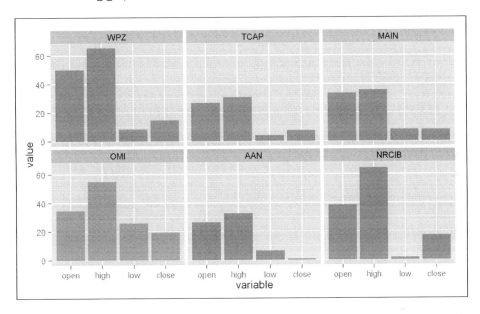

How it works...

Daily stock price charts are very "spiky" or volatile, and this sometimes makes them difficult to read. Moving averages smooth out the price fluctuations of a stock so that you can get a better sense of whether the stock is moving up or down over time.

Moving averages are also used to time investment in stocks. In other words, they are used as a guide to determine whether to invest in a stock now or to wait. There are varying opinions about what signals the best time, but one example is when the stock's 50-day moving average is below its 200-day moving average but is trending up. For more on moving averages, please see http://www.investopedia.com/university/movingaverage/.

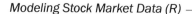

The combined historical price chart we generated in this section shows us the degree to which our target stocks' prices move in tandem. If you are looking to invest in multiple stocks, it can be good to invest in ones where the prices are not too highly correlated. You can also visualize how volatile one stock has been when compared to another. In our graph, you can see that the symbols **WPZ** and **NRCIB** have been fairly volatile, while the other symbols have been somewhat less volatile.

Another way to look at the price comparisons is by examining the price summaries' bar chart we created. This chart shows the opening, high, low, and closing prices for the period analyzed. The opening price is the very first price the stock traded at, the closing price is the very last price the stock has traded at thus far, the high price is the highest price the stock has been at during the period, and the low price is the lowest price the stock has been at during the period. The volatility mentioned previously can be viewed in a different way on this graph, as you can clearly see the difference between the highs and the lows of our two most volatile stocks. This chart also lets you see where the stock's closing price is relative to its all-time high and all-time low, which might help to give you a clue of the fairness of its current valuation.

5
Visually Exploring Employment Data (R)

In this chapter, we will cover:

- ▶ Preparing for analysis
- ▶ Importing employment data into R
- ▶ Exploring the employment data
- ▶ Obtaining and merging additional data
- ▶ Adding geographical information
- ▶ Extracting state- and county-level wage and employment information
- ▶ Visualizing geographical distributions of pay
- ▶ Exploring where the jobs are, by industry
- ▶ Animating maps for a geospatial time series
- ▶ Benchmarking performance for some common tasks

Introduction

This project will introduce you to the US employment data provided by the **Bureau of Labor Statistics** (**BLS**) of the United States government. The BLS is the federal agency responsible for measuring labor market activity and working conditions and prices in the US economy. Its mission is the collection, analysis, and dissemination of essential economic information to support public and private decision-making. In this project, we will use the aggregate annual data on employment and pay, stratified by geography and industry, from 2012, derived from the **Quarterly Census of Employment and Wages** (**QCEW**). This data can be downloaded as a compressed **comma-separated value** (**csv**) file at http://www.bls.gov/cew/data/files/2012/csv/2012_annual_singlefile.zip, which contains the single file 2012.annual.singlefile.csv. This file has 15 columns and about 3.5 million rows.

The QCEW is a quarterly collection of data, via the corporate tax collection system, related to employment and wages reported by employers. This census covers about 98 percent of the US civilian jobs, and excludes proprietors, unincorporated self-employed, unpaid family members, and some farm and domestic workers. The data is available as the aggregate data by county, metropolitan area (MSA), state, and national levels by industry. This government program has been in place since the 1930s in some form, and the current form has been in existence since 2003. The data is based on corporate reports to federal and local governments that are required by law, so it should be relatively free of reporting bias. This data gives a snapshot, in aggregate, of the wages and employment levels in the country by geography and industry.

The basic questions that we will address in this chapter are the geographical distribution of pay and employment in the US in 2012 and the last available full year of data at the time of writing this book. We will look at state and county levels as well as drill down to a few industries. We will also look at the temporal change in the geographical distribution of pay for the period 2003-2012 and what this reveals about the changing employment landscape in the US.

The goal of this chapter, is to guide you through the data science pipeline using a step-by-step example, which, in this case, is the exploration of government employment data freely available at the U.S. Government's BLS. We will work through ingesting the data into R, transforming and manipulating the data, creating subsets of the data, and generating visualizations that might provide some insight about patterns in the data. We hope that this example will serve as another exemplar that you can transfer to other projects for similar purposes.

 Please be aware that the content in this chapter is more advanced than some of the previous chapters.

We assume that you have already gone through *Chapter 1, Preparing Your Data Science Environment*, and have RStudio readily available on the computer that you will use to complete the recipes in this chapter.

Preparing for analysis

This recipe will prepare the groundwork with the tools you need to complete this project. If you do not have R installed on your computer, please see the instructions in *Chapter 1, Preparing Your Data Science Environment*.

Getting ready

You need a computer with R installed and an Internet connection.

How to do it...

The following steps will get you prepared for the remainder of this chapter by downloading the dataset from the BLS website and ensuring that we have the needed R packages:

1. Download the 27.5 MB compressed data from `http://www.bls.gov/cew/data/files/2012/csv/2012_annual_singlefile.zip`, and save it to a location that you will remember.

2. Uncompress the file by right-clicking on it in Explorer or Finder, and use the appropriate menu item.

 If you are familiar with the command line in the terminal in Linux/Mac OS X, you can easily uncompress the downloaded file using `unzip 2012_annual_singlefile.zip`.

3. Launch the RStudio IDE on your computer (or just plain R for purists).

4. Load the R packages we will need for this project:
```
library(data.table)
library(plyr)
library(dplyr)
library(stringr)
library(ggplot2)
library(maps)
library(bit64)
library(RColorBrewer)
library(choroplethr)
```

If you do not have one of these packages installed on your machine, you can easily install it using the following command, exchanging `data.table` for the package name to be installed:

```
install.packages('data.table',repos='http://cran.r-
project.org')
```

The R package repository, known as CRAN, has several mirrors around the world. A "mirror," in this usage, is a duplicate copy of the software repository that is run on a server in a different region, providing faster access for individuals near the location. You can, and should, choose a mirror geographically closest to your location to speed up the package download. In the preceding code snippet, you change `http://cran.r-project.org` to the URL of your preferred CRAN mirror.

5. Finally, set your working directory to the path where you have saved the file. This will tell R where you want it to look for the file:

```
setwd('path')
```

How it works...

We will primarily use three different R packages that are extremely useful in importing, manipulating, and transforming large datasets.

The package `data.table` improves upon the `data.frame` object in R, making operations faster and allowing the specification of an index variable in a dataset, a concept familiar to database experts. It also allows the fast aggregation of large data, including very fast-ordered joins. We will primarily use the `data.table` package for its function `fread`, which allows (very) fast importing of large-structured datasets into R. We will also investigate the relative performance of functions in this package against other functions we use in the benchmarking recipe later in this chapter.

The `stringr` package provides tools for text and string manipulation. This package streamlines and syntactically unifies available string manipulation functionalities available in R, making tasks involving string search, manipulation, and extraction much easier. We will need these functionalities here.

The `dplyr` package is the next iteration of the popular package, `plyr`, by Dr. Hadley Wickham. It is targeted at rectangular data and allows very fast aggregation, transformation, summarization, column selection, and joins. It also provides syntactical sugar to allow commands to be strung together, piping the results of one command into the next. This will be our workhorse in this project.

The `ggplot2` package will be our visualization workhorse. It implements the Grammar of Graphics paradigm in R and provides a very flexible means of creating visualizations.

The `maps` package provides geographical information about the US that we will use in our visualizations.

See also

▶ Refer to the `dplyr` reference material available at `https://github.com/hadley/dplyr/blob/master/README.md`, which has links to vignettes and other reference materials

▶ Refer to the `ggplot2` reference manual available at `http://cran.r-project.org/web/packages/ggplot2/ggplot2.pdf`

▶ Refer to the `sqldf` reference materials available at `https://code.google.com/p/sqldf/`

Importing employment data into R

Our first step in this project is to import the employment data into R so that we can start assessing the data and perform some preliminary analysis.

Getting ready

You should be ready to go ahead after completing the previous recipe.

How to do it...

The following steps will guide you through two different ways of importing the CSV file:

1. We can directly load the data file into R (even from the compressed version) using the following command:

   ```
   ann2012 <-
   read.csv(unz('2012_annual_singlefile.zip','2012.annual.singlef
   ile.csv'),stringsAsFactors=F)
   ```

   However, you will find that this takes a very long time with this file. There are better ways.

2. We chose to import the data directly into R since there are further manipulations and merges we will do later. We will use the `fread` function from the `data.table` package to do this:

   ```
   library(data.table)
   ```

   ```
   ann2012 <- fread('data/2012.annual.singlefile.csv')
   ```

   That's it. Really! It is also many times faster than the other method. It will not convert character variables to factors by default, so if you need factors later, you will have to convert them, but that is, in our opinion, a desirable feature in any case.

How it works...

We were familiar with `read.csv` from *Chapter 2, Driving Visual Analysis with Automobile Data (R)*. It basically reads the data line by line, separating columns by commas. As the data we are using for this project is 3.5 million rows, it is still small enough to fit into the memory of most modern personal computers, but will take quite some time to import using `read.csv()`.

The `fread` function from the `data.table` package uses an underlying C-level function to figure out, from the file, the length, number of fields, data types, and delimiters in the file, and it then reads the file using the parameters it has learned. As a result, it is significantly faster than `read.csv`. There is an extensive description of the details of `fread` in the R documentation.

There's more...

One of the limitations currently in R is that data imported into R needs to fit into the memory of the host computer. For large datasets, using a SQL-based database for data storage and manipulation takes advantage of the speed of the SQL-based database and circumvents R's memory limitation. Often, in enterprise environments, data is stored in Oracle, SAP, MySQL or PostgreSQL databases.

The `sqldf` package is extremely useful if you are from a SQL background, and many entering the world of data science have such a background. This package allows you to use SQL commands and queries within R, and treats `data.frame` objects in R just as you would treat tables in a SQL database. It also allows you to connect with most SQL-based databases that you have access to, including SQLite, MySQL, and PostgreSQL, among others.

As a demonstration, we can import data into a SQLite database, and then read and manipulate it there:

```
sqldf('attach blsdb as new')
read.csv.sql('data/2012.annual.singlefile.csv',
sql='create table main.ann2012 as select * from file',
dbname='blsdb')
```

 You must have SQLite installed and available on your machine for the preceding code to work. We will leave the installation to you.

This will also take some time, but you'll have the data in SQLite. The preceding command actually doesn't ingest the data into R, but just imports it into SQLite.

You can import the data into R using the following command:

```
ann2012<- sqldf("select * from main.ann2012", dbname='blsdb')
```

You can also choose to do your manipulations using SQL within SQLite with `sqldf`. For some users, it will be easier to manipulate the data using SQL, and then merely import the munged data into R.

As the first part of the book is focused on R, we will not delve deeper into the use of `sqldf` beyond what was presented here. However, if you are more familiar with SQL, you are welcome to replicate the steps presented in R in the various recipes with SQL commands, but we'll leave this as an exercise for you.

See also

▶ Refer to the SQLite documentation available at `http://www.sqlite.org`
▶ Refer to the `data.table` documentation available at `http://datatable.r-forge.r-project.org/`

Exploring the employment data

Now that the data is imported into R and we have learned some strategies to import larger datasets into R, we will do some preliminary analysis of the data. The purpose is to see what the data looks like, identify idiosyncrasies, and ensure that the rest of the analysis plan can move forward.

Getting ready

If you completed the last recipe, you should be ready to go.

How to do it...

The following steps will walk you through this recipe to explore the data:

1. First, let's see how large this data is:

```
>dim(ann2012)
[1] 3556289      15
```

Good, it's only 15 columns.

2. Let's take a peek at the first few rows so that we can see what the data looks like:

```
head(ann2012)
```

You can refer to the following screenshot:

What are the variables `own_code`, `industry_code`, and so on, and what do they mean? We might need more data to understand this data.

3. There is also a weird idiosyncrasy in this data. Some of the values for `total_annual_wages`, `taxable_annual_wages` and `annual_contributions` look impossibly small. A peek at the actual data shows that these numbers don't appear to be correct. However, `fread` actually gives an indication of what is going on:

```
ann2012 <- fread('data/2012.annual.singlefile.csv', sep=',',
colClasses=c('character', 'integer', 'integer', 'integer',
'integer', 'integer', 'character',rep('integer',8)))
```

You can refer to the following screenshot:

4. This points to the fact that the `bit64` package might be needed to properly display these large numbers. Installing and loading this package, and then reimporting the data corrects the problem, as seen in the following command lines:

```
install.packages('bit64')
library('bit64')
```

```
ann2012 <- fread('data/2012.annual.singlefile.csv', sep=',',
colClasses=c('character', 'integer', 'integer', 'integer',
'integer', 'integer', 'character',rep('integer',8)))
```

You can refer to the following screenshot:

```
> head(ann2012)
   area_fips own_code industry_code agglvl_code size_code year qtr disclosure_code
1:    01000         0            10          50         0 2012   A
2:    01000         1            10          51         0 2012   A
3:    01000         1           102          52         0 2012   A
4:    01000         1          1021          53         0 2012   A
5:    01000         1          1022          53         0 2012   A
6:    01000         1          1023          53         0 2012   A
   annual_avg_estabs_count annual_avg_emplvl total_annual_wages taxable_annual_wages
1:                  116233           1828248        76768801894           13424728725
2:                    1252             56031         4194319351                     0
3:                    1252             56031         4194319351                     0
4:                     599             11734          719641114                     0
5:                       2                13             436204                     0
6:                      17               161           12253089                     0
   annual_contributions annual_avg_wkly_wage avg_annual_pay
1:            419383612                  808          41990
2:                    0                 1440          74857
3:                    0                 1440          74857
4:                    0                 1179          61330
5:                    0                  662          34437
6:                    0                 1468          76343
```

How it works...

The `head` command displays the first few lines (the default is the top six lines) of a data frame. We notice that some of the headings are self-explanatory, but some allude to codes that we currently don't have access to. We will have to obtain additional data in order to make a meaningful analysis. We could have looked at the data without importing it into R. The UNIX command, `less`, and the Windows PowerShell command, `type`, could have shown us the same thing as `head` did.

See also

  ▸   Refer to the documentation for the dataset available at http://www.bls.gov/
       cew/doc/layouts/csv_annual_layout.htm

Obtaining and merging additional data

In the previous recipe, we found that additional data was needed to understand what the data in the csv file actually represents, and this recipe will directly address this need.

Getting ready

We can find additional data on the BLS website at `http://www.bls.gov/cew/datatoc.htm` under the header **Associated Codes and Titles**. There are five files there, which we will download to our computer. They are as follows:

- ▶ `agglevel_titles.csv` (http://www.bls.gov/cew/doc/titles/agglevel/agglevel_titles.csv)
- ▶ `area_titles.csv` (http://www.bls.gov/cew/doc/titles/area/area_titles.csv)
- ▶ `industry_titles.csv` (http://www.bls.gov/cew/doc/titles/industry/industry_titles.csv)
- ▶ `ownership_titles.csv` (http://www.bls.gov/cew/doc/titles/ownership/ownership_titles.csv)
- ▶ `size_titles.csv` (http://www.bls.gov/cew/doc/titles/size/size_titles.csv)

We download them to our computer, remembering where we stored them. We need to get ready to import them into R and merge them with our original data.

How to do it...

The following steps will lead you through loading these files into R and joining them into a larger data frame:

1. We will now import these data files into R using the following command lines:

```
for(u in c('agglevel','area','industry',
'ownership','size')){
assign(u,read.csv(paste('data/',u,'_titles.csv',sep=''),
stringsAsFactors=F))
}
```

This is an example of code that makes it easier for us to do repeated tasks.

2. Each of these datasets has exactly one variable (column header) in common with our original data, which is `ann2012`, as shown in the following screenshot:

```
> intersect(names(agglevel),names(ann2012))
[1] "agglvl_code"
> intersect(names(industry), names(ann2012))
[1] "industry_code"
> intersect(names(area), names(ann2012))
[1] "area_fips"
> intersect(names(ownership),names(ann2012))
[1] "own_code"
> intersect(names(size), names(ann2012))
[1] "size_code"
```

So, it should be fairly easy to put the datasets together. We'll join four of these datasets with `ann2012` now, and save `area`, that is, the data from `area_titles.csv`, for the next recipe, since we want to manipulate it a bit:

```
codes <- c('agglevel','industry','ownership','size')

ann2012full <- ann2012

for(i in 1:length(codes)){

eval(parse(text=paste('ann2012full <- left_join(ann2012full,
',codes[i],')', sep='')))

}
```

The end result is shown in the following screenshot:

```
> head(ann2012full)
  area_fips own_code industry_code agglvl_code size_code year qtr disclosure_code
1    01000        0            10          50         0 2012   A
2    01000        1            10          51         0 2012   A
3    01000        1           102          52         0 2012   A
4    01000        1          1021          53         0 2012   A
5    01000        1          1022          53         0 2012   A
6    01000        1          1023          53         0 2012   A
  annual_avg_estabs_count annual_avg_emplvl total_annual_wages taxable_annual_wages
1                  116233           1828248         76768801894          13424728725
2                    1252             56031          4194319351                    0
3                    1252             56031          4194319351                    0
4                     599             11734           719641114                    0
5                       2                13              436204                    0
6                      17               161            12253089                    0
  annual_contributions annual_avg_wkly_wage avg_annual_pay
1            419383612                  808          41990
2                    0                 1440          74857
3                    0                 1440          74857
4                    0                 1179          61330
5                    0                  662          34437
6                    0                 1468          76343
                                   agglvl_title                         industry_title
1                           State, Total Covered                 Total, all industries
2              State, Total -- by ownership sector                 Total, all industries
3             State, by Domain -- by ownership sector                    Service-providing
4 State, by Supersector -- by ownership sector Trade, transportation, and utilities
5 State, by Supersector -- by ownership sector                            Information
6 State, by Supersector -- by ownership sector                   Financial activities
                own_title              size_title
1        Total Covered All establishment sizes
2 Federal Government All establishment sizes
3 Federal Government All establishment sizes
4 Federal Government All establishment sizes
5 Federal Government All establishment sizes
6 Federal Government All establishment sizes
```

How it works...

In step 1 of the *How to do it...* section, we want to assign each dataset to its own object. We can write an individual line of code for each import, but this code allows us to do this much faster, and it will be easier to maintain in the future. The `assign` command takes two basic inputs: a variable name and a value to be assigned to the variable name. The `for` loop here doesn't iterate over numbers, but over objects. At the first iteration, u takes the value `agglevel`. The `assign` function takes the name `agglevel` and assigns it the result of the `read.csv` command. Within the `paste` command, we again use the value of u, since all the files we are importing have the same naming convention. It is this common naming convention that allows us to use this type of coding. Thus, the first iteration gives `assign('agglevel', read.csv('data/agglevel_title.csv'))`, and so forth.

In step 2, we join the datasets together. We first copy the original data to a new name, `ann2012full`, so that we can build up this new dataset without corrupting the original data in case something goes wrong. We then use a macro-like construct to join all the new datasets to the original one, iterating over numbers in the `for` loop and the indices of the vector code.

Let's work our way inside out in this complex command (a sound strategy to understand complex code in general). Within the `paste` command, we create the command we would like evaluated. We want to do a `left_join` (this is from the `dplyr` package), joining `ann2012full` with `agglevel` in the first iteration. The `left_join` ensures that all the rows of `ann2012full` are preserved, and the rows of `agglevel` are appropriately replicated to match the number of rows in `ann2012full`. Since there is only one common variable in the two datasets, `left_join` automatically chooses to join using this.

In general, `left_join` will join the two datasets using all the variable names it finds common between the two. If you do not want this, you can specify which variables you want to use for the join by specifying, for example, `left_join(ann2012full, agglevel, by="agglvl_code ")`.

The `eval` statement then evaluates the command we constructed using the `paste` command. We iterate over the names in code so that each of the four datasets gets joined with `ann2012full`.

A quick check will show that the number of rows in `ann2012full` after the joins, and in `ann2012`, is the same.

Adding geographical information

The main purpose of this chapter is to look at the geographical distribution of wages across the US. Mapping this out requires us to first have a map. Fortunately, maps of the US, both at the state-and county-levels, are available in the maps package, and the data required to make the maps can be extracted. We will align our employment data with the map data in this recipe so that the correct data is represented at the right location on the map.

Getting ready

We already have the area dataset imported into R, so we are ready to go.

How to do it...

The following steps will guide you through the process of creating your first map in R:

1. Let's first look at the data in area:

   ```
   head (area)
   ```

   The output is shown in the following screenshot:

   ```
   > head(area)
     area_fips                                     area_title
   1    US000                                      U.S. TOTAL
   2    USCMS      U.S. Combined Statistical Areas (combined)
   3    USMSA  U.S. Metropolitan Statistical Areas (combined)
   4    USNMS  U.S. Nonmetropolitan Area Counties (combined)
   5    01000                            Alabama -- Statewide
   6    01001                        Autauga County, Alabama
   ```

   We see that there is something called area_fips here. **Federal Information Processing Standards** (**FIPS**) codes are used by the Census Bureau to designate counties and other geographical areas in the US.

2. We want to capitalize all the names, according to the conventions. We'll write a small function to do this:

   ```
   simpleCap <-function(x){
   if(!is.na(x)){
   s <- strsplit(x,' ')[[1]]
   paste(toupper(substring(s,1,1)), substring(s,2),
   sep='', collapse=' ')
   } else {NA}
   }
   ```

3. The `maps` package contains two datasets that we will use; they are `county.fips` and `state.fips`. We will first do some transformations. If we look at `county.fips`, we notice that the FIPS code there is missing a leading `0` on the left for some of the codes. All the codes in our employment data comprise five digits:

    ```
    > data(county.fips)
    > head(county.fips)
      fips          polyname
    1 1001 alabama,autauga
    2 1003 alabama,baldwin
    3 1005 alabama,barbour
    4 1007    alabama,bibb
    5 1009 alabama,blount
    6 1011 alabama,bullock
    ```

4. The `stringr` package will help us out here:

    ```
    county.fips$fips <- str_pad(county.fips$fips, width=5,
    pad="0")
    ```

5. We want to separate the county names from the `polyname` column in `county.fips`. We'll get the state names from `state.fips` in a minute:

    ```
    county.fips$polyname <- as.character(county.fips$polyname)
    county.fips$county <- sapply(
      gsub('[a-z\ ]+,([a-z\ ]+)','\\1',county.fips$polyname),
      simpleCap)
    county.fips <- unique(county.fips)
    ```

6. The `state.fips` data involves a lot of details:

    ```
    > data(state.fips)
    ```

    The output is shown in the following screenshot:

    ```
    > head(state.fips)
      fips ssa region division abb    polyname
    1    1   1      3        6  AL      alabama
    2    4   3      4        8  AZ      arizona
    3    5   4      3        7  AR     arkansas
    4    6   5      4        9  CA   california
    5    8   6      4        8  CO     colorado
    6    9   7      1        1  CT  connecticut
    ```

7. We'll again pad the `fips` column with a `0`, if necessary, so that they have two digits, and capitalize the state names from `polyname` to create a new `state` column. The code is similar to the one we used for the `county.fips` data:

```
state.fips$fips <- str_pad(state.fips$fips, width=2, pad="0",
side='left')
state.fips$state <- as.character(state.fips$polyname)
state.fips$state <-
    gsub("([a-z\ ]+):[a-z\ \\']+","\\1",state.fips$state)
state.fips$state <- sapply(state.fips$state, simpleCap)
```

8. We make sure that we have unique rows. We need to be careful here, since we only need to have uniqueness in the `fips` and `state` values, and not in the other code:

```
mystatefips <-unique(state.fips[,c('fips','abb','state')])
```

The `unique function`, when applied to a `data.frame` object, returns the unique rows of the object. You might be used to using `unique` on a single vector to find the unique elements in the vector.

9. We get a list of the lower 48 state names. We will filter our data to look only at these states:

```
lower48 <-
setdiff(unique(state.fips$state),c('Hawaii','Alaska'))
```

 The `setdiff` set operation looks for all the elements in the first set that are not in the second set.

10. Finally, we put all this information together into a single dataset, `myarea`:

```
myarea <- merge(area, county.fips,
by.x='area_fips',by.y='fips', all.x=T)
myarea$state_fips <- substr(myarea$area_fips, 1,2)
myarea <- merge(myarea,
mystatefips,by.x='state_fips',by.y='fips', all.x=T)
```

11. Lastly, we join the geographical information with our dataset, and filter it to keep only data on the lower 48 states:

```
ann2012full <- left_join(ann2012full, myarea)
ann2012full <- filter(ann2012full, state %in% lower48)
```

12. We now store the final dataset in an R data (`rda`) file on disk. This provides an efficient storage mechanism for R objects:

```
save(ann2012full, file='data/ann2014full.rda',compress=T)
```

How it works...

The 12 steps of this recipe covered quite a bit of material, so let's dive into some of the details, starting with step 2. The `simpleCap` function is an example of a function in R. We use functions to encapsulate repeated tasks, reducing code duplication and ensuring that errors have a single point of origin. If we merely repeat code, changing the input values manually, we can easily make errors in transcription, break hidden assumptions, or accidentally overwrite important variables. Further, if we want to modify the code, we have to do it manually at every duplicate location. This is tedious and error-prone, and so we make functions, a best practice that we strongly encourage you to follow.

The `simpleCap` function uses three functions: `strsplit`, `toupper` and `substring`. The `strsplit` function splits strings (or a vector of strings) whenever it finds the string fragment to split on (in our case, ' ' or a space). The `substring` function extracts substrings from strings between the character locations specified. Specifying only one character location implies extracting from this location to the end of the string. The `toupper` function changes the case of a string from lowercase to uppercase. The reverse operation is done by `tolower`.

From step 3, packages often have example data bundled with them. `county.fips` and `state.fips` are examples of datasets that have been bundled into the `maps` package.

The `stringr` package, used in step 4, is another package by Dr. Wickham, which provides string manipulation functions. Here, we use `str_pad`, which pads a string with a character (here, `0`) to give the string a particular width.

In step 5, we use the inbuilt regular expression (regex) capabilities in R. We won't talk about regular expressions too much here. The `gsub` function looks for the first pattern and substitutes the second pattern in the string specified as third. Here, the pattern we're looking for comprises one or more letters or spaces (`[a-z\ ]+`), then a comma, and then one or more letters or spaces. The second set of letters and spaces is what we want to keep, so we put parentheses around it. The `\\1` pattern says to replace the entire pattern with the first pattern we used parentheses around. This replacement happens for every element of the `polyname` field.

Since we want capitalization for every element in `polyname`, we can use a `for` loop, but choose to use the more efficient `sapply` instead. Every element in `polyname` is passed through the `simpleCap` function, and is thus capitalized in step 7.

In step 10, we join the `area`, `county.fips`, and `mystatefips` datasets together. We use the `merge` function rather than `left_join`, since the variables we want to join on have different names for different `data.frame` objects. The `merge` function in the R standard library allows this flexibility. To ensure a left join, we specify `all.x=TRUE`.

In step 11, we join the `myarea` data frame to our `ann2014full` dataset. We then use the `filter` function to subset the data, restricting it to data from the lower 48 states. The `filter` function is from the `dplyr` package. We'll speak about the functionalities in `dplyr` in the next recipe.

See also

- ▶ Read about regular expressions in R at http://stat.ethz.ch/R-manual/R-patched/library/base/html/regex.html
- ▶ Refer to information about the stringr library available at http://journal.r-project.org/archive/2010-2/RJournal_2010-2_Wickham.pdf

Extracting state- and county-level wage and employment information

So far, we worked to get the data into shape for analysis. We'll now start with looking at the geographical distribution of the average annual pay per state and per county.

Getting ready

If you have thoroughly followed the recipes in this chapter till now, you will have the data in a form from where you can extract information at different levels. We're good to go!

How to do it...

We will first extract data from ann2014full at the state-level. We need to perform the following steps:

1. We look at the aggregate state-level data. A peek at agglevel tells us that the code for the level of data that we want is 50. Also, we only want to look at the average annual pay (avg_annual_pay) and the average annual employment level (annual_avg_emplvl), and not the other variables:

   ```
   d.state <- filter(ann2014full, agglvl_code==50)
   d.state <- select(d.state, state, avg_annual_pay,
   annual_avg_emplvl)
   ```

2. We create two new variables, wage and empquantile, which discretizes the pay and employment variables:

   ```
   d.state$wage <- cut(d.state$avg_annual_pay,
   quantile(d.state$avg_annual_pay, c(seq(0,.8, by=.2), .9, .95,
   .99, 1)))
   d.state$empquantile <- cut(d.state$annual_avg_emplvl,
   quantile(d.state$annual_avg_emplvl,
   c(seq(0,.8,by=.2),.9,.95,.99,1)))
   ```

3. We also want the levels of these discretized variables to be meaningful. So, we run the following commands:

```
x <- quantile(d.state$avg_annual_pay, c(seq(0,.8,by=.2),.9,
.95, .99, 1))

xx <- paste(round(x/1000),'K',sep='')

Labs <- paste(xx[-length(xx)],xx[-1],sep='-')

levels(d.state$wage) <- Labs


x <- quantile(d.state$annual_avg_emplvl,
c(seq(0,.8,by=.2),.9, .95, .99, 1))

xx <- ifelse(x>1000, paste(round(x/1000),'K',sep=''),
round(x))

Labs <- paste(xx[-length(xx)],xx[-1],sep='-')

levels(d.state$empquantile) <- Labs
```

4. We repeat this process at the county-level. We will find that the appropriate aggregation level code is `70` (`agglvl_code==70`). Everything else will be the same. Let's try to be a bit smarter this time around. First of all, we will discretize our variables the same way, and then change the labels to match. A function might be a good idea! The following command lines depict this:

```
Discretize <- function(x, breaks=NULL){
  if(is.null(breaks)){
    breaks <- quantile(x, c(seq(0,.8,by=.2),.9, .95, .99, 1))
    if (sum(breaks==0)>1) {
      temp <- which(breaks==0, arr.ind=TRUE)
      breaks <- breaks[max(temp):length(breaks)]
    }
  }
  x.discrete <- cut(x, breaks, include.lowest=TRUE)
  breaks.eng <- ifelse(breaks > 1000,
                       paste0(round(breaks/1000),'K'),
                       round(breaks))
  Labs <- paste(breaks.eng[-length(breaks.eng)], breaks.eng[-
1],
               sep='-')
  levels(x.discrete) <- Labs
  return(x.discrete)
}
```

5. We alluded to the syntactic sugar of `dplyr` before; now, we see it in action. The `dplyr` package allows you to string together different operations, piping the results of one operation as input for the next, using the `%.%` operator. We'll describe the main operations of `dplyr` in the next recipe. Using some function encapsulation, the following code achieves everything that we spent significantly more lines of code to achieve in steps 1-3:

```
d.cty <- filter(ann2012full, agglvl_code==70)%.%
select(state,county,abb, avg_annual_pay, annual_avg_emplvl)%.%
mutate(wage=Discretize(avg_annual_pay),
empquantile=Discretize(annual_avg_emplvl))
```

We now have the basic datasets we need to visualize the geographic patterns in the data.

How it works...

The preceding five steps covered a lot of R code, so let's start breaking things down. The two functions `filter` and `select` are from `dplyr`. The `dplyr` package provides five basic functions, which are as follows:

- ▸ `filter`: This creates subsets of the data based on specified criteria
- ▸ `select`: This selects columns or variables from the dataset
- ▸ `mutate`: This creates new columns or variables in a dataset, which are derived from other variables in the dataset
- ▸ `group_by`: This splits the data by a variable or set of variables, and subsequent functions operate on each component defined by a unique variable value or combination
- ▸ `arrange`: This rearranges the data (or sorts it) according to variable(s) in the dataset

Each of these functions can operate on a `data.frame`, `data.table`, or `tbl` object, which is part of `dplyr`.

The `cut` function discretizes a continuous variable based on specified breakpoints or thresholds. Here, we specify the thresholds based on quantiles of the variable. We specify which quantiles we want by a sequence of fractions:

```
c(seq(0, .8, by=.2), .9, .95, .99, 1)
```

This is done using the `seq` function to create a regular sequence of numbers with a start value, an end value, and the difference between two successive values.

In step 3, we take the specified thresholds and format them. Numbers above 1,000 are truncated at the thousands place and appended with a K, as is conventionally seen. Using `round` without specifying the number of decimal places implies no decimal places.

Further, in step 3, we want our labels to represent a range. So, we need to create the labels by putting a dash (-) between successive values of our formatted thresholds. One way of doing this is to create two copies of the vector of thresholds, one without the last element and another without the first element. We then paste them together with -. Notice that this trick allows successive thresholds to be aligned and pasted together. If you're not convinced, print out `xx[-length(xx)]` and `xx[-1]`, and see for yourself.

The `Discretize` function encapsulates the work we were doing in discretizing our outcomes and formatting their labels.

This code snippet uses the syntax of `dplyr` to string together functions. We first subset the original data, keeping only data that has `agglvl_code=50` (note the `==` in the code). We then pipe the resulting reduced data into the second function, `select`, which keeps only the four variables we're interested in. This further reduces data, and it is then inputted into the `mutate` function, which then creates two new variables in the data object. This final object is then stored with the variable name `d.cty`.

See also

▶   Get more details about `dplyr` at `http://blog.rstudio.org/2014/01/17/introducing-dplyr/`

Visualizing geographical distributions of pay

We created datasets that contain the data we need to visualize average pay and employment by county and state. In this recipe, we will visualize the geographical distribution of pay by shading the appropriate areas of the map with a color that maps to a particular value or range of values. This is commonly referred to as a chlropleth map; this visualization type has become increasingly popular over the last few years as it has become much simpler to make such maps, especially online. Other geographic visualizations will overlay a marker or some other shape to denote data; there is no need to fill specific shapes with geographically meaningful boundaries.

Getting ready

After the last recipe, you should be ready to use the datasets we created to visualize geographical distributions. We will use the `ggplot2` package to generate our visualizations. We will also use the `RColorBrewer` package, which provides "palettes" of colors that are visually appealing. If you don't currently have `RColorBrewer`, install it using `install.packages('RColorBrewer', repos='http://cran.r-project.org')`.

How to do it...

The following steps walk you through the creation of this geospatial data visualization:

1. We first need to get some data on the map itself. The `ggplot2` package provides a convenient function, `map_data`, to extract this from data bundled in the `maps` package:

```
library(ggplot2)
library(RColorBrewer)
state_df <- map_data('state')
county_df <- map_data('county')
```

2. We now do a bit of transforming to make this data conform to our data:

```
transform_mapdata <- function(x){
    names(x)[5:6] <- c('state','county')
    for(u in c('state','county')){
      x[,u] <- sapply(x[,u],simpleCap)
    }
    return(x)
}
state_df <- transform_mapdata(state_df)
county_df <- transform_mapdata(county_df)
```

3. The `data.frame` objects, `state_df` and `county_df`, contain the latitude and longitude of points. These are our primary graphical data and need to be joined with the data we created in the previous recipe, which contains what is in effect the color information for the map:

```
chor <- left_join(state_df, d.state, by='state')
ggplot(chor, aes(long,lat,group=group))+
geom_polygon(aes(fill=wage))+geom_path(color='black',size=0.2)
+ scale_fill_brewer(palette='PuRd') +
theme(axis.text.x=element_blank(),
axis.text.y=element_blank(), axis.ticks.x=element_blank(),
axis.ticks.y=element_blank())
```

This gives us the following figure that depicts the distribution of average annual pay by state:

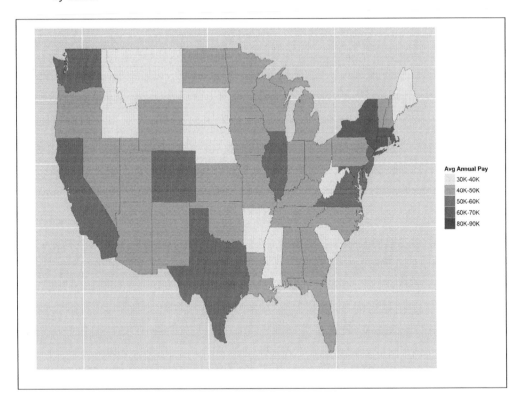

4. We can similarly create a visualization of the average annual pay by county, which will give us a much more granular information about the geographical distribution of wages:

```
chor <- left_join(county_df, d.cty)
ggplot(chor, aes(long,lat, group=group))+
  geom_polygon(aes(fill=wage))+
  geom_path( color='white',alpha=0.5,size=0.2)+
  geom_polygon(data=state_df, color='black',fill=NA)+
  scale_fill_brewer(palette='PuRd')+
  labs(x='',y='', fill='Avg Annual Pay')+
  theme(axis.text.x=element_blank(), axis.text.y=element_blank(),
axis.ticks.x=element_blank(), axis.ticks.y=element_blank())
```

This produces the following figure showing the geographical distribution of average annual pay by county:

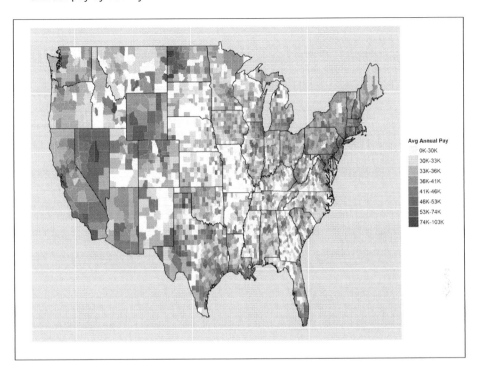

Avg Annual Pay
- 0K-30K
- 30K-33K
- 33K-36K
- 36K-41K
- 41K-46K
- 46K-53K
- 53K-74K
- 74K-103K

It is evident from the preceding figure that there are well-paying jobs in western North Dakota, Wyoming, and northwestern Nevada, most likely driven by new oil exploration opportunities in these areas. The more obvious urban and coastal areas also show up quite nicely.

How it works...

Let's dive into the explanation of how the preceding 4 steps work. The `map_data` function is provided by `ggplot2` to extract map data from the `maps` package. In addition to county and state, it can also extract data for the `france`, `italy`, `nz`, `usa`, `world`, and `world2` maps provided by the `maps` package.

The columns that contain state and county information in `county_df` and `state_df` are originally named `region` and `subregion`. In step 2, we need to change their names to `state` and `county`, respectively, to make joining this data with our employment data easier. We also capitalize the names of the states and counties to conform to the way we formatted the data in our `employment` dataset.

For the creation of the map in step 3, we create the plotting dataset by joining `state_df` and `d.state` using the name of the state. We then use `ggplot` to draw the map of the US and fill in each state with a color corresponding to the level of wage and the discretized average annual pay created in the previous recipe. To elaborate, we establish that the data for the plot comes from `chor`, and we draw polygons (`geom_polygon`) based on the latitude and longitude of the borders of each state, filling them with a color depending on how high wage is, and then we draw the actual boundaries of the states (`geom_path`) in black. We specify that we will use a color palette that starts at white, goes through purple, and has red corresponding to the highest level of wage. The remainder of the code is formatted by specifying labels and removing axis annotations and ticks from the plot.

For step 4, the code is essentially the same as step 3, except that we draw polygons for the boundaries of the counties rather than the states. We add a layer to draw the state boundaries in black (`geom_polygon(data=state_df, color='black', fill=NA)`), in addition to the county boundaries in white.

See also

> ▸ Refer to the `ggplot2` documentation available at `http://www.ggplot2.org`

Exploring where the jobs are, by industry

In the previous recipe, we saw how to visualize the top-level aggregate data on pay. The employment dataset has more granular data, divided by public/private sectors and types of jobs. The types of jobs in this data follow a hierarchical coding system called **North American Industry Classification System** (**NIACS**). In this recipe, we will consider four particular industries and look at visualizing the geographical distribution of employment in these industries, restricted to private sector jobs.

We will look at four industrial sectors in this recipe:

> ▸ Agriculture, forestry, fishing, and hunting (NIACS 11)

> ▸ Mining, quarrying, and oil and gas extraction (NIACS 21)

> ▸ Finance and insurance (NIACS 52)

> ▸ Professional and technical services (NIACS 54)

How to do it...

We need to create a subset of the employment data, including the data for industrial sectors, but restricting it to the private sector, by performing the following steps:

1. We start by filtering the data by the conditions we are imposing on the industry and private sectors, and keep only relevant variables:

```
d.sectors <- filter(ann2012full, industry_code %in%
c(11,21,54,52),

own_code==5, # Private sector

agglvl_code == 74 # county-level

) %.%

select(state,county,industry_code, own_code,agglvl_code,
        industry_title, own_title, avg_annual_pay,
        annual_avg_emplvl)%.%

mutate(wage=Discretize(avg_annual_pay),

emplevel=Discretize(annual_avg_emplvl))

d.sectors <- filter(d.sectors, !is.na(industry_code))
```

 Here, our selection is based on a set of industry codes, and we restrict ourselves to county-level data. This code is different from before since we're now looking at industry-specific data.

2. We now create the visualization using `ggplot2`. This visualization will be an array of four panels, one for each industrial sector. Each panel will have a county-level map of the US, with colors signifying the level of employment in each county in 2012 in each particular industry. We will also choose a blue-dominated palette for this visualization:

```
chor <- left_join(county_df, d.sectors)
ggplot(chor, aes(long,lat,group=group))+
  geom_polygon(aes(fill=emplevel))+
  geom_polygon(data=state_df, color='black',fill=NA)+
  scale_fill_brewer(palette='PuBu')+
  facet_wrap(~industry_title, ncol=2, as.table=T)+
  labs(fill='Avg Employment Level',x='',y='')+
  theme(axis.text.x=element_blank(),
axis.text.y=element_blank(),
    axis.ticks.x=element_blank(),
axis.ticks.y=element_blank())
```

This produces the following visualization, showing geographical distribution of employment by industry:

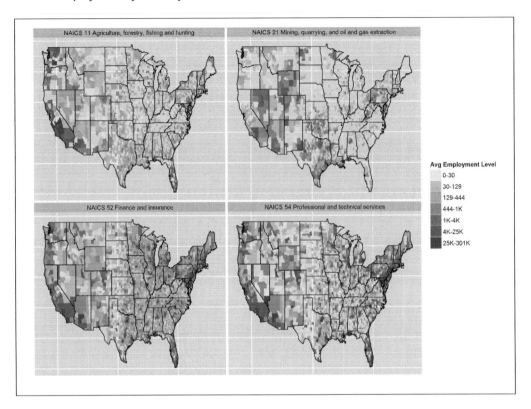

How it works...

In this recipe, we used the `dplyr` functions for data munging. One of our filter criteria was that the `industry_code` variable should have one of the values out of 11, 21, 52, or 54. This was achieved by the `%in%` operator, which is a set operations. It asks if an element on the left is a member of the set on the right. We have multiple criteria in the `filter` statement, separated by commas. This implies an AND relationship in that all of the criteria must be satisfied in order for the data to pass the filter.

We noticed that there were some missing values in the industry code. This resulted in an extra panel in the visualization, corresponding to data where the industry code was missing. We didn't want this, so we filtered out this data in this first step.

In the second step, the command to create the visualization is essentially the same as in the previous recipe, except for the following line:

```
facet_wrap(~industry_title, ncol=2)
```

This command splits the data up by the value of `industry_title`, creates separate visualizations for each value of `industry_title`, and puts them back onto a grid with two columns and an appropriate number of rows. We also used `industry_title` instead of `industry_code` here (they give the same visualization) so that the labeling of the panels is understandable, rather than comprising just some numbers that require the reader to look up their meaning.

There's more...

This recipe is the tip of the iceberg for this dataset. There are many levels that can be explored with this data, both in terms of private/public sectors and in terms of drilling down into different industries. The additional quarterly data from 2012 is also available and can shed light on temporal patterns. The annual and quarterly data is available from 1990 onwards. Further analyses are possible association of temporal patterns of employment with other socioeconomic events. The `choroplethr` and `rMaps` packages provide ways of creating animations over time for this type of data.

See also

- Read about the `rMaps` package at `http://rmaps.github.io` and `http://rmaps.github.io/blog/posts/animated-choropleths/`
- Read about the `choroplethr` package at `https://github.com/trulia/choroplethr`
- Have a look at the choropleth challenge results at `http://blog.revolutionanalytics.com/2009/11/choropleth-challenge-result.html`
- Look at examples of animated maps at `http://www.r-bloggers.com/animated-choropleths-using-animation-ggplot2-rcharts-googlevis-and-shiny-to-visualize-violent-crime-rates-in-different-us-states-across-5-decades/`

Animating maps for a geospatial time series

One of the real interests in this project is to see how wage patterns, as a surrogate for income patterns, changed over time. The QCEW site provides data from 2003 to 2012. In this recipe, we will look at the overall average annual pay by county for each of these years and create an animation that displays the changes in the pay pattern over this period.

Getting ready

For this recipe, we need to download the annual data for the years 2003 to 2011 from the BLS website, at `http://www.bls.gov/cew/datatoc.htm`. You will need to download the files corresponding to these years for the QCEW NIACS-based data files in the column **CSVs Single Files-Annual Averages**. Store these files (which are compressed `.zip` files) in the same location as the zipped 2012 data you downloaded at the beginning of this project. Don't unzip them! You must also download and install the `choroplethr` package using `install.packages('chloroplethr')`, if you haven't already done so.

> Note that this recipe is relatively memory-intensive. Those running on 32-bit machines might face out-of-memory issues.

How to do it...

What we need to do is import the data for all the years from 2003 through 2012 and extract data for the county-level (`agglvl_code==70`) average annual pay (`avg_annual_pay`) for each county, plot it, and then string the pay values together in an animation. Since we basically need to do the same things for each year's data, we can do this in a `for` loop, and we can create functions to encapsulate the repeated actions. We start by writing code for a single year, performing the following steps:

1. We import the data from the ZIP file that we call `zipfile` in this prototype code. In reality, the file names are of the pattern `2003_annual_singlefile.zip`, and the CSV files in them are of the pattern `2003.annual.singlefile.csv`. We will use the common patterns in the ZIP and CSV files in our code to automate the process. For me, the data lies in a folder called `data`, which is reflected in the following code:

    ```
    unzip(file.path('data',zipfile), exdir='data') # unzips the
    file
    csvfile <- gsub('zip','csv', zipfile) # Change file name
    csvfile <- gsub('_','.',csvfile) # Change _ to . in name
    dat <- fread(file.path('data', csvfile)) # read data
    ```

2. We now join the employment data with the geographical data from `myarea`:

    ```
    dat <- left_join(dat, myarea)
    ```

3. We then use the `dplyr` functions to extract the county-level aggregate pay data, keeping the state and county information:

```
dat <- filter(dat, agglvl_code==70) %.% # County-level
aggregate
select(state, county, avg_annual_pay) # Keep variables
```

4. We then encapsulate the actions in steps 1 through 3 in a function:

```
get_data <- function(zipfile){
unzip(file.path('data',zipfile), exdir='data') # unzips the
file
csvfile <- gsub('zip','csv', zipfile) # Change file name
csvfile <- gsub('_','.',csvfile) # Change _ to . in name
dat <- fread(file.path('data', csvfile)) # read data
dat <- left_join(dat, myarea)
dat <- filter(dat, agglvl_code==70) %.% # County-level
aggregate
select(state, county, avg_annual_pay) # Keep variables
return(dat)
}
```

5. We now have to repeat this for each of the 10 years and store the data. For this type of data, a list object usually makes sense:

```
files <- dir('data', pattern='annual_singlefile.zip') # file
names
n <- length(files)
dat_list <- vector('list',n) # Initialize the list
for(i in 1:n){
dat_list[[i]]<- get_data(files[i])   # ingest data
names(dat_list)[i] <- substr(files[i],1,4) #label list with
years
}
```

6. Next, we start creating the visualizations. Since we are essentially creating 10 visualizations, the colors need to mean the same thing on all of them for comparison purposes. So, the discretization needs to be the same for all the years:

```
annpay <- ldply(dat_list) # puts all the data together
breaks <- quantile(annpay$avg_annual_pay,
   c(seq(0,.8,.2),.9,.95,.99,1)) # Makes a common set of
breaks
```

7. We will create the same visualization for each year, using the same breaks. Let's create a function for this common visualization to be produced. We will use ggplot2 for the visualizations. The input values are the data that we create using get_data, and the output is a plot object that can create the visualization:

```
mychoro <- function(d, fill_label=''){
# d has a variable "outcome" that
# is plotted as the fill measure
chor <- left_join(county_df, d)
plt <- ggplot(chor, aes(long,lat, group=group))+
geom_polygon(aes(fill=outcome))+
geom_path(color='white',alpha=0.5,size=0.2)+
geom_polygon(data=state_df, color='black',fill=NA)+
scale_fill_brewer(palette='PuRd')+
labs(x='',y='', fill=fill_label)+
theme(axis.text.x=element_blank(),
axis.text.y=element_blank(),
axis.ticks.x=element_blank(),axis.ticks.y=element_blank())
return(plt)
}
```

8. We now create plot objects for each year using a for loop. We store these objects in a list, with each element corresponding to each year. In the process, we create a new variable, outcome, which is the discretized pay variable, using the common breaks. This variable needs to be called outcome because of the way we designed the mychoro function:

```
plt_list <- vector('list',n)
for(i in 1:n){
dat_list[[i]] <- mutate(dat_list[[i]],
outcome=Discretize(avg_annual_pay,breaks=breaks))
plt_list[[i]] <-
mychoro(dat_list[[i]])+ggtitle(names(dat_list)[i])
}
```

9. The choroplethr package has the utility function, choroplethr_animate, which takes a list of plot objects created with ggplot2 and makes a web page with an animated GIF, layering the plots we created in order. The default web file is animated_choropleth.html:

```
library(choroplethr)
choroplethr_animate(plt_list)
```

We extract three panels from this animation here to give you a flavor of what the animation looks like:

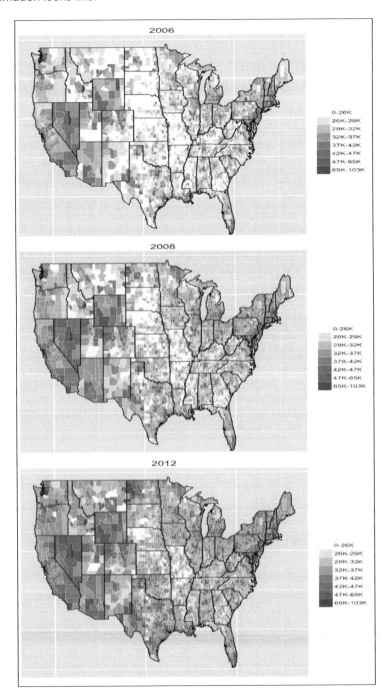

Even from this limited view of the data, we can see the striking growth of employment and wealth in western North Dakota, Wyoming and northeast Nevada, probably due to the discovery, exploration, and mining of shale oil in this region. We can also see that generally, over the 8 years shown here, pay has risen across the country; however, regions throughout the heart of the continental United States have seen almost no change in average pay over this period. We also see a clear increase and expansion of high pay in both California and the northeast. Recall that all three plots are on the same color scale, and so, the interpretation is consistent across them.

How it works...

We covered the individual functionality used in this recipe in previous recipes and so will not repeat them. However, looking at the big picture here shows us two key points worth noting. First, we had to run through a common set of steps multiple times to create a single image. As we had to go through the same steps to create each image used in the final animation, we started to "operationalize" the code a bit, refactoring repeated code blocks into functions.

Secondly, the set of steps needed to create each image is another demonstration of the stages of the data science pipeline. In stage one, we acquire the data through the ingestion of CSV files. Our understanding of the dataset has been built in previous recipes, so the exploration and understanding stage (stage 2 of the pipeline) is a bit light. We join disparate datasets and filter them for stage 3, the munging, wrangling, and manipulation stage. For stage 4, analysis and modeling, we simply discretize the data and then map it to a particular but consistent color scale. Finally, the final data product, the animated choropleth, is used to communicate the vast amount of data in a concise and quickly understandable fashion.

There is more...

The R package `choroplethr` can directly create the individual choropleths using the `choropleth` function, which uses `ggplot2`. However, we didn't like the default appearance of the output, and customization was easier using `ggplot2` directly.

Dr. Vaidyanathan, the creator of the popular `rCharts` package, also created the `rMaps` package. It creates choropleths from R using JavaScript visualization libraries for presentation on the Web, and it can also create animated choropleths using the function `ichoropleth`. However, the package is still in development at the time of writing this book, so we didn't have the facility to create county-level maps. An example with state-level maps is shown in the `rMaps` blog at `http://rmaps.github.io/blog/posts/animated-choropleths/`.

Benchmarking performance for some common tasks

R and its package ecosystem often provide several alternative ways of performing the same task. R also promotes users to create their own functions for particular tasks. When execution time is important, benchmarking performance is necessary to see which strategy works best. We will concentrate on speed in this recipe. The two tasks we will look at are loading the data into R and joining two data objects based on a common variable. All tests are done on a Windows 7 desktop running a 2.4 GHz Intel processor with 8 GB of RAM.

Getting ready

We will use the `ann2012full` and `industry` data objects for our performance experiments here, along with the 2012 annual employment data CSV file for data loading. Since you already have these, you are good to go. If you don't, you will need to install the two functions, `rbenchmark` and `microbenchmark`, using the `install.packages()` command.

How to do it...

The following steps will walk us through benchmarking two different tasks in R:

1. Our first task is to load the employment data into R. The `2012.annual.singlefile.csv` file has 3,556,289 lines of data and 15 columns. While we used `fread` in this chapter, there are many other possible ways of importing this data, which are as follows:

    ❑ The first and most standard way is to use `read.csv` to read the CSV file

    ❑ You can also unzip the original `2012_annual_singlefile.zip` data file on the fly and read the data using `read.csv`

    ❑ We can save the data to an `RData` file the first time we load it, and also subsequent times we load this file, to import the data into R

2. The most basic way to benchmark speed is using the `system.time` function, which measures the time (both elapsed and actual computing time) taken for the task to be performed:

```
> system.time(fread('data/2012.annual.singlefile.csv'))
   user  system elapsed
 14.817   0.443   15.23
```

Note that the times you see will be different than those listed in the preceding command.

3. However, there are packages in R that make benchmarking and comparing different functions much easier. We will introduce the `rbenchmark` package, which provides the `benchmark` function that allows the simultaneous comparison of different functions:

```
library(rbenchmark)

opload <- benchmark(
    CSV=read.csv('data/2012.annual.singlefile.csv',
      stringsAsFactors=F),
    CSVZIP=read.csv(unz('data/2012_annual_singlefile.zip',
      '2012.annual.singlefile.csv'), stringsAsFactors=F),
    LOAD = load('data/ann2012full.rda'),
    FREAD = fread('data/2012.annual.singlefile.csv'),
    order='relative', # Report in order from shortest to longest
    replications=5
)
```

You can refer to the following screenshot for the output of the preceding commands:

```
> opload
    test replications elapsed relative user.self sys.self user.child sys.child
4  FREAD            5   16.29    1.000     15.85     0.43         NA        NA
3   LOAD            5   79.67    4.891     79.10     0.50         NA        NA
1    CSV            5  189.30   11.621    160.82     2.54         NA        NA
2 CSVZIP            5  212.02   13.015    182.46     1.55         NA        NA
```

Note that the results are ordered, and the relative times are recorded under the `relative` column. This shows that `fread` is quite a bit faster than reading using `read.csv`. The very interesting thing is that, on an average, it is 4 times faster than loading the data from an RData file, which is the usual storage method for R data. It is apparently faster to load the data from the file using `fread` than storing the data in R's own serialized format!

4. Our second task is to perform a left outer join of two data objects. We'll look at a task that we have already performed—a left join of the employment data with the industry codes. A left join ensures that the rows of data on the *left* of the operation will be preserved through the operation, and the other data will be expanded by repetition or missing data to have the same number of rows. We used `left_join` in this chapter, but there are three other strategies we can take, which are as follows:

   ❏ The `merge` function available in R's standard library

   ❏ The `join` function from the `plyr` package

   ❏ The `merge` function from the `data.table` package, first transforming the data into `data.table` objects

5. We will again use the `benchmark` function to compare these strategies with `left_join`:

```
ann2012full_dt <- data.table(ann2012full, key='industry_code')

industry_dt <- data.table(industry, key='industry_code')

op <- benchmark(
    DT = data.table::merge(ann2012full_dt, industry_dt,
                by='industry_code', all.x=T),
    PLYR = plyr::join(ann2012full, industry,
              by='industry_code',type='left'),
    DPLYR = dplyr::left_join(ann2012full, industry),
    DPLYR2 = dplyr::left_join(ann2012full_dt, industry_dt),
    MERGE = merge(ann2012full, industry,
                by='industry_code', all.x=T),
    order='relative',
    replications=5
)
```

You can refer to the following screenshot for the output of the preceding commands:

```
> op
     test replications elapsed relative user.self sys.self user.child sys.child
1      DT            5    0.41    1.000      0.41     0.00         NA         NA
4  DPLYR2            5    4.90   11.951      4.24     0.63         NA         NA
3   DPLYR            5    5.40   13.171      4.52     0.86         NA         NA
2    PLYR            5   97.70  238.293     95.46     1.67         NA         NA
5   MERGE            5  207.14  505.220    204.14     2.54         NA         NA
```

Here, we see that the `data.table` method is a lot faster than any other strategy. Using `dplyr` is about 12 times slower for this particular task, `plyr` is about 100 times slower, and the standard `merge` method is 200 times slower. There is a bit of overhead in converting the `data.frame` objects to `data.table` objects, but the margin of advantage in this task overcomes this overhead.

How it works...

The basic workhorse of time benchmarking in R is the `system.time` function. This function records the time when evaluation of an expression starts, runs the expression, and then notes the time when it finishes. It then reports the difference of the two times. By default, garbage collection takes place before each evaluation so that the results are more consistent and maximal memory is freed for each evaluation.

The `benchmark` function in the `rbenchmark` package provides additional flexibility. It wraps the `system.time` function and allows several expressions to be evaluated in a single run. It also does some basic computations, such as relative times, to simplify reporting.

In terms of our tasks here, `fread` uses a powerful optimized C function to read the data, resulting in a high degree of speed optimization. The `read.csv` function just reads the datafile line by line and parses the fields by the comma separator. We can get some speed improvements in our experiments by specifying the column types in `read.csv`, using the `colClasses` option, since determining data types consumes some execution time. The `load` function reads the data from the `RData` files created using the `save` function, which stores binary representations of R objects. It compresses the size of the data a lot, but we see that there are more efficient ways of reading data than loading the `RData` file.

The second task we set ourselves to benchmark is a left outer join of the employment data `ann2014full`, with the data object of the `industry` industry codes. The former has 3,556,289 rows and 15 columns, and the latter has 2,469 rows and 2 columns. They are merged based on the common variable, `industry_code`. In a left join, all the rows of `ann2014full` will be preserved. For this, the `merge` commands will use the `all.x=T` option. The `join` function has the `type='left'` option for a left join. For the `data.table` merge, we first convert the `data.frame` objects to `data.table` objects, specifying that each has the same key variable, (think *index* in a database) `industry_code`. The `data.table` objects are then merged using this key variable.

There is a bit of new code formatting in this code snippet. We use `plyr::join` and `dplyr::left_join`, rather than just `join` and `left_join`. This style of coding explicitly specifies that we are using a particular function from a particular package to avoid confusion. Sometimes, this style of coding is useful when you have functions with the same name in two different packages that are both loaded in R.

There's more...

The `data.table` package provides very fast tools for data loading, munging, and joining. The `data.table` object is a derivative object of the `data.frame` package, and many of the functions in R that input `data.frame` objects can also import `data.table` objects. It is for this reason that the `data.table` object becomes your default container for rectangular data.

See also

▸   Hadley Wickham has a very nice exposition on benchmarking that is part of his online book, available at `http://adv-r.had.co.nz/Performance.html`. He promotes the `microbenchmark` package for benchmarking purposes.

6

Creating Application-oriented Analyses Using Tax Data (Python)

In this chapter, we will cover:

- ▸ Preparing for the analysis of top incomes
- ▸ Importing and exploring the world's top incomes dataset
- ▸ Analyzing and visualizing the top income data of the US
- ▸ Furthering the analysis of the top income groups of the US
- ▸ Reporting with Jinja2

Introduction

So far in the book, we've taken a practical approach to data analysis with R. With relative ease, we've been able to answer questions about particular datasets, produce models, and export visualizations. For this reason, R is an excellent choice for rapid prototyping and analytics; it is a domain-specific language designed for statistical data analysis, and it does its job well.

In the next half of the book, we will take a look at a different approach to analytics, one that is more geared toward production environments and applications. The data science pipeline of hypothesis, acquisition, cleaning and munging, analysis, modeling, visualization, and application is not a clean and linear process by any means. Moreover, when the analysis is meant to be reproducible at scale in an automated fashion, many new considerations and requirements enter into the picture. Thus, many data applications require a broader toolkit. This toolkit should still provide rapid prototyping, be generally available on all systems, and provide full support for a range of computing operations, including network operations, data operations, and scientific operations. Given these requirements, Python becomes a clear contender as the tool of choice for application-oriented analyses.

Python is an interpreted language (sometimes referred to as a scripting language), much like R. It requires no special IDE or software compilation tools and is therefore as fast as R to develop with and prototype. Like R, it also makes use of C shared objects to improve computational performance. Additionally, Python is a default system tool on Linux, Unix, and Mac OS X machines and is available on Windows. Python comes with "batteries included," which means that the standard library is widely inclusive of many modules, from multiprocessing to compression toolsets. Python is a flexible computing powerhouse that can tackle any problem domain. If you find yourself in need of libraries that are outside of the standard library, Python also comes with a package manager (like R) that allows the download and installation of other code bases.

Python's computational flexibility means that some analytical tasks take more lines of code than their counterpart in R. However, Python does have the tools that allow it to perform the same statistical computing. This leads to an obvious question: "When do we use R over Python and vice versa?" This chapter attempts to answer this question by taking an application-oriented approach to statistical analyses.

An introduction to application-oriented approaches

Data applications and data products are interminably becoming part of our everyday lives. These products have much farther reach than simple, data-driven web applications, which include all manner of frontend web and mobile applications that are backed by a database and include middleware to handle transactions. By this definition, a simple blog is not fundamentally different from a large-scale e-commerce site. Instead, data products and appliances acquire their value from the data itself and create more data as a result. These types of applications can be utilized to enrich traditional applications, such as semantic tagging for the blog or recommendation engines for an e-commerce site. On the other hand, they can be standalone data products in their own right, including everything from quantified self devices to self-driving vehicles.

The treatment and analyses of data in a live or streaming context seem to be the defining characteristic of application-oriented analyses, unlike more traditional data mining or statistical evaluations of a static dataset. In order to deal with such data, a fair amount of programmatic nimbleness or dynamic approaches are required, and flexibility is precisely where Python shines in the data science context.

Consider a specific example for a reporting task. Taking a snapshot of a data window and manually compiling a report from gathered analytics with charting graphics and visualizations is good practice to understand changing data and get a feel for larger patterns. When this report needs to be run daily on lower data volumes, schedulers could merely dump the report out to a file every day. However, when the reporting task becomes hourly, or on demand, it means the visualization application has become a static web application and will probably require a central location. As this task and the data size grow, adding constraints or queries on the report becomes important. This is a typical life cycle for data applications, and Python development is well suited to handle these changing requirements.

In this chapter, we will repeat the task of one of the first chapters in R to perform analyses of a dataset to discover interesting trends and features. We will describe, model, and visualize a dataset that contains the world's top incomes and discuss the statistical toolkit in Python. However, as we go through this chapter, we will also include notes on how the analyses and methodologies we are utilizing can be framed in an application-oriented context.

Preparing for the analysis of top incomes

For the following recipes, you will need Python installed on your computer and you will need the world's top incomes dataset. This recipe will help ensure you have set up everything you need to complete this analysis project.

Getting ready

To step through this recipe, you will need a computer with access to the Internet.

Make sure you have downloaded and installed Python and the necessary Python libraries to complete this project.

 Refer to *Chapter 1, Preparing Your Data Science Environment*, to set up a Python development environment using virtualenv and install the required libraries for matplotlib and NumPy.

How to do it...

The following steps will guide you to download the world's top incomes dataset and install the necessary Python libraries to complete this project:

 The original dataset for the world's top incomes can be downloaded from `http://topincomes.g-mond.parisschoolofeconomics.eu/`. However, the site has been updated several times, which has changed the output format of the data (from `.csv` to `.xlsx`). This recipe assumes a `.csv` file format.

This chapter's repository contains the properly formatted version of the input data file.

1. Save the world's top incomes dataset to a location on your computer where you will be able to find it.

2. Open up a terminal window and start a Python interpreter.

3. Check to make sure that the following three libraries, NumPy, matplotlib, and Jinja2, are installed; try to import each:

   ```
   >>> import numpy as np
   >>> import jinja2
   >>> import matplotlib as plt
   ```

4. Each of the preceding libraries should import without a comment or remark from Python. If they do, you are good to go. If not, refer to *Chapter 1, Preparing Your Data Science Environment*, to set up your system.

How it works...

NumPy is the fundamental scientific computing library for Python; it is therefore essential to any data science toolkit, and we will leverage it in many places throughout the Python chapters. However, since NumPy is an external library that must be compiled for your system, we will discuss alternative native-Python approaches alongside the NumPy approach.

Importing and exploring the world's top incomes dataset

Once you have downloaded and installed everything in the previous recipe, you can read the dataset with Python and then start doing some preliminary analysis to get a sense of what the data you have looks like.

The dataset that we'll explore in this chapter was created by *Alvaredo, Facundo, Anthony B. Atkinson, Thomas Piketty*, and *Emmanuel Saez, The World Top Incomes Database,* http://topincomes.g-mond.parisschoolofeconomics.eu/, *10/12/2013*. It contains global information about the highest incomes per country for approximately the past 100 years, gleaned from tax records.

Getting ready

If you've completed the previous recipe, you should have everything you need to continue.

How to do it...

Let's use the following sequence of steps to import the data and start our exploration of this dataset in Python:

1. With the following snippet, we create a Python list in memory that contains dictionaries of each row, where the keys are the column names (the first row of the CSV contains the header information) and the values are the values for that particular row:

    ```
    #Reading this data is straightforward with the built
    in csv module:

    import csv

    data_file = "../data/income_dist.csv"

    with open(data_file, 'r') as csvfile:
        reader = csv.DictReader(csvfile)
        data = list(reader)
    ```

     Note that the input file, income_dist.csv, might be in a different directory on your system depending on where you place it.

2. We perform a quick check with `len` to reveal the number of records:

    ```
    len(data)
    2180
    ```

3. When utilizing CSV data with headers, we check the field names on the CSV reader itself, as well as getting the number of variables:

    ```
    print reader.fieldnames
    ['Country', 'Year', 'Top 10% income share', ...]

    len(reader.fieldnames)
    354
    ```

4. While this data is not too large, let's start using best practices when accessing it. Rather than holding all of the data in memory, we use a generator to access the data one row at a time.

Generators are Python expressions that allow you to create functions that act as iterables; rather than returning all of the data, they yield data one "part" at a time in a memory-efficient iteration context. As our datasets get larger, it's useful to use generators to perform filtering on demand and clean data as you read it.

```python
def dataset(path):
    with open(path, 'r') as csvfile:
        reader = csv.DictReader(csvfile)
        for row in reader:
            yield row
```

Also, take note of the `with open(path, 'r') as csvfile` statement. This statement ensures that the CSV file is closed when the `with` block is exited, even (or especially) if there is an exception. Python `with` blocks replace the `try`, `except`, and `finally` statements, and are syntactically brief while semantically more correct programming constructs.

5. Using our new function, we can take a look to determine which countries are involved in our dataset:

```python
print set([row["Country"] for row in dataset(data_file)])
set(['Canada', 'Italy', 'France', 'Netherlands', 'Ireland',
...])
```

6. We can also inspect the range of years that this dataset covers, as follows:

```python
print min(set([int(row["Year"]) for row in
dataset(data_file)]))
```
```
1875
```
```python
print max(set([int(row["Year"]) for row in
dataset(data_file)]))
2010
```

In both of these previous examples, we used a Python list comprehension to generate a set. A comprehension is a concise statement that generates an iterable, much like the earlier memory-safe generators. The output variable (or variables) is specified, along with the `for` keyword, and the iterable to express the variable, along with an optional `if` condition. In Python 2.7, set and dictionary comprehensions also exist. The previous country set could also be expressed as follows:

```python
{row["Country"] for row in dataset(data_file)}
set(['Canada', 'Italy', 'France', 'Netherlands', 'Ireland',
...])
```

7. Finally, let's filter just the data for the United States so we can analyze it exclusively:

```
filter(lambda row: row["Country"] == "United States",
              dataset(data_file))
```

The Python `filter` function creates a list from all of the values of a sequence or iterable (the second parameter) that make the function specified by the first parameter true. In this case, we use an anonymous function (a `lambda` function) to check whether the value in the specified row's `Country` column is equal to `United States`.

8. With this initial discovery and exploration of the dataset, we can now take a look at some of the data using matplotlib, one of the main scientific plotting packages available for Python and very similar to the plotting capabilities of MATLAB:

```
import csv
import numpy as np
import matplotlib.pyplot as plt


def dataset(path, filter_field=None, filter_value=None):
    with open(path, 'r') as csvfile:
        reader = csv.DictReader(csvfile)
        if filter_field:
            for row in filter(lambda row:
                row[filter_field]==filter_value, reader):
                yield row
        else:
            for row in reader:
                yield row


def main(path):
    data  = [(row["Year"], float(row["Average income per tax
        unit"]))

            for row in dataset(path, "Country", "United
                States")]

    width = 0.35
    ind   = np.arange(len(data))
    fig   = plt.figure()
    ax    = plt.subplot(111)
```

```
ax.bar(ind, list(d[1] for d in data))
ax.set_xticks(np.arange(0, len(data), 4))
ax.set_xticklabels(list(d[0] for d in data)[0::4],
    rotation=45)
ax.set_ylabel("Income in USD")
plt.title("U.S. Average Income 1913-2008")


plt.show()


if __name__ == "__main__":
    main("income_dist.csv")
```

The preceding snippet will give us the following output:

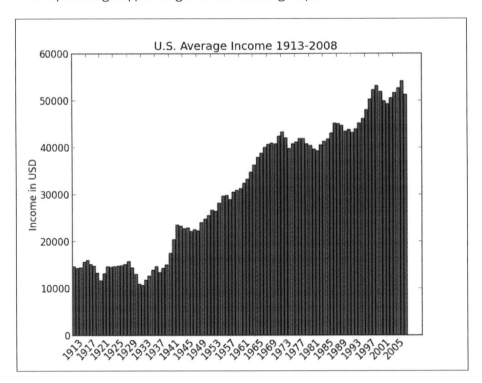

The preceding example of data exploration with Python should seem familiar from many of the R chapters. Loading the dataset, filtering, and computing ranges required a few more lines of code and specific typecasting, but we quickly created analyses in a memory-safe fashion.

9. When we moved on to creating charts, we started using NumPy and matplotlib a bit more. NumPy can be used in a very similar fashion to R, to load data from a CSV file to an array in memory and dynamically determine the type of each column. To do this, the following two module functions can be used:

   ❑ genfromtext: This function creates an array from tabular data stored in a text file with two main loops. The first converts each line of the file to string sequences, and the second converts each string to an appropriate datatype. It is a bit slower and not as memory efficient, but the result is a convenient data table stored in memory. This function also handles missing data, which other faster and simpler functions cannot.

   ❑ recfromcsv: This function is a helper function based on genfromtext that has default arguments set to provide access to a CSV file.

Have a look at the following snippet:

```
import numpy as np
dataset = np.recfromcsv(data_file, skip_header=1)
dataset
array([[          nan,   1.93200000e+03,             nan, ...,
                nan,   1.65900000e+00,   2.51700000e+00],
       [          nan,   1.93300000e+03,             nan, ...,
                nan,   1.67400000e+00,   2.48400000e+00],
       [          nan,   1.93400000e+03,             nan, ...,
                nan,   1.65200000e+00,   2.53400000e+00],
       ...,
       [          nan,   2.00600000e+03,   4.52600000e+01, ...,
          1.11936337e+07,   1.54600000e+00,   2.83000000e+00],
       [          nan,   2.00700000e+03,   4.55100000e+01, ...,
          1.19172976e+07,   1.53000000e+00,   2.88500000e+00],
       [          nan,   2.00800000e+03,   4.56000000e+01, ...,
          9.14119000e+06,   1.55500000e+00,   2.80300000e+00]])
```

The first argument to the function should be the data source. It should be either a string that points to a local or remote file or a file-like object with a read method. URLs will be downloaded to the current working directory before they are loaded. Additionally, the input can be either text or a compressed file. The function recognizes gzip and bzip2. These files need to have the .gz or .bz2 extensions to be readable. Notable optional arguments to genfromtext include the delimiter, , (comma) by default in recfromcsv; skip_header and skip_footer, which take an optional number of lines to skip from the top or bottom respectively; and dtype, which specifies the datatype of the cells. By default, the dtype is None, and NumPy will attempt to detect the correct format.

10. We can now get an overall sense of the scope of our data table:

```
dataset.size
```

```
771720
```

```
dataset.shape
```

```
(2179, 354)
```

 Depending on your version of NumPy, you might see slightly different output. The `dataset.size` statement might report back the number of rows of data `(2179)`, and the shape might output as `(2179,)`.

The `size` property on `ndarray` returns the number of elements in the matrix. The shape property returns a tuple of the dimensions in our array. CSVs are naturally two-dimensional, therefore the `(m, n)` tuple indicates the number of rows and columns, respectively.

However, there are a couple of gotchas with using this method. First, note that we had to skip our header line; `genfromtxt` does allow named columns by setting the keyword argument names to `True` (and in this case, you won't set `skip_headers=1`). Unfortunately, in this particular dataset, the column names might contain commas. The CSV reader deals with this correctly since the strings that contain commas are quoted, but `genfromtxt` is not a CSV reader in general. To fix this, either the headers have to be fixed, or some other names need to be added. Secondly, the `Country` column has been reduced to NaN, and the `Year` column has been turned into a floating point integer, which is not ideal.

11. A manual fix on the dataset is necessary, and this is not uncommon. Since we know that there are 354 columns and the first two columns are `Country` and `Year`, we can precompute our column names and datatypes:

```
names = ["country", "year"]
names.extend(["col%i" % (idx+1) for idx in xrange(352)])
dtype = "S64,i4," + ",".join(["f18" for idx in xrange(352)])


dataset = np.genfromtxt(data_file, dtype=dtype, names=names,
delimiter=",", skip_header=1, autostrip=2)
```

We name the first two columns `country` and `year`, respectively, and assign them datatypes of `S64` or string-64, then assign the `year` column as `i4` or integer-4. For the rest of the columns, we assign them the name `coln`, where `n` is an integer from 1 to 352, and the datatype is `f18` or float-18. These character lengths allow us to capture as much data as possible, including exponential floating point representations.

Unfortunately, as we look through the data, we can see a lot of nan values that represent Not a Number, a fixture in floating point arithmetic used to represent values that are not numbers nor are equivalent to infinity. Missing data is a very common issue in the data wrangling and cleaning stage of the pipeline. It appears that the dataset contains many missing or invalid entries, which makes sense given the historical data, and countries that may not have had effective data collection for given columns.

12. In order to clean the data, we use a NumPy masked array, which is actually a combination of a standard NumPy array and a mask, a set of Boolean values that indicate whether the data in that position should be used in computations or not. This can be done as follows:

```
import numpy.ma as ma

ma.masked_invalid(dataset['col1'])

masked_array(data = [-- -- -- ..., 45.2599983215332
45.5099983215332 45.599998474121094],

mask = [ True   True   True ..., False False False],fill_value =
1e+20)
```

How it works...

Our dataset function has been modified to filter on a single field and value if desired. If no filter has been specified, it generates the entire CSV. The main piece of interest is what happens in the main function. Here, we generate a bar chart of average incomes in the United States per year using matplotlib. Let's walk through the code.

We collect our data as (year, avg_income) tuples in a list comprehension that utilizes our special dataset method to filter data only for the United States.

> We have to cast the average income per tax unit to a float in order to compute on it. In this case, we leave the year as a string since it simply acts as a label; however, in order to perform datetime computations, we might want to convert that year to a date using datetime.strptime (row['Year'], '%Y').date().

After we have performed our data collection, filtering, and conversions, we set up the chart. The width is the maximum width of a bar. An ind iterable (ndarray) refers to the x axis locations for each bar; in this case, we want one location for every data point in our set. A NumPy np.arange function is similar to the built-in xrange functions; it returns an iterable (ndarray) of evenly spaced values in the given interval. In this case, we provide a stop value that is the length of the list and use the default start value of 0 and step size of 1, but these can also be specified. The use of arange allows floating point arguments, and it is typically much faster than simply instantiating the full array of values.

The `figure` and `subplot` module functions utilize the `matplotlib.pyplot` module to create the base figure and axes, respectively. The `figure` function creates a new figure, or returns a reference to a previously created figure. The `subplot` function returns a subplot axis positioned by the grid definition with the following arguments: the number of rows, number of columns, and plot number. This function has a convenience when all three arguments are less than 10; simply supply a three-digit number with the respective values, for example, `plot.subplot (111)` creates 1 x 1 axes in subplot 1.

We then use the subplot to create a bar chart from our data. Note the use of another comprehension that passes the values of the incomes from our dataset along with the indices we created with `np.arange`. On setting the x axis labels, however, we notice that if we add all years as individual labels, the x axis is unreadable. Instead, we add ticks for every 4 years, starting with the first year. In this case, you can see that we use a step size of 4 in `np.arange` to set our ticks, and similarly, in our labels, we use slices on the Python list to step through every four labels. For example, for a given list, we will use:

```
mylist[s:e:t]
```

The slice of the list starts at `s`, ends at `e`, and has the step size `t`. Negative numbers are also supported in slices to be iterated from the end of the list; for example, `mylist [-1]` will return the last item of the list.

There's more...

NumPy is an incredibly useful and powerful library, but we should note some very important differences. The list datatype in Python is wildly different from the `numpy` array. The Python list can contain any number of different datatypes, including lists. Thus, the following example list is perfectly valid:

```
python_list = ['bob' , 5.1, True, 1, [5, 3, 'sam'] ]
```

Underneath the hood, the Python list contains pointers to the memory locations of the elements of the list. To access the first element of the list, Python goes to the memory location for the list and grabs the first value stored there. This value is a memory address for the first element. Python then jumps to this new memory location to grab the value for the actual first element. Thus, "grabbing" the first element of the list requires two memory lookups.

NumPy arrays are very much like C. They must contain a single datatype, and this allows the array to be stored in a contiguous block of memory, which makes reading the array significantly faster. When reading the first element of the array, Python goes to the appropriate memory address that contains the actual value to be retrieved. When the next element in the array is needed, it is right next to the location of the first element in memory, which makes reading much faster.

See also

▶ The NumPy documentation at `http://docs.scipy.org/doc/numpy/reference/`

▶ A strong tutorial on NumPy and SciPy at `http://www.engr.ucsb.edu/~shell/che210d/numpy.pdf`

Analyzing and visualizing the top income data of the US

Now that we've imported and explored the top incomes dataset a bit, let's drill down on a specific country and conduct some analyses on their income distribution data. In particular, the United States has excellent data relating to the top incomes by percentile, so we'll use the data of the United States in the following exercises. If you choose other countries to leverage their datasets, beware that you may need to use different fields to get the same analyses.

Getting ready

In order to conduct our analyses, we're going to create a few helper methods that we will use continually throughout this chapter. Application-oriented analyses typically produce reusable code that performs singular tasks in order to adapt quickly to changing data or analysis requirements. In particular, let's create two helper functions: one that extracts data by a particular country and one that creates a time series from a set of particular rows:

```
def dataset(path, country="United States"):
    """
    Extract the data for the country provided. Default is United
      States.
    """

    with open(path, 'r') as csvfile:
        reader = csv.DictReader(csvfile)
        for row in filter(lambda row: row["Country"]==country,
          reader):
            yield row


def timeseries(data, column):
    """
    Creates a year based time series for the given column.
    """
```

```
    for row in filter(lambda row: row[column], data):
        yield (int(row["Year"]), row[column])
```

The first function iterates through the dataset using the `csv.DictReader` filter on a particular country using Python's built-in `filter` function. The second function leverages the fact that there is a `Year` column to create a time series for the data, a generator that yields `(year, value)` tuples for a particular column in the dataset. Note that this function should be passed in a generator created by the `dataset` function. We can now utilize these two functions for a series of analyses across any column for a single country.

How to do it...

Generally speaking, the data for the United States is broken up into six groups:

- ▸ Top 10 percent income share
- ▸ Top 5 percent income share
- ▸ Top 1 percent income share
- ▸ Top 0.5 percent income share
- ▸ Top 0.1 percent income share
- ▸ Average income share

These groups reflect aggregations for data points collected in those specific bins. An easy and quick first analysis is to simply plot these percentages of income shares over time for each of the top income groups. Since plotting several time series is going to be a common task, let's once again create a `helper` function that wraps matplotlib and generates a line chart for each time series that is passed to it:

```
def linechart(series, **kwargs):
    fig = plt.figure()
    ax  = plt.subplot(111)

    for line in series:
        line  = list(line)
        xvals = [v[0] for v in line]
        yvals = [v[1] for v in line]
        ax.plot(xvals, yvals)

    if 'ylabel' in kwargs:
        ax.set_ylabel(kwargs['ylabel'])
```

```
    if 'title' in kwargs:
        plt.title(kwargs['title'])


    if 'labels' in kwargs:
        ax.legend(kwargs.get('labels'))


    return fig
```

This function is very simple. It creates a `matplotlib.pyplot` figure as well as the axis subplot. For each line in the series, it gets the x axis values (remember that the first item in our time series time tuple is `Year`) as the first item of the tuple and the y axis, which is the second value. It splits these into separate generators and then plots them on the figure. Finally, any options we want for our chart, such as labels or legends, we can simply pass as keyword arguments, and our function will handle them for us! The following steps will walk you through this recipe of application-oriented analysis:

1. In order to generate our chart, we simply need to use our `timeseries` function on the columns we would like and pass them to the `linechart` function. This simple task is now repeatable, and we'll use it a few times for the next few charts:

```
def percent_income_share(source):
    """
    Create Income Share chart
    """
    columns = (
        "Top 10% income share",
        "Top 5% income share",
        "Top 1% income share",
        "Top 0.5% income share",
        "Top 0.1% income share",
    )
    source   = list(dataset(source))

    return linechart([timeseries(source, col) for col in
        columns],
                        labels=columns,
                        title="U.S. Percentage Income Share",
                        ylabel="Percentage")
```

Note that I wrapped the generation of this chart in a function as well; this way, we modify the chart as needed, and the function wraps the configuration and generation of the chart itself. The function identifies the columns for the line series and then fetches the dataset. For each column, it creates a time series and then passes these time series to our `linechart` function with our configuration options.

2. To generate the plot, we define the input parameter to the `percent_income_source` function:

```
percent_income_share(data_file)

plt.show()
```

The following screenshot shows the result, and you will use a similar pattern in the rest of the chapter to use the functions to create the needed plots:

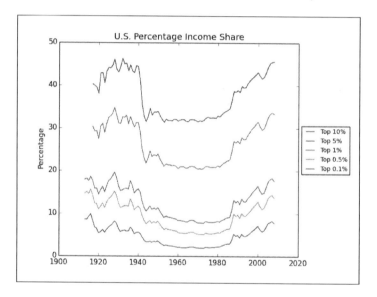

This graph tells us that the raw percentages for the income groups tend to move in the same direction. When one group's income increases, the other groups' incomes also increase. This seems like a good sanity check as folks who are in the top 0.1 percent income bracket are also in the top 10 percent income bracket, and they contribute a lot to the overall mean for each bin. There is also a clear, persistent difference between each of the lines.

3. Looking at the raw percentages is useful, but we may also want to consider how the percentages have changed over time, relative to what the average percentage has been for that income group. In order to do this, we can calculate the means of each group's percentages and then divide all of the group's values by the mean we just calculated.

   Since mean normalization is another common function that we might want to perform on a range of datasets, we will once again create a function that will accept a time series as input and return a new time series whose values are divided by the mean:

```
def normalize(data):
    """
    Normalizes the data set. Expects a timeseries input
    """
    data =  list(data)
    norm =  np.array(list(d[1] for d in data), dtype="f8")
    mean =  norm.mean()
    norm /= mean
        return zip((d[0] for d in data), norm)
```

4. We can now easily write another function that takes these columns and computes the mean normalized time series:

```
def mean_normalized_percent_income_share(source):
    columns = (
        "Top 10% income share",
        "Top 5% income share",
        "Top 1% income share",
        "Top 0.5% income share",
        "Top 0.1% income share",
    )
    source  = list(dataset(source))


    return linechart([normalize(timeseries(source, col)) for
        col in columns],
                        labels=columns,
                        title="Mean Normalized U.S. Percentage
                            Income Share",
                        ylabel="Percentage")
mean_normalized_percent_income_share(data_file)
plt.show()
```

Note how the following command snippet is very similar to the previous function, except when it performs the normalization:

```
>>> fig = mean_normalized_percent_income_
share(DATA)
>>> fig.show()
```

The preceding commands give us the following graph:

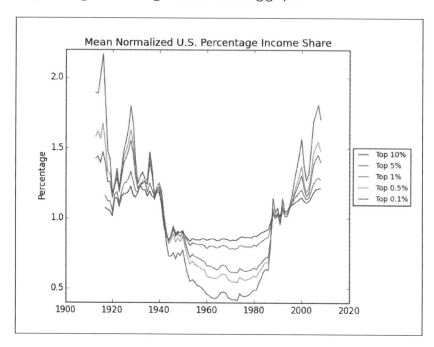

This graph shows us that the wealthier the group, the larger the percentage-wise swings we tend to see in their incomes.

5. The dataset also breaks the group's income into categories, such as income that includes capital gains versus income without capital gains. Let's take a look at how each group's capital gains income fluctuates over time.

Another common functionality is to compute the difference between two columns and plot the resulting time series. Computing the difference between two NumPy arrays is also very easy, and since it is common for our task, we write yet another function to do the job:

```
def delta(first, second):
    """
    Returns an array of deltas for the two arrays.
    """

    first   = list(first)
    years   = yrange(first)
    first   = np.array(list(d[1] for d in first), dtype="f8")
    second  = np.array(list(d[1] for d in second), dtype="f8")


    # Not for use in writing
    if first.size != second.size:
        first = np.insert(first, [0,0,0,0], [None, None, None,
            None])


    diff    = first - second
    return zip(years, diff)
```

Furthermore, the following is an appropriate helper function:

```
def yrange(data):
    """
    Get the range of years from the dataset
    """

    years = set()
    for row in data:
        if row[0] not in years:
            yield row[0]
            years.add(row[0])
```

This function once again creates NumPy arrays from each dataset, casting the datatype to floats. Note that we need to get the list of years from one of the datasets, so we gather it from the first dataset.

6. We also need to keep in mind that `first.size` needs to be the same as `second.size`, for example, that each array shares the same dimensionality. The difference is computed and the years are once again zipped to the data to form a time series:

```python
def capital_gains_lift(source):
    """
    Computes capital gains lift in top income percentages over
      time chart
    """
    columns = (
        ("Top 10% income share-including capital gains", "Top
          10% income share"),
        ("Top 5% income share-including capital gains", "Top
          5% income share"),
        ("Top 1% income share-including capital gains", "Top
          1% income share"),
        ("Top 0.5% income share-including capital gains", "Top
          0.5% income share"),
        ("Top 0.1% income share-including capital gains", "Top
          0.1% income share"),
        ("Top 0.05% income share-including capital gains",
          "Top 0.05% income share"),
    )

    source  = list(dataset(source))
    series  = [delta(timeseries(source, a), timeseries(source,
      b)) for a, b in columns]

    return linechart(series,labels=list(col[1] for col in
      columns), title="U.S. Capital Gains Income Lift",
      ylabel="Percentage Difference")
capital_gains_lift(data_file)
plt.show()
```

The preceding code stores the columns as tuples of two columns—first and second—and then uses the `delta` function to compute the difference between the two. Like our previous graphs, it then creates a line chart as shown:

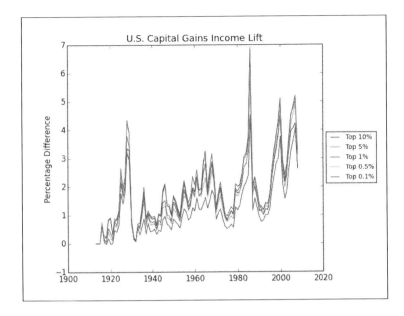

This is interesting as the graph shows the volatility of the capital gains income over time. If you are familiar with U.S. financial history, you can see the effect on the capital gains income of the well-known stock market booms and busts in this chart.

How it works...

The easiest way to perform operations on big datasets is to use NumPy's `array` class. As we've already seen, this class allows us to perform common operations, including basic mathematical operations between a scalar and an array. Converting the generator to an array, however, requires us to load the data into memory. Python's built-in `list` function takes an iterator and returns a list. This is required because the NumPy array must know the length of the data in order to allocate the correct amount of memory. With the array, it is easy enough to calculate the mean and then perform the divide equals scalar operation across the entire array. This broadcasts the division operation so that each element in the array is divided by the mean. We are, in essence, normalizing the elements of the array by their mean. We can then zip together our years with the newly computed data and return the time series.

Furthering the analysis of the top income groups of the US

So far in this chapter, we have focused on the analysis of income percentages over time. Next, we will continue our analysis by taking a look at some of the other interesting figures that we have in our dataset, specifically the actual income figures and income categories that comprise these figures.

Getting ready

If you've completed the previous recipe, you should have everything you need to continue.

How to do it...

With the following steps, we dive deeper into the dataset and examine additional income figures:

1. The dataset also contains the average incomes by year of the different groups. Let's graph these and see how they have changed over time, relative to each other:

```python
def average_incomes(source):
    """
    Compares percentage average incomes
    """
    columns = (
        "Top 10% average income",
        "Top 5% average income",
        "Top 1% average income",
        "Top 0.5% average income",
        "Top 0.1% average income",
        "Top 0.05% average income",
    )

    source = list(dataset(source))

    return linechart([timeseries(source, col) for col in columns], labels=columns, title="U.S. Average Income",
    ylabel="2008 US Dollars")

average_incomes(data_file)

plt.show()
```

Since we have the foundation in place to create line charts, we can immediately analyze this new dataset with the tools we already have. We simply choose a different collection of columns and then customize our chart accordingly! The following is the resulting graph:

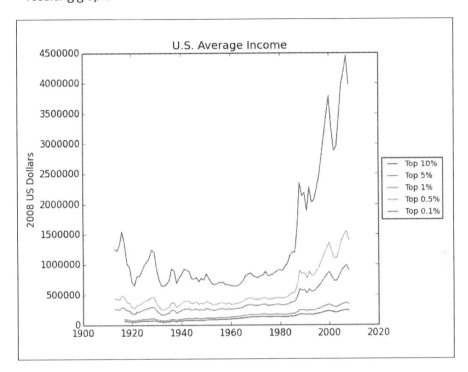

The results shown by this graph are quite fascinating. Until the 1980s, the wealthy have been about $1-1.5 million richer than the lower income groups. From the 1980s forward, the disparity has increased dramatically.

2. We can also use the `delta` functionality to see how much richer the rich are than the average American:

```
def average_top_income_lift(source):
    """
    Compares top percentage avg income over total avg
    """

    columns = (
        ("Top 10% average income", "Top 0.1% average income"),
        ("Top 5% average income", "Top 0.1% average income"),
        ("Top 1% average income", "Top 0.1% average income"),
```

```
    ("Top 0.5% average income", "Top 0.1% average
        income"),
    ("Top 0.1% average income", "Top 0.1% average
        income"),
)
source  = list(dataset(source))
series  = [delta(timeseries(source, a), timeseries(source,
    b)) for a, b in columns]


return linechart(series,
                    labels=list(col[0] for col in columns),
                    title="U.S. Income Disparity",
                    ylabel="2008 US Dollars")
```

We still haven't written new code other than the selection of our columns and utilization of the functionality that we have already added to our project. This reveals the following:

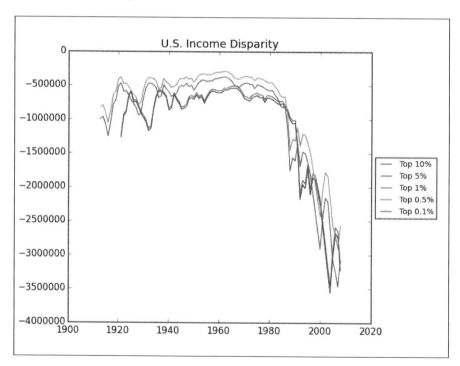

3. In our last analysis, we'll show off a different kind of chart to look at the composition of the income of the wealthiest Americans. Since the composition is a percentage-based time series, a good chart for this task is a stacked area. Once again, we can utilize our time series code and simply add a function to create stacked area charts as follows:

```
def stackedarea(series, **kwargs):
    fig = plt.figure()
    axe = fig.add_subplot(111)

    fnx = lambda s: np.array(list(v[1] for v in s), dtype="f8")
    yax = np.row_stack(fnx(s) for s in series)
    xax = np.arange(1917, 2008)

    polys = axe.stackplot(xax, yax)
    axe.margins(0,0)

    if 'ylabel' in kwargs:
        axe.set_ylabel(kwargs['ylabel'])

    if 'labels' in kwargs:
        legendProxies = []
        for poly in polys:
            legendProxies.append(plt.Rectangle((0, 0), 1, 1,
                fc=poly.get_facecolor()[0]))

        axe.legend(legendProxies, kwargs.get('labels'))

    if 'title' in kwargs:
        plt.title(kwargs['title'])

    return fig
```

The preceding function expects a group of time series, the total percentages of which add up to 100. We create a special, anonymous function that will convert each series into a NumPy array. The NumPy `row_stack` function creates a sequence of arrays stacked vertically; this is what will generate our stackplot using the `subplot.stackplot` function. The only other surprise in this function is the requirement to use a legend proxy to create rectangles with the fill color from the stackplot in the legend.

4. Now, we can take a look at the income composition of the wealthiest Americans:

```python
def income_composition(source):
    """

    Compares income composition
    """


    columns = (
        "Top 10% income composition-Wages, salaries and
          pensions",
        "Top 10% income composition-Dividends",
        "Top 10% income composition-Interest Income",
        "Top 10% income composition-Rents",
        "Top 10% income composition-Entrepreneurial income",
    )


    source  = list(dataset(source))
    labels  = ("Salary", "Dividends", "Interest", "Rent",
      "Business")
    return stackedarea([timeseries(source, col) for col in
      columns], labels=labels, title="U.S. Top 10% Income
      Composition", ylabel="Percentage")
```

The preceding code generates the following plot:

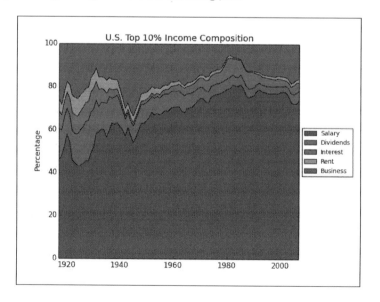

As you can see, the top 10 percent of American earners make most of their money from a salary income; however, business income also plays a large role. Dividends played a bigger role earlier in the century than they do towards the end of the century, which is true for interest and rent as well. Interestingly, for the first part of the 20th century, the percentage of income that is related to entrepreneurial income declines, until the 1980s, when it starts to grow again, possibly because of the technology sector.

How it works...

This recipe really helps to demonstrate the value of the application-oriented approach. We continue to abstract out portions of code that perform singular tasks and use them as functions. As our library of functions increases, our analysis, often filled with repeated but slightly different tasks, becomes more composition than creation. Even better, these individual pieces are much easier to test and evaluate. Over time, with additional analyses, we will build a rich and fully customized library of tools that will drastically speed up future investigations.

This recipe also reveals how Python code can be created to construct more R-like analyses. As we performed further evaluations, we leveraged functions and tools that we had already built for our dataset and created new ones, such as the stacked area function that built off our older tools. However, unlike an analysis-oriented approach, these tools now exist in a data-specific library of code that can be used to build applications and reports, as we'll see in the next recipe.

Reporting with Jinja2

Visualizations and graphs are excellent for identifying obvious patterns in the dataset. However, as trends emerge from multiple sources, more in-depth reporting is required, as well as descriptions of the techniques used for those not directly involved in the project. Instead of creating these reports by hand, application-oriented analyses make use of template languages to dynamically construct documents at the time of analysis. Jinja2 is a Python library that is used to generate documents by combining a template—usually an HTML file, but can be any kind of text file—with a context, a data source that is used to fill in the template. This combination is ideal to report on the analyses that we're performing.

Getting ready

The Jinja2 template library should be installed and ready to use.

How to do it...

The following steps will walk us through using the Jinja2 templating library to create flexible and appealing reporting output:

1. Jinja2 is simple and has familiar Python-esque syntax (though it is not Python). Templates can include logic or control flow, including iteration, conditionals, and formatting, which removes the need to have the data adapt to the template. A simple example is as follows:

```
>>> from jinja2 import Template
>>> template = Template(u'Greetings, {{ name }}!')
>>> template.render(name='Mr. Praline')
Greetings, Mr. Praline!
```

2. However, we should decouple our templates from our Python code, and instead, store the templates as text files on our system. Jinja2 provides a central `Environment` object, which is used to store configurations and global objects to load templates either from the filesystem or other Python packages:

```
from jinja2 import Environment, PackageLoader, , FileSystemLoader
# 'templates' should be the path to the templates folder
# as written, it is assumed to be in the current directory
jinjaenv = Environment(loader = FileSystemLoader('templates'))
template = jinjaenv.get_template('report.html')
```

Here, the Jinja2 environment is configured to look for template files in the `templates` directory of our Python module. Another recommended loader is `FileSystemLoader`, which should be provided a search path to look for template files. In this case, the template called `report.html` is fetched from the Python module and is ready to be rendered.

Rendering can be as simple as `template.render(context)`, which will return a Unicode string of generated output. The context should be a Python dictionary whose keys are the variable names that will be used in the template. Alternatively, the context can be passed in as keyword arguments; `template.render({'name':'Terry'})` is equivalent to `template.render(name='Terry')`. However, for large templates (and large datasets) it is far more efficient to use the `Template.stream` method; it does not render the entire template at once, but evaluates each statement sequentially and yields it as a generator.

3. The stream can then be passed to a file-like object to be written to disk or serialized over the network:

```
template.stream(items=['a', 'b', 'c'],
name='Eric').dump('report-2013.html')
```

This seemingly simple technique is incredibly powerful, especially when combined with the JSON module. JSON data can be dumped directly into JavaScript snippets for interactive charting and visualization libraries on the Web, such as D3, Highcharts, and Google Charts.

4. Let's take a look at a complete example using the world's top incomes dataset:

```
import csv
import json

from datetime import datetime
from jinja2 import Environment, PackageLoader, FileSystemLoader
from itertools import groupby
from operator import itemgetter

def dataset(path, include):
    column = 'Average income per tax unit'

    with open(path, 'r') as csvfile:
        reader = csv.DictReader(csvfile)
        key = itemgetter('Country')

        # Use groupby: memory efficient collection by country
        for key, values in groupby(reader, key=key):
            # Only yield countries that are included
            if key in include:
                yield key, [(int(value['Year']),
                    float(value[column]))
                        for value in values if value[column]]

def extract_years(data):
    for country in data:
        for value in country[1]:
            yield value[0]
```

```python
def extract_series(data, years):
    for country, cdata in data:
        cdata  = dict(cdata)
        series = [cdata[year] if year in cdata else None for
          year in years]
        yield {
            'name': country,
            'data': series,
        }


def write(context):
    path = "report-%s.html" %datetime.now().strftime("%Y%m%d")
    jinjaenv = Environment(loader = FileSystemLoader('templates'))
    template = jinjaenv.get_template('report.html')
    template.stream(context).dump(path)


def main(source):
    # Select countries to include
    include = ("United States", "France", "Italy",
               "Germany", "South Africa", "New Zealand")

    # Get dataset from CSV
    data = list(dataset(source, include))
    years = set(extract_years(data))

    # Generate context
    context = {
        'title': "Average Income per Family, %i - %i" %
          (min(years), max(years)),
        'years': json.dumps(list(years)),
        'countries': [v[0] for v in data],
        'series': json.dumps(list(extract_series(data, years))),
    }

    # Write HTML with template
    write(context)
```

```
if __name__ == '__main__':
    source = '../data/income_dist.csv'
    main(source)
```

This is a lot of code, so let's go through it step by step. The `dataset` function reads our CSV file for the `Average income` column and filters based on a set of included countries. It uses a functional iteration helper, `groupby`, that collects the rows of our CSV file by the `Country` field, which means that we get a dataset per country. Both the `itemgetter` and `groupby` functions are common, memory-safe helper functions in Python that do a lot of heavy lifting during large-scale data analyses.

After we extract the dataset, we have two helper methods. The first, `extract_years`, generates all the year values from every country. This is necessary because not all countries have values for every year in the dataset. We'll also use this function to determine the range of years for our template. This brings us to the second function, `extract_series`, that normalizes the data, replacing empty years with `None` values to ensure our time series is correct.

The write method wraps the template-writing functionality. It creates a file called `report-{date}.html`, adding the current date for reference. It also loads the `Environment` object, finds the report template, and writes the output to disk. Finally, the `main` method gathers all the data and context together and connects the functions.

5. The report template is as follows:

```html
<html>
<head>
    <title>{{ title }}</title>
</head>
<body>
    <div class="container">
        <h1>{{ title }}</h1>
        <div id="countries">
            <ul>
            {% for country in countries %}
                <li>{{ country }}<li>
            {% endfor %}
            </ul>
        </div>
        <div id="chart"></div>
    </div>
```

```
    <script type="text/javascript"
src="http://codeorigin.jquery.com/jquery-
2.0.3.min.js"></script>

    <script src="http://code.highcharts.com/highcharts.js">
    </script>

    <script type="text/javascript">
        $.noConflict();

        jQuery(document).ready(function($) {
            $('#chart').highcharts({
                xAxis: {
                    categories: JSON.parse('{{ years }}'),
                    tickInterval: 5,
                },
                yAxis: {
                    title: {
                        text: "2008 USD"
                    }
                },
                plotOptions: {
                    line: {
                        marker: {
                            enabled: false
                        }
                    }
                },
                series: JSON.parse('{{ series }}')
            });
        });
    </script>
</body>
</html>
```

The preceding template fills in the title in the correct spot, then creates an unordered list of the countries included in our dataset. Additionally, it uses Highcharts to create an interactive chart. Highcharts is an option-based, JavaScript chart library. Note that we're using `JSON.parse` to parse the JSON data that we dumped in Python. This will ensure there are no conflicts when converting Python datatypes to JavaScript ones. When you open up the report in a browser, it should look something like the following screenshot:

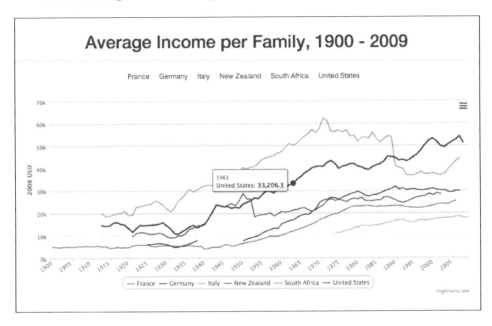

How it works...

Performing analytics and data mining in Python parallels R closely, especially when using the NumPy library. NumPy, like R, is designed for scientific computing and has a similar set of functionality when dealing with multidimensional arrays. However, as a general rule, Python takes more lines of code, especially when creating charts with matplotlib. This is caused by Python's generic approach to data, particularly because it is used in many problem domains, not specifically statistical analyses, and this is also Python's strength.

In particular, data analyses with Python tend to have an application-oriented approach, typically involving live or streaming data that is routinely updated, rather than analyses on a single dataset. This usually means that analyses performed in Python leverage fast prototyping and statistical exploration with tools such as NumPy, but then leverage an extremely inclusive standard library to handle the data in all phases of the data pipeline.

There's more...

There are several different Python template languages, each with a different approach to combining a predefined template with data to form human-readable output. Many of these template languages are intended as the backbone of web application frameworks, such as Django and Flask, that are used to construct dynamic web pages from a database. Since these languages are well suited to generate HTML, reporting with these tools creates an easy transition, from one-off reporting, to scheduled reporting, to on-demand reporting from a web application. Jinja2 is the primary template language for Flask and has a Django-like syntax, making it an excellent choice for future implementations.

See also

- ▸ For the data source, go to
  `http://topincomes.g-mond.parisschoolofeconomics.eu/`

- ▸ The *Templating in python* article at
  `https://wiki.python.org/moin/Templating`

- ▸ The *What is Data Science?* article at
  `http://radar.oreilly.com/2010/06/what-is-data-science.html`

- ▸ The *Setting up Python and Matplotlib in OSX Mountain Lion* article at
  `http://www.tapir.caltech.edu/~dtsang/python.html`

7

Driving Visual Analyses with Automobile Data (Python)

In this chapter, we will cover:

- ▸ Getting started with IPython
- ▸ Exploring IPython Notebook
- ▸ Preparing to analyze automobile fuel efficiencies
- ▸ Exploring and describing fuel efficiency data with Python
- ▸ Analyzing automobile fuel efficiency over time with Python
- ▸ Investigating the makes and models of automobiles with Python

Introduction

In the first chapter on R (*Chapter 2, Driving Visual Analysis with Automobile Data (R)*), we walked through an analysis project that examined automobile fuel economy data using the R statistical programming language. This dataset, available at `http://www.fueleconomy.gov/feg/epadata/vehicles.csv.zip`, contains fuel efficiency performance metrics over time for all makes and models of automobiles in the United States of America. This dataset also contains numerous other features and attributes of the automobile models other than fuel economy, providing an opportunity to summarize and group the data so that we can identify interesting trends and relationships.

Unlike the first chapter on R, we will perform the entire analysis using Python. However, we will ask the same questions and follow the same sequence of steps as before, again following the data science pipeline. With study, this will allow you to see the similarities and differences between the two languages for a mostly identical analysis.

In *Chapter 6, Creating Application-oriented Analyses Using Tax Data (Python)*, we used mostly pure Python with some help from NumPy and SciPy, either straight from the Python command line—also known as **Read-Eval-Print Loop** (**REPL**)—or from executable script files. In this chapter, we will take a very different approach using Python as a scripting language in an interactive fashion that is more similar to R. We will introduce the reader to the unofficial interactive environment of Python, IPython, and the IPython notebook, showing how to produce readable and well-documented analysis scripts. Further, we will leverage the data analysis capabilities of the relatively new but powerful pandas library and the invaluable data frame data type that it offers. pandas often allows us to complete complex tasks with fewer lines of code. The drawback to this approach is that while you don't have to reinvent the wheel for common data manipulation tasks, you do have to learn the API of a completely different package, which is pandas.

The goal of this chapter is not to guide you through an analysis project that you have already completed but to show you how that project can be completed in another language. More importantly, we want to get you, the reader, to become more introspective with your own code and analysis. Think not only about how something is done but why something is done that way in that particular language. How does the language shape the analysis?

Getting started with IPython

IPython is the interactive computing shell for Python that will change the way you think about interactive shells. It brings to the table a host of very useful functionalities that will most likely become part of your default toolbox, including magic functions, tab completion, easy access to command-line tools, and much more. We will only scratch the surface here and strongly recommend that you keep exploring what can be done with IPython.

Getting ready

If you have completed the installation instructions in the first chapter, you should be ready to tackle the following recipes. Note that IPython 2.0, which is a major release, was launched in 2014.

How to do it...

The following steps will get you up and running with the IPython environment:

1. Open up a terminal window on your computer and type `ipython`. You should be immediately presented with the following text:

   ```
   Python 2.7.5 (default, Mar  9 2014, 22:15:05)
   Type "copyright", "credits" or "license" for more information.


   IPython 2.1.0 -- An enhanced Interactive Python.
   ?           -> Introduction and overview of IPython's features.
   %quickref -> Quick reference.
   help        -> Python's own help system.
   object?     -> Details about 'object', use 'object??' for extra
   details.
   In [1]:
   ```

   Note that your version might be slightly different than what is shown in the preceding command-line output.

2. Just to show you how great IPython is, type in `ls`, and you should be greeted with the directory listing! Yes, you have access to common Unix commands straight from your Python prompt inside the Python interpreter.

3. Now, let's try changing directories. Type `cd` at the prompt, hit space, and now hit *Tab*. You should be presented with a list of directories available from within the current directory. Start typing the first few letters of the target directory, and then, hit *Tab* again. If there is only one option that matches, hitting the *Tab* key automatically will insert that name. Otherwise, the list of possibilities will show only those names that match the letters that you have already typed. Each letter that is entered acts as a filter when you press *Tab*.

4. Now, type `?`, and you will get a quick introduction to and overview of IPython's features.

5. Let's take a look at the *magic* functions. These are special functions that IPython understands and will always start with the `%` symbol. The `%paste` function is one such example and is amazing for copying and pasting Python code into IPython *without* losing proper indentation.

6. We will try the `%timeit` magic function that intelligently benchmarks Python code. Enter the following commands:

```
n = 100000
%timeit range(n)
%timeit xrange(n)
```

We should get an output like this:

```
1000 loops, best of 3: 1.22 ms per loop
1000000 loops, best of 3: 258 ns per loop
```

This shows you how much faster `xrange` is than `range` (`1.22` milliseconds versus `2.58` nanoseconds!) and helps show you the utility of generators in Python.

7. You can also easily run system commands by prefacing the command with an exclamation mark. Try the following command:

```
!ping www.google.com
```

You should see the following output:

```
PING google.com (74.125.22.101): 56 data bytes
64 bytes from 74.125.22.101: icmp_seq=0 ttl=38 time=40.733 ms
64 bytes from 74.125.22.101: icmp_seq=1 ttl=38 time=40.183 ms
64 bytes from 74.125.22.101: icmp_seq=2 ttl=38 time=37.635 ms
```

8. Finally, IPython provides an excellent command history. Simply press the up arrow key to access the previously entered command. Continue to press the up arrow key to walk backwards through the command list of your session and the down arrow key to come forward. Also, the magic `%history` command allows you to jump to a particular command number in the session. Type the following command to see the first command that you entered:

```
%history 1
```

9. Now, type `exit` to drop out of IPython and back to your system command prompt.

How it works...

There isn't much to explain here and we have just scratched the surface of what IPython can do. Hopefully, we have gotten you interested in diving deeper, especially with the wealth of new features offered by IPython 2.0, including dynamic and user-controllable data visualizations.

See also

- ▸ IPython at `http://ipython.org/`
- ▸ The *IPython* Cookbook at `https://github.com/ipython/ipython/wiki?path=Cookbook`
- ▸ *IPython: A System for Interactive Scientific Computing* at `http://fperez.org/papers/ipython07_pe-gr_cise.pdf`
- ▸ *Learning IPython for Interactive Computing and Data Visualization, Cyrille Rossant, Packt Publishing*, available at `http://www.packtpub.com/learning-ipython-for-interactive-computing-and-data-visualization/book`
- ▸ The future of IPython at `http://www.infoworld.com/print/236429`

Exploring IPython Notebook

IPython Notebook is the perfect complement to IPython. As per the IPython website:

> *"The IPython Notebook is a web-based interactive computational environment where you can combine code execution, text, mathematics, plots and rich media into a single document."*

While this is a bit of a mouthful, it is actually a pretty accurate description. In practice, IPython Notebook allows you to intersperse your code with comments and images and anything else that might be useful. You can use IPython Notebooks for everything from presentations (a great replacement for PowerPoint) to an electronic laboratory notebook or a textbook.

Getting ready

If you have completed the installation instructions in the first chapter, you should be ready to tackle the following recipes.

How to do it...

These steps will get you started with exploring the incredibly powerful IPython Notebook environment. We urge you to go beyond this simple set of steps to understand the true power of the tool.

1. Type `ipython notebook --pylab=inline` in the command prompt. The `--pylab=inline` option should allow your plots to appear inline in your notebook. You should see some text quickly scroll by in the terminal window, and then, the following screen should load in the default browser (for me, this is Chrome). Note that the URL should be `http://127.0.0.1:8888/`, indicating that the browser is connected to a server running on the local machine at port `8888`.

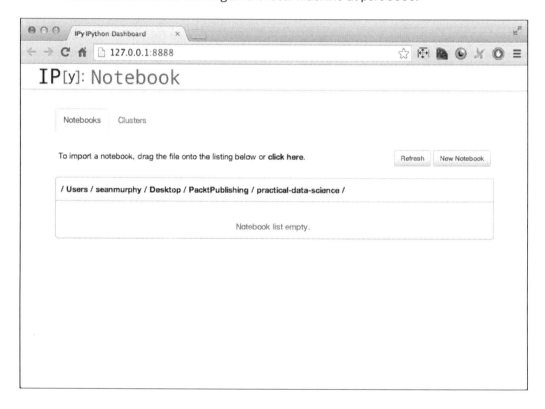

2. You should not see any notebooks listed in the browser (note that IPython Notebook files have a `.ipynb` extension) as IPython Notebook searches the directory you launched it from for notebook files. Let's create a notebook now. Click on the **New Notebook** button in the upper right-hand side of the page. A new browser tab or window should open up, showing you something similar to the following screenshot:

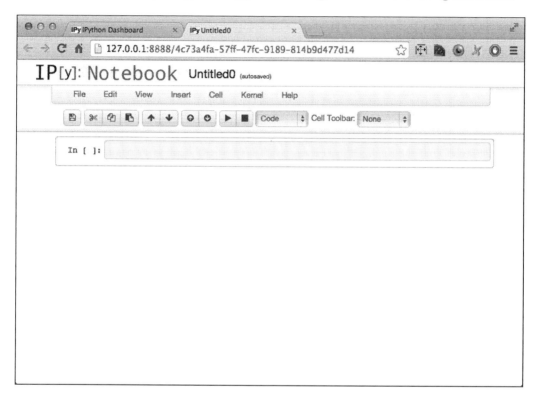

3. From the top down, you can see the text-based menu followed by the toolbar for issuing common commands, and then, your very first cell, which should resemble the command prompt in IPython.

4. Place the mouse cursor in the first cell and type `5+5`. Next, either navigate to **Cell | Run** or press *Shift + Enter* as a keyboard shortcut to cause the contents of the cell to be interpreted. You should now see something similar to the following screenshot. Basically, we just executed a simple Python statement within the first cell of our first IPython Notebook.

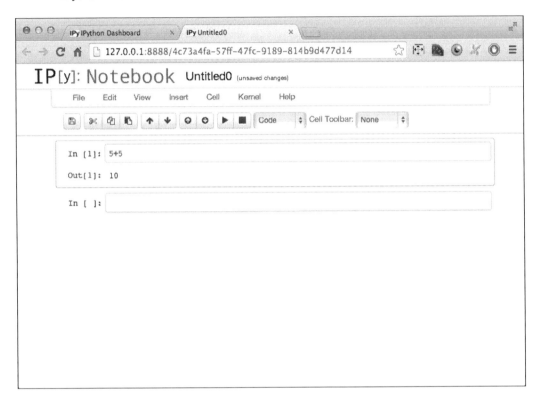

5. Click on the second cell, and then, navigate to **Cell | Cell Type | Markdown**. Now, you can easily write `markdown` in the cell for documentation purposes.

6. Close the two browser windows or tabs (the notebook and the notebook browser).

7. Go back to the terminal in which you typed `ipython notebook`, hit *Ctrl + C*, then hit *Y*, and press *Enter*. This will shut down the IPython Notebook server.

How it works...

For those of you coming from either more traditional statistical software packages, such as Stata, SPSS, or SAS, or more traditional mathematical software packages, such as MATLAB, Mathematica, or Maple, you are probably used to the very graphical and feature-rich interactive environments provided by the respective companies. From this background, IPython Notebook might seem a bit foreign but hopefully much more user friendly and less intimidating than the traditional Python prompt. Further, IPython Notebook offers an interesting combination of interactivity and sequential workflow that is particularly well suited for data analysis, especially during the prototyping phases. R has a library called `Knitr` (http://yihui.name/knitr/) that offers the report-generating capabilities of IPython Notebook.

When you type in `ipython notebook`, you are launching a server running on your local machine, and IPython Notebook itself is really a web application that uses a server-client architecture. The IPython Notebook server, as per `ipython.org`, uses a two-process kernel architecture with ZeroMQ (http://zeromq.org/) and Tornado. ZeroMQ is an intelligent socket library for high-performance messaging, helping IPython manage distributed compute clusters among other tasks. Tornado is a Python web framework and asynchronous networking module that serves IPython Notebook's HTTP requests. The project is open source and you can contribute to the source code if you are so inclined.

IPython Notebook also allows you to export your notebooks, which are actually just text files filled with JSON, to a large number of alternative formats using the command-line tool called `nbconvert` (http://ipython.org/ipython-doc/rel-1.0.0/interactive/nbconvert.html). Available export formats include HTML, LaTex, reveal.js HTML slideshows, Markdown, simple Python scripts, and reStructuredText for the Sphinx documentation.

Finally, there is IPython Notebook Viewer (`nbviewer`), which is a free web service where you can both post and go through static, HTML versions of notebook files hosted on remote servers (these servers are currently donated by Rackspace). Thus, if you create an amazing `.ipynb` file that you want to share, you can upload it to http://nbviewer.ipython.org/ and let the world see your efforts.

There's more...

We will try not to sing too loudly the praises of Markdown, but if you are unfamiliar with the tool, we strongly suggest that you try it out. Markdown is actually two different things: a syntax for formatting plain text in a way that can be easily converted to a structured document and a software tool that converts said text into HTML and other languages. Basically, Markdown enables the author to use any desired simple text editor (VI, VIM, Emacs, Sublime editor, TextWrangler, Crimson Editor, or Notepad) that can capture plain text yet still describe relatively complex structures such as different levels of headers, ordered and unordered lists, and block quotes as well as some formatting such as bold and italics. Markdown basically offers a very human-readable version of HTML that is similar to JSON and offers a very human-readable data format.

See also

▶ IPython Notebook at `http://ipython.org/notebook.html`

▶ The IPython Notebook documentation at `http://ipython.org/ipython-doc/stable/interactive/notebook.html`

▶ An interesting IPython Notebook collection at `https://github.com/ipython/ipython/wiki/A-gallery-of-interesting-IPython-Notebooks`

▶ The IPython Notebook development retrospective at `http://blog.fperez.org/2012/01/ipython-notebook-historical.html`

▶ Setting up a remote IPython Notebook server at `http://nbviewer.ipython.org/github/Unidata/tds-python-workshop/blob/master/ipython-notebook-server.ipynb`

▶ The Markdown home page at `https://daringfireball.net/projects/markdown/basics`

Preparing to analyze automobile fuel efficiencies

In this recipe, we are going to start our Python-based analysis of the automobile fuel efficiencies data.

Getting ready

If you completed the first chapter successfully, you should be ready to get started.

How to do it...

The following steps will see you through setting up your working directory and IPython for the analysis for this chapter:

1. Create a project directory called `fuel_efficiency_python`.

2. Download the automobile fuel efficiency dataset from `http://fueleconomy.gov/feg/epadata/vehicles.csv.zip` and store it in the preceding directory. Extract the `vehicles.csv` file from the zip file into the same directory.

3. Open a terminal window and change the current directory (`cd`) to the `fuel_efficiency_python` directory.

4. At the terminal, type the following command:

```
ipython notebook
```

5. Once the new page has loaded in your web browser, click on **New Notebook**.

6. Click on the current name of the notebook, which is **untitled0**, and enter in a new name for this analysis (mine is `fuel_efficiency_python`).

7. Let's use the top-most cell for `import` statements. Type in the following commands:

```
import pandas as pd
import numpy as np
from ggplot import *
%matplotlib inline
```

Then, hit *Shift + Enter* to execute the cell. This imports both the `pandas` and `numpy` libraries, assigning them local names to save a few characters while typing commands. It also imports the `ggplot` library. Please note that using the `from ggplot import *` command line is not a best practice in Python and pours the `ggplot` package contents into our default namespace. However, we are doing this so that our `ggplot` syntax most closely resembles the R `ggplot2` syntax, which is strongly not Pythonic. Finally, we use a magic command to tell IPython Notebook that we want `matploblib` graphs to render in the notebook.

8. In the next cell, let's import the data and look at the first few records:

```
vehicles = pd.read_csv("vehicles.csv")
vehicles.head
```

Then, press *Shift + Enter*. The following text should be shown:

```
/Library/Python/2.7/site-packages/pandas/io/parsers.py:1139: DtypeWarning: Columns (22,23,70,71,72,73) have mixed types. Specify dtyp
e option on import or set low_memory=False.
  data = self._reader.read(nrows)
Out[2]: <bound method DataFrame.head of    barrels08  barrelsA08  charge120  charge240  city08  city08U  cityA08  \
0       15.689436           0           0         19        0        0
1       29.950562           0           0          9        0        0
2       12.195570           0           0         23        0        0
3       29.950562           0           0         10        0        0
4       17.337486           0           0         17        0        0
5       14.964294           0           0         21        0        0
6       13.184400           0           0         22        0        0
7       13.733750           0           0         23        0        0
8       12.657024           0           0         23        0        0
9       13.184400           0           0         23        0        0
10      12.657024           0           0         23        0        0
11      15.689436           0           0         18        0        0
12      13.733750           0           0         21        0        0
13      15.689436           0           0         18        0        0
14      25.336022           0           0         12        0        0
```

However, notice that a red warning message appears as follows:

```
/Library/Python/2.7/site-packages/pandas/io/parsers.py:1070:
DtypeWarning: Columns (22,23,70,71,72,73) have mixed types.
Specify dtype option on import or set low_memory=False.    data
= self._reader.read(nrows)
```

This tells us that columns 22, 23, 70, 71, 72, and 73 contain mixed data types. Let's find the corresponding names using the following commands:

```
column_names = vehicles.columns.values
column_names[[22, 23, 70, 71, 72, 73]]

array([cylinders, displ, fuelType2, rangeA, evMotor, mfrCode],
dtype=object)
```

 Mixed data types sounds like it could be problematic so make a mental note of these column names. Remember, data cleaning and wrangling often consume 90 percent of project time.

How it works...

With this recipe, we are simply setting up our working directory and creating a new IPython Notebook that we will use for the analysis. We have imported the pandas library and very quickly read the `vehicles.csv` data file directly into a data frame. Speaking from experience, pandas' robust data import capabilities will save you a lot of time.

Although we imported data directly from a comma-separated value file into a data frame, pandas is capable of handling many other formats, including Excel, HDF, SQL, JSON, Stata, and even the clipboard using the reader functions. We can also write out the data from data frames in just as many formats using writer functions accessed from the data frame object.

Using the bound method `head` that is part of the `Data Frame` class in pandas, we have received a very informative summary of the data frame, including a per-column count of non-null values and a count of the various data types across the columns.

There's more...

The data frame is an incredibly powerful concept and data structure. Thinking in data frames is critical for many data analyses yet also very different from thinking in array or matrix operations (say, if you are coming from MATLAB or C as your primary development languages).

With the data frame, each column represents a different variable or characteristic and can be a different data type, such as floats, integers, or strings. Each row of the data frame is a separate observation or instance with its own set of values. For example, if each row represents a person, the columns could be `age` (an integer) and `gender` (a category or string). Often, we will want to select the set of observations (rows) that match a particular characteristic (say, all males) and examine this subgroup. The data frame is conceptually very similar to a table in a relational database.

See also

▸ Data structures in pandas at `http://pandas.pydata.org/pandas-docs/stable/dsintro.html`

▸ Data frames in R at `http://www.r-tutor.com/r-introduction/data-frame`

Exploring and describing fuel efficiency data with Python

Now that we have imported the automobile fuel efficiency dataset into IPython and witnessed the power of pandas, the next step is to replicate the preliminary analysis performed in R from the earlier chapter, getting your feet wet with some basic pandas functionality.

Getting ready

We will continue to grow and develop the IPython Notebook that we started in the previous recipe. If you've completed the previous recipe, you should have everything you need to continue.

How to do it...

1. First, let's find out how many observations (rows) are in our data using the following command:

    ```
    len(vehicles)
    34287
    ```

    If you switch back and forth between R and Python, remember that in R, the function is `length` and in Python, it is `len`.

2. Next, let's find out how many variables (columns) are in our data using the following command:

    ```
    len(vehicles.columns)
    74
    ```

3. Let's get a list of the names of the columns using the following command:

```
print(vehicles.columns)

Index([u'barrels08', u'barrelsA08', u'charge120',
u'charge240', u'city08', u'city08U', u'cityA08', u'cityA08U',
u'cityCD', u'cityE', u'cityUF', u'co2', u'co2A',
u'co2TailpipeAGpm', u'co2TailpipeGpm', u'comb08', u'comb08U',
u'combA08', u'combA08U', u'combE', u'combinedCD',
u'combinedUF', u'cylinders', u'displ', u'drive', u'engId',
u'eng_dscr', u'feScore', u'fuelCost08', u'fuelCostA08',
u'fuelType', u'fuelType1', u'ghgScore', u'ghgScoreA',
u'highway08', u'highway08U', u'highwayA08', u'highwayA08U',
u'highwayCD', u'highwayE', u'highwayUF', u'hlv', u'hpv',
u'id', u'lv2', u'lv4', u'make', u'model', u'mpgData',
u'phevBlended', u'pv2', u'pv4', u'range', u'rangeCity',
u'rangeCityA', u'rangeHwy', u'rangeHwyA', u'trany', u'UCity',
u'UCityA', u'UHighway', u'UHighwayA', u'VClass', u'year',
u'youSaveSpend', u'guzzler', u'trans_dscr', u'tCharger',
u'sCharger', u'atvType', u'fuelType2', u'rangeA', u'evMotor',
u'mfrCode'], dtype=object)
```

 The u letter in front of each string indicates that the strings are represented in Unicode (`http://docs.python.org/2/howto/unicode.html`)

4. Let's find out how many unique years of data are included in this dataset and what the first and last years are using the following command:

```
len(pd.unique(vehicles.year))
31
min(vehicles.year)
1984
max(vehicles["year"])
2014
```

 Note that again, we have used two different syntaxes to reference individual columns within the `vehicles` data frame.

5. Next, let's find out what types of fuel are used as the automobiles' primary fuel types. In R, we have the `table` function that will return a count of the occurrences of a variable's various values. In pandas, we use the following:

```
pd.value_counts(vehicles.fuelType1)
```

```
Regular Gasoline       24587
Premium Gasoline        8521
Diesel                  1025
Natural Gas               57
Electricity               56
Midgrade Gasoline         41
dtype: int64
```

6. Now if we want to explore what types of transmissions these automobiles have, we immediately try the following command:

```
pd.value_counts(vehicles.trany)
```

However, this results in a bit of unexpected and lengthy output:

```
In [3]: pd.value_counts(vehicles.trany)

Out[3]: Automatic 4-spd                    11029
        Manual 5-spd                        8213
        Automatic 3-spd                     3151
        Automatic 5-spd                     2149
        Manual 6-spd                        2009
        Automatic (S6)                      1877
        Manual 4-spd                        1483
        Automatic 6-spd                     1093
        Automatic (S5)                       813
        Automatic (variable gear ratios)     534
        Automatic 7-spd                      493
        Automatic (S8)                       366
```

What we really want to know is the number of cars with automatic and manual transmissions. We notice that the `trany` variable always starts with the letter A when it represents an automatic transmission and M for manual transmission. Thus, we create a new variable, `trany2`, that contains the first character of the `trany` variable, which is a string:

```
vehicles["trany2"] = vehicles.trany.str[0]
```

```
pd.value_counts(vehicles.trany2)
```

The preceding command yields the answer that we wanted or twice as many automatics as manuals:

```
A    22451
M    11825
dtype: int64
```

How it works...

In this recipe, we looked at some basic functionality in Python and pandas. We have used two different syntaxes (`vehicles['trany']` and `vehicles.trany`) to access variables within the data frame. We have also used some of the core pandas functions to explore the data, such as the incredibly useful `unique` and the `value_counts` function.

There's more...

In terms of the data science pipeline, we have touched on two stages in a single recipe: data cleaning and data exploration. Often, when working with smaller datasets where the time to complete a particular action is quite short and can be completed on our laptop, we will very quickly go through multiple stages of the pipeline and then loop back, depending on the results. In general, the data science pipeline is a highly iterative process. The faster we can accomplish steps, the more iterations we can fit into a fixed time, and often, we can create a better final analysis.

See also

▸ The pandas API overview at `http://pandas.pydata.org/pandas-docs/stable/api.html`

Analyzing automobile fuel efficiency over time with Python

In this recipe, we are going to look at some of the fuel efficiency metrics over time and in relation to other data points. To do so, we are going to have to replicate the functionality of two very popular R libraries, which are `plyr` and `ggplot2`, in Python. The split-apply-combine data analysis capabilities that are so handily covered by the `plyr` R library are handled equally well but in a slightly different fashion by pandas right out of the box. The data visualization abilities of `ggplot2`—an R library implementation of the grammar of graphics—are not handled as readily, as we shall see in this recipe.

Getting ready

If you've completed the previous recipe, you should have almost everything you need to continue. However, we are going to use a Python clone of the ggplot2 library for R, which is conveniently named ggplot. If you didn't complete the entire setup chapter and haven't yet installed the ggplot package, open up a terminal and type the following:

```
pip install ggplot (or sudo pip install ggplot)
```

This should work on Windows machines as well.

Wait for the installation to complete. After you do this, you will have to restart the IPython Notebook server to be able to import this newly installed ggplot library.

How to do it...

We dive into the analysis stage with the following steps:

1. Let's start by looking at whether there is an overall trend of how mpg changes over time on average. We first want to group the data by year:

   ```
   grouped = vehicles.groupby("year")
   ```

2. Next, we want to compute the mean of three separate columns by the previous grouping:

   ```
   averaged = grouped['comb08',  'highway08',
   'city08'].agg([np.mean])
   ```

   This produces a new data frame with three columns containing the mean of comb08, highway08, and city08 variables, respectively. Notice that we are using the mean function supplied by NumPy (np).

3. To make life easier, we will rename the columns and then create a new column named year, which contains the data frame's index:

   ```
   averaged.columns = ['comb08_mean','highway08_mean',
   'city08_mean']
   ```
   ```
   averaged['year'] = averaged.index
   ```

   Note how easy renaming columns is compared to what we had to do in R! The columns attribute of the data frame contains the name of the columns and what we need to modify in order to rename the columns.

4. Finally, we want to plot the results as a scatter plot using the new `ggplot` package for the Python library:

```
print ggplot(averaged, aes('year', 'comb08_mean')) +
geom_point(color='steelblue') + xlab("Year") + ylab("Average
MPG") + ggtitle("All cars")
```

Refer to the following graph:

This plot might be misleading as hybrid cars with excellent mileage have recently become more popular. Let's see whether we can screen out these automobile makes. Astute observers will recognize that this figure does not include the `geom_smooth()` method of the matching image in the R chapter. While the current `ggplot` library (0.4.7 as of February 11, 2014) has the potentially equivalent `stat_smooth()` method, the current version still has some bugs that caused erroneous results to be plotted (and not shown).

5. To remove hybrid cars, we create three Boolean arrays. The `criteria1` array selects those rows of the data frame where `fuelType1` is `Regular Gasoline`, `Premium Gasoline`, or `Midgrade Gasoline`. The `criteria2` array makes sure that the rows contain a null for `fuelType2`, and `criteria3` ensures that the `atvType` is not `Hybrid`. We can perform the logical AND operation over these three Boolean arrays together to select only the desired rows from the data frame:

```
criteria1 = vehicles.fuelType1.isin(["Regular Gasoline",
"Premium Gasoline", "Midgrade Gasoline"])

criteria2 = vehicles.fuelType2.isnull()

criteria3 = vehicles.atvType != "Hybrid"

vehicles_non_hybrid = vehicles[criteria1 & criteria2 &
criteria3]

len(vehicles_non_hybrid)

31659
```

6. We group the resulting data frame by year and then compute the mean combination fuel efficiency for each year, resulting in the following data frame:

```
grouped = vehicles_non_hybrid.groupby(['year'])

averaged = grouped['comb08'].agg([np.mean])

print(averaged)
```

The preceding command results in this output:

```
          mean
year
1984   19.121622
1985   19.394686
1986   19.320457
1987   19.164568
1988   19.367607
1989   19.141964
...
2007   18.987512
2008   19.191781
2009   19.738095
2010   20.466736
2011   20.961755
2012   21.496767
2013   22.335118
2014   22.248027
```

Based on the preceding data, we see that there is still a marked rise in the average miles per gallon even after eliminating hybrids.

7. The next question that we can ask is whether there have been fewer cars with large engines built more recently? If this is true, it could explain the increase in average miles per gallon. First, let's verify that larger engine cars have poorer miles per gallon. To look at this, we need to dig into the `displ` variable that represents the engine displacement in liters. Remember, pandas gave us a warning about this variable containing multiple data types, so let's compute the unique `displ` values:

```
pd.unique(vehicles_non_hybrid.displ)
array([2.0, 4.9, 2.2, 5.2, 1.8, 1.6, 2.3, 2.8, 4.0, 5.0, 3.3,
3.1, 3.8,
       4.6, 3.4, 3.0, 5.9, 2.5, 4.5, 6.8, 2.4, 2.9, 5.7, 4.3,
3.5, 5.8,
       3.2, 4.2, 1.9, 2.6, 7.4, 3.9, 1.5, 1.3, 4.1, 8.0, 6.0,
3.6, 5.4,
       5.6, 1.0, 2.1, 1.2, 6.5, 2.7, 4.7, 5.5, 1.1, 5.3, 4.4,
3.7, 6.7,
       4.8, 1.7, 6.2, 8.3, 1.4, 6.1, 7.0, 8.4, 3.3, 3.8, 3.5,
4.5, 5.0,
       4.6, 4.2, 5.5, 6.0, 3.0, 1.5, 2.0, 2.8, 2.4, 2.7, 2.3,
3.2, 2.5,
       4.0, 4.7, 5.4, 5.7, 4.3, 3.7, 4.8, 2.2, 1.8, 6.5, 3.6,
6.1, 6.2,
       1.6, 1.0, 4.4, 5.9, 1.3, 6.7, 5.6, 3.4, 7.0, 5.2, 3.9,
5.3, 4.9,
       2.9, 5.8, 3.1, 8.4, 1.1, 2.1, 2.6, 1.4, 6.8, 1.7, 4.1,
1.9, 8.0,
       6.3, nan, 6.6, 6.4, 1.2, 7.4], dtype=object)
```

8. We see that there are some values that might not be numeric, including the `nan` value. Let's remove all rows from the `vehicles_non_hybrid` data frame that have `nan displ` values and then do the same for the `comb08` variable. In the process, let's use the `astype` method to ensure that each value is of type `float`, just in case:

```
criteria = vehicles_non_hybrid.displ.notnull()

vehicles_non_hybrid = vehicles_non_hybrid[criteria]

vehicles_non_hybrid.displ =
vehicles_non_hybrid.displ.astype('float')


criteria = vehicles_non_hybrid.comb08.notnull()

vehicles_non_hybrid = vehicles_non_hybrid[criteria]

vehicles_non_hybrid.comb08 =
vehicles_non_hybrid.comb08.astype('float')
```

9. Finally, we will produce a scatter plot of the results again using the `ggplot` library:

```
print ggplot(vehicles_non_hybrid, aes('displ', 'comb08')) +
geom_point(color='steelblue') + xlab("Engine Displacement") +
ylab("Average MPG") + ggtitle("Gasoline cars")
```

Refer to the following graph:

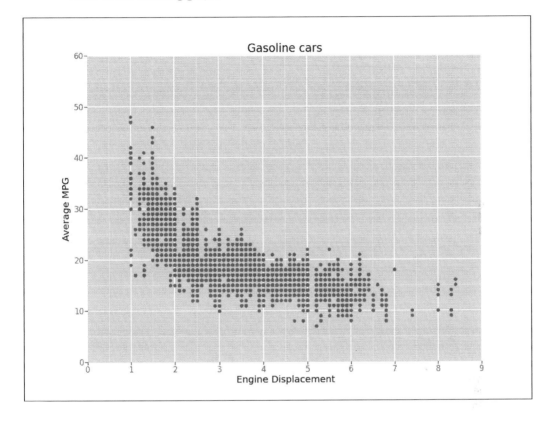

The preceding plot seems to confirm a negative relationship between fuel economy and engine displacement.

Now, have there been fewer cars with large engines made recently?

10. Let's see whether smaller cars were made in later years on average:

```
grouped_by_year = vehicles_non_hybrid.groupby(['year'])
avg_grouped_by_year = grouped_by_year['displ',
'comb08'].agg([np.mean])
```

11. Next, let's plot both the average `displ` value and the average `comb08` value by year on the same plot to look for trends. To do this, we need to reshape the `avg_grouped_by_year` data frame to convert it from the wide format to the long format:

```
avg_grouped_by_year['year'] = avg_grouped_by_year.index
melted_avg_grouped_by_year = pd.melt(avg_grouped_by_year,
id_vars='year')
```

Then, let's create our faceted plot:

```
p = ggplot(aes(x='year', y='value', color = 'variable_0'),
data=melted_avg_grouped_by_year)
p + geom_point() + facet_wrap("variable_0")
```

Refer to the following graph:

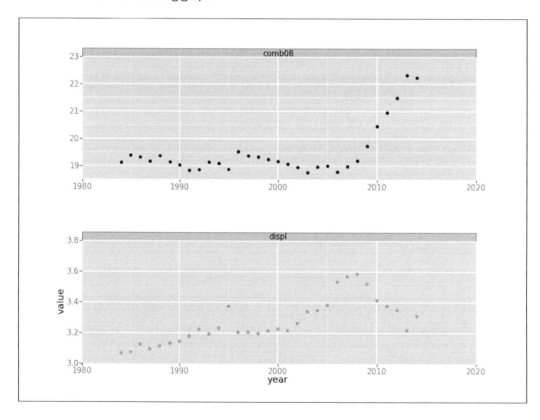

How it works...

Let's ignore the actual findings of the analysis, as they are the same as the ones in the chapter using R. The truly interesting part is the numerous important data analysis techniques that were used in this chapter. Let's break each technique down individually.

First and foremost, let's take a look at the general data analysis pattern known as split-apply-combine, which was previously mentioned in the companion R chapter. When analyzing a dataset, it is often desirable to group the data by one or more characteristics, perform an operation on the grouped subsets of data, and then put the results together. In this chapter, we grouped our data by year, computed averages on different variables, and then combined these results. In the previous chapter, we used the `plyr` package by Hadley Wickham. With `plyr`, we called the `ddply` function passing in the data frame to be analyzed, the characteristic or set of characteristics to group by, and then the functions to be used on the group data. The `ddply` function then returns the resulting data frame. One line of code performs the split-apply-combine pattern.

The pandas library in Python takes a slightly different approach and splits up the functionality that is subsumed in a single function call in `plyr`. First, we can group a pandas object such as a data frame by a specified characteristic as in this line of code—`grouped_by_year = vehicles_non_hybrid.groupby(['year'])`—where we are grouping the rows of the `vehicles_non_hybrid` data frame by the `year` variable. Note that we are not limited to grouping by a single variable and can create groupings with multiple characteristics (year and car company, for example).

Once we have the `grouped_by_year` object, we can iterate through the groups if we wanted to:

```
for (name, group) in grouped_by_year:
    print name
    print group
```

This will print out each group name and the resulting data frame. Next, we use the `aggregrate` method on the `GroupBy` object using the `mean` function from the NumPy library (`np.mean`). In the following code, we are choosing to only aggregate a single variable, which is `comb08`, from the `grouped_by_year` data frame:

```
averaged = grouped['comb08'].agg([np.mean])
```

In pandas, this very robust split-apply-combine functionality is built into the library, and we have only scratched the surface of what it is capable of.

There's more...

We have also used the `ggplot` package from yhat instead of the venerable matplotlib. *The Grammar of Graphics* offers a very concise, although highly non-Pythonic, way of describing graphs. The back cover of the seminal book, *The Grammar of Graphics, Leland Wilkinson, Springer* states that:

> "*The Grammar of Graphics presents a unique foundation for producing almost every quantitative graphic found in scientific journals, newspapers, statistical packages, and data visualization systems. While the tangible results of this work have been several visualization software libraries, this book focuses on the deep structures involved in producing quantitative graphics from data. What are the rules that underlie the production*
> *of pie charts, bar charts, scatterplots, function plots, maps, mosaics, and radar charts?*"

The `ggplot2` package in R is one of R's greatest assets, and Python now has a functioning `ggplot` clone. Unfortunately, as shown by some of the experiences in this chapter, the `ggplot` Python library is not quite feature-complete at this time.

As the Python `ggplot` library is still under development (and we had a few issues with the smoothing functionality), you might be interested to know that there is a Python library that allows you to use R from within your Python program. The `rpy2` package, at `http://rpy.sourceforge.net/rpy2.html`, offers both a low-level and a high-level interface to R from Python. The low-level interface is somewhat similar to R's C API. The high-level interface exposes R objects as instances of Python classes. In order to use `rpy2`, ensure that you have R installed on your system. Any packages that you call from Python must be available in R!

See also

- pandas: indexing and selecting data at `http://pandas.pydata.org/pandas-docs/stable/indexing.html`

- The *Matplotlib and the Future of Visualization in Python* article at `http://jakevdp.github.io/blog/2013/03/23/matplotlib-and-the-future-of-visualization-in-python/`

- The home page of Hadley Wickham at `http://had.co.nz/`

- The `ggplot` package for Python at `http://blog.yhathq.com/posts/ggplot-for-python.html`

- More `ggplot` for Python at `http://blog.yhathq.com/posts/aggregating-and-plotting-time-series-in-python.html`

- The article *The Split-Apply-Combine Strategy fro Data Analysis, Hadley Wickham, Journal of Statistical Software* at `http://www.jstatsoft.org/v40/i01/paper`

Investigating the makes and models of automobiles with Python

To continue our investigation of this dataset, we are going to examine the makes and models of the various automobiles more closely, repeating many of the steps from the previous chapter while translating from R to Python.

Getting ready

If you've completed the previous recipe, you should have everything you need in order to continue.

How to do it...

The following steps will lead us through our investigation:

1. Let's look at how makes and models of cars inform us about fuel efficiency over time. First, let's look at the frequency of makes and models of cars available in the U.S., concentrating on 4-cylinder cars. To select the 4-cylinder cars, we first make the `cylinders` variable unique to see what the possible values are:

    ```
    pd.unique(vehicles_non_hybrid.cylinders)
    array([4.0, 12.0, 8.0, 6.0, 5.0, 10.0, 2.0, 3.0, 16.0, 6, 8,
    12, 4, 3, 5, 2, 10, 16, nan], dtype=object)
    ```

     Both 4.0 and 4 are listed as unique values; this fact should raise your suspicion. Remember, when we imported the data, pandas warned us that several variables were mixed types, and one of these variables was `cylinders`.

2. Let's convert the `cylinders` variable to `float` so that we can then easily subset the data frame:

    ```
    vehicles_non_hybrid.cylinders =
    vehicles_non_hybrid.cylinders.astype('float')

    pd.unique(vehicles_non_hybrid.cylinders)
    array([  4.,  12.,   8.,   6.,   5.,  10.,   2.,   3.,  16.,
    nan])

    vehicles_non_hybrid_4 =
    vehicles_non_hybrid[(vehicles_non_hybrid.cylinders == 4.0)]
    ```

3. Now, let's look at the numbers of makes that have 4-cylinder cars over the time frame that is available:

```
import matplotlib.pyplot as plt
%matplotlib inline


grouped_by_year_4_cylinder =
vehicles_non_hybrid_4.groupby(['year']).make.nunique()
fig = grouped_by_year_4_cylinder.plot()
fig.set_xlabel('Year')
fig.set_ylabel('Number of 4-Cylinder Makes')
print fig
```

Note that we have switched from `ggplot` to `matplotlib` as we are trying to plot a series object. In Python, it is considered bad form to have your code littered with random `import` statements. Therefore, we will move the `import` statement to the top of our IPython Notebook. Remember, if you restart your IPython Notebook, make sure that you execute the `import` statements at the top of the Notebook first so that the rest of your code will run.

Refer to the following graph:

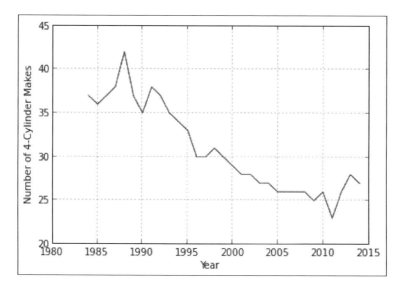

We can see in the preceding graph that there has been a decline in the number of makes with 4-cylinder engines available since 1980. However, as a caveat, this plot could be misleading, as we do not know if the total number of available makes per year has changed over the same period of time.

4. Can we look at the makes that have been available every year of this study? First, we want to find a list of the automobile makes with 4-cylinder engines that were present in every year of this study. To do this, we first compute the unique list of makes per model year:

```
grouped_by_year_4_cylinder =
vehicles_non_hybrid_4.groupby(['year'])

unique_makes = []
for name, group in grouped_by_year_4_cylinder:
    unique_makes.append(set(pd.unique(group['make'])))

unique_makes = reduce(set.intersection, unique_makes)
print unique_makes

Set(['Dodge', 'Mitsubishi', 'Jeep', 'Chevrolet', 'Nissan',
'Honda', 'Toyota', 'Volkswagen', 'Mazda', 'Subaru',
'Chrysler', 'Ford'])
```

We find that there are only 12 manufacturers that made 4-cylinder cars every year during this period.

5. Now, we ask the question how these car manufacturers' models have performed over time in terms of fuel efficiency. To do this, we decide to take the long way. First, we create an empty list that will eventually be populated by Booleans. We then iterate over each row in the data frame using the `iterrows` generator that yields both an index and row (we choose to do nothing with the index in the loop). We then test whether the make of the current row is in the `unique_makes` set computed previously and append the Boolean to the `Boolean_mask` set. After the loop is completed, we subset the data frame to contain only rows with a make within the set of `unique_makes`:

```
boolean_mask = []
for index, row in vehicles_non_hybrid_4.iterrows():
    make = row['make']
    boolean_mask.append(make in unique_makes)

df_common_makes = vehicles_non_hybrid_4[boolean_mask]
```

6. Next, we must group the data frame by both `year` and `make` and then compute the mean for each grouping:

```
df_common_makes_grouped =
df_common_makes.groupby(['year','make']).agg(np.mean).reset_in
dex()
```

7. Finally, we display the results of our efforts using a faceted plot, courtesy of `ggplot`:

```
ggplot(aes(x='year', y='comb08'), data =
df_common_makes_grouped) + geom_line() + facet_wrap('make')
```

Refer to the following graph:

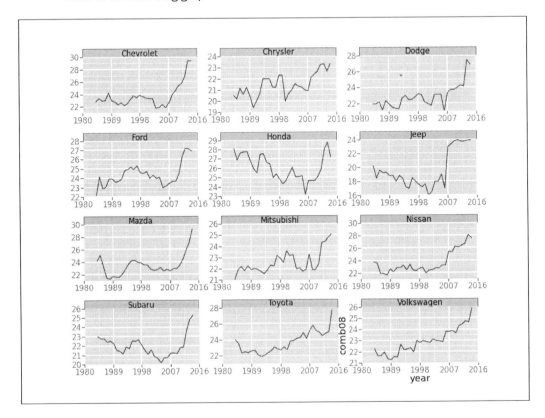

How it works...

A lot of the steps were spelled out in detail during the recipe itself, so we won't belabor the points here. However, there are a few things that are certainly worth pointing out. First, did you notice the `.reset_index()` call at the end of the last split-apply-combine step? The following command shows this:

```
df_common_makes.groupby(['year','make']).agg(np.mean).reset_index()
```

When performing the `groupby` step, pandas returns the key by which rows were grouped as an index and not as a simple data column. In the case of multiple grouping keys, pandas returns a multilevel index. Unfortunately, this will not work for `ggplot`, and we need to tell pandas to treat these indices as data columns with the `.reset_index()` method.

Second, we used a `for` loop, iterating over the rows of the data frame to determine whether the make was in the list of `unique_makes` of interest. If this block of code seemed a bit verbose, it is because it was. Pandas has an incredible amount of functionalities built in, and we could have performed the row selection using the `.isin()` method, as shown in the following command:

```
test =
vehicles_non_hybrid_4[vehicles_non_hybrid_4['make'].isin(unique_makes
)]
```

If there is a data analysis step that you wish to perform on your data frame, chances are there is a method that has already been built to do this.

From a performance standpoint, we committed a very obvious sin in the `for` loop by appending the loop to a list, thus growing the size of the list with each iteration. To speed this up, we should have pre-allocated the list to the size of the number of rows in the data frame filled with false Boolean values. Preallocating arrays is a very general technique that speeds up code in most languages; this trick is especially powerful in `matplotlib`.

To perform the set intersection that we used in order to identify all of the makes present in every year of the data, we needed the `sets` Python package that is part of the Python distribution. Again, we would move this import statement to the top of our script in order to follow best Python practices.

See also

- ▶ The matplotlib home page at `http://matplotlib.org/`
- ▶ The `groupby` documentation at `http://pandas.pydata.org/pandas-docs/stable/groupby.html`

8
Working with Social Graphs (Python)

In this chapter, we will cover:

- ▶ Preparing to work with social networks in Python
- ▶ Importing networks
- ▶ Exploring subgraphs within a heroic network
- ▶ Finding strong ties
- ▶ Finding key players
- ▶ Exploring characteristics of entire networks
- ▶ Clustering and community detection in social networks
- ▶ Visualizing graphs

Introduction

Social networks have become a fixture of modern life, thanks to social networking sites such as Facebook and Twitter. Social networks themselves are not new, however. The study of such networks dates back to the early twentieth century, particularly in the fields of sociology and anthropology. It is their prevalence in mainstream applications that has moved these types of studies to the purview of data science.

It turns out that social networks are extremely interesting as models for human behavior. Human civilization stems from tribal societies, and as a result, Dunbar's number—a hypothesis that at any given time we can only have 150 people in our extended social network—has famously been proven through the analysis of the most active networks. Latent social networks exist everywhere, not just in popular Web 2.0 applications. We manage our lives through connections to various networks, and, because of that, we generate a lot of related, rich data that can be used to make predictions about ourselves and our relationships.

Networks, like the ones we'll discuss in this chapter, take a relationship-centered view of the world. By leveraging an existing data structure of people-to-people relationships (a social network), we can produce analyses about the larger network with clustering techniques to discover communities, reveal insights into the role of important members of the graph, and even generate behavioral predictions through relational inference. These analyses have a number of practical applications from law enforcement to election prediction and recommendations to application optimization.

The mathematical underpinnings of these analyses stem from graph theory. Therefore, the techniques for the analyses in this chapter will focus on the cardinality, traversal, and clustering of graphs. To introduce these techniques, we will make use of an excellent Python graph library, NetworkX. We'll go through several analyses at various levels of the network, such as pairwise comparisons at the individual level, community detection at the group level, and cohesion analyses at the network level. Finally, we'll look at visualizing and drawing our graphs and subgraphs with various tools.

Understanding graphs and networks

The basis for the analyses in this chapter comes from graph theory—the mathematical study of the application and properties of graphs, originally motivated by the study of games of chance. Generally speaking, this involves the study of network encoding and measuring properties of a graph. Graph theory can be traced back to Euler's work on the Seven Bridges of Königsberg problem in the year 1735. However, in recent decades, the rise of the social network has influenced the discipline, particularly with computer science graph data structures and databases.

Let's start with a point of contention. What is the difference between a network and a graph? The term graph can be used to imply visual representations of variables and functions, the mathematical concept of a set of nodes and edges, or the data structure based on that concept. Similarly, the term network has multiple definitions; it can be an interconnected system or a specialized type of mathematical graph. Therefore, either term, social network or social graph, is appropriate in this case, particularly as we are referring to the mathematical concept and data structure.

A **graph** is a symbolic representation of a network that is composed of a set of vertices (nodes) and their connections (relationships or edges). More formally, a graph can be defined as: G = (V, E), an entity consisting of a finite set of nodes denoted by V (vertices) or V(G) and a collection E (edges) or E(G) of unordered pairs {u, v} where u, v ∈ V. A visual example, as shown in the following figure, should be familiar to the reader:

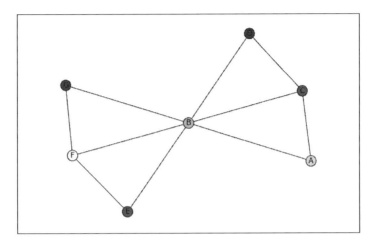

Graphs can be either directed or undirected. Directed graphs have ordered relationships; undirected graphs can be seen as bidirectional directed graphs. A directed graph in a social network tends to have directional semantic relationships, for example, "friends", where Abe might be friends with Jane, but Jane might not reciprocate. Undirected social networks have more general semantic relationships, for example, "knows". Any directed graph can easily be converted to the more general undirected graph. In this case, the adjacency matrix becomes symmetric; every relationship is reciprocal.

Adjacency matrices are two-dimensional graph representations, where each cell or element (i, j) is 1 if the ith node and jth node are connected; it is 0 otherwise. This is certainly not the most compact manner of storing information about graphs; a byte must be stored for every pair of nodes, even if the majority of nodes do not share an edge with most other nodes. However, this representation is computationally effective and is used for many graph algorithms. Consider that a node can be represented in this scheme as a vector of its edges. An example of a small adjacency matrix for an undirected graph with four nodes is shown in the following figure:

	A	B	C	D
A	–	1	1	0
B	1	–	1	0
C	1	1	–	1
D	0	0	1	–

A few final terms will help us in our discussion. The cardinality of vertices is called the order of the graph, whereas the cardinality of the edges is called the size. In the graph pictured in the preceding figure, the order is 7 and the size is 10. Two nodes are adjacent if they share an edge; if this is true, they are also called neighbors. The neighborhood of a vertex is the set of all vertices that the vertex is connected to. The degree of a vertex is the size of its neighborhood, the number of nodes that share an edge with the vertex.

With this in mind, graph problems generally fall into a few categories. Existence problems attempt to determine if a node, path, or subgraph exists, particularly if there is a constraint. Construction problems focus on the construction of a graph, given a set of nodes and paths, within given constraints. Enumeration problems attempt to determine the list of vertices and relationships within a set of constraints. Finally, optimization problems determine the shortest path between two nodes.

Preparing to work with social networks in Python

One of Python's key advantages that merits repeating is the number of excellent premade packages available for the language; fortunately for us, network analysis is no exception. This short recipe will walk you through installing the libraries you'll need for the rest of this chapter.

Getting ready

The required external libraries for the tasks in this chapter are as follows:

- NetworkX
- matplotlib
- python-louvain

How to do it...

We will use the following steps that should be familiar at this point to prepare for the remaining recipes:

1. Open a new terminal or command prompt and change to your project directory.

2. If you are using a virtual environment, activate your virtual environment and type the following:

    ```
    pip install networkx
    ```

    If you are not using a virtual environment, you will most likely need to use `sudo`, as follows:

    ```
    sudo pip install networkx
    ```

3. Now, we must install the `python-louvain` package:

    ```
    pip install python-louvain
    ```

How it works...

NetworkX is a well-maintained Python library for the creation, manipulation, and study of the structure of complex networks. Its tools allow for the quick creation of graphs, and the library also contains many common graph algorithms. In particular, NetworkX complements Python's scientific computing suite of SciPy/NumPy, matplotlib, and Graphviz and can handle graphs in memory of 10M's of nodes and 100M's of links. NetworkX should be part of every data scientist's toolkit.

NetworkX and Python are the perfect combination to do social network analysis. NetworkX is designed to handle data at scale. The core algorithms that are included are implemented on extremely fast legacy code. Graphs are hugely flexible (nodes can be any hashable type), and there is an extensive set of native IO formats. Finally, with Python, you'll be able to access or use a myriad of datasources from databases on the Internet.

Python-louvain is a small Python library built for a singular purpose, which is to use the Louvain method for community detection, as described in the *Fast unfolding of communities in large networks* paper (Journal of Statistical Mechanics: Theory and Experiment, 2008 (10)). A C++ implementation is also available.

There's more...

While we will use NetworkX exclusively in this chapter, there are a number of excellent alternative social network analysis libraries that are worth mentioning. First, igraph (`http://igraph.org/redirect.html`) can be programmed and used from R, Python, and C/C++, with the underlying tools built in C/C++ for performance. The second library to take a look at is graph-tool (`http://graph-tool.skewed.de/`). Underneath its Python usability, it can also be implemented in C++, but with the added benefit of leveraging OpenMP for parallelization across multicore machines.

Importing networks

The dataset we will explore in this chapter is fun. It's the Marvel Universe Social Graph dataset constructed by Cesc Rosselló, Ricardo Alberich, and Joe Miro as part of their research on disordered systems and neural networks (`http://bioinfo.uib.es/~joemiro/marvel.html`). They created the network by compiling characters with the comic books in which they appear; as it turns out, the network actually mimics a real-world social network. Since then, there have been many visualizations of, and other mashups using this famous dataset (as well as extensions). In this recipe, we will import the needed data into our Python environment.

Getting ready

Once you have installed the needed libraries from the preceding recipe, you will need to use the dataset provided with the chapter.

How to do it...

Perform the following steps to import the data:

1. In order to get this graph into a NetworkX graph representation, iterate over the dataset and add edges (which automatically creates the nodes) for each hero pair:

```python
import networkx as nx
import unicodecsv as csv

def graph_from_csv(path):
    graph = nx.Graph(name="Heroic Social Network")
    with open(path, 'rU') as data:
        reader = csv.reader(data)
        for row in reader:
```

```
        graph.add_edge(*row)
    return graph
```

Each row is a (hero, hero) tuple. Using the `*row` notation, we expand the tuple so that the function definition is actually `graph.add_edge(hero, hero)`.

2. The dataset is large, weighing in at 21 MB, and takes a second or two to load into memory; you can compute the size and the order of the graph as follows:

```
>>> graph.order()  # graph.number_of_nodes()
6426
>>> graph.size()   # graph.number_of_edges()
167219
```

Keep this function handy; we'll need it to get the graph for most of the rest of the chapter!

3. The alternate dataset, from which the social network was derived, includes the comics in which the characters appeared. A slightly different graph generation mechanism is necessary for this format:

```
def graph_from_gdf(path):
    graph = nx.Graph(name="Characters in Comics")
    with open(path, 'rU') as data:
        reader = csv.reader(data)
        for row in reader:
            if 'nodedef' in row[0]:
                handler = lambda row,G: G.add_node(row[0],
                    TYPE=row[1])
            elif 'edgedef' in row[0]:
                handler = lambda row,G: G.add_edge(*row)
            else:
                handler(row, graph)
    return graph
```

In this **tab-separated value** (**TSV**) file, there is a banner that says `nodedef` or `edgedef` before the rows of nodes or edge definitions. While we loop through each row, we create a handler function, `lambda`, depending on whether we've seen the banner. Then, for every row under the banner, we use the defined handler as we're in the section for either nodes or edges.

4. At this point, we can calculate some quick information for the graph using built-in methods from NetworkX:

```
>>> nx.info(graph)
Name: Heroic Social Network
Type: Graph
Number of nodes: 6426
Number of edges: 167219
Average degree:  52.0445
```

Note that the name for the graph was added when we instantiated `nx.Graph`, an optional feature that makes it easier to track multiple graphs in your code.

How it works...

Data import can be a challenge in any data science project and graph data can come in a variety of formats. For this recipe, the data is simple; it is a TSV file of hero-to-hero connections with the implied "knows" relationship.

There is also an alternate dataset that expands the "knows" relationship by including the source of their relationship, the comic book that the heroes appear in together. This expansion adds additional hops between the hero-to-hero network by expanding the comic-to-hero network via "appears in" relationships. This expanded network might allow us to compute the strength of the "knows" relationships; for example, the more comics that heroes appear in together, the better they probably know each other. It is interesting to note that this type of dataset has been shown to be effective at community discovery and relationship clustering.

The `graph_from_gdf` function determines whether we're reading edges or nodes, and it handles each line of the TSV file appropriately by implementing a new handler via a `lambda` function when it sees a row banner called `nodedef` or `edgedef`, indicating that the rows below it are nodes or edges, respectively. This function also gives us the opportunity to create a property graph.

A property graph extends our current graph definition with the inclusion of key/value pairs on nodes and edges, and even potentially on the graph itself. Property graphs are more expressive, and they are the basis of many graph databases because they can hold more information per node and per relationship (thus making it a possible replacement for traditional relational databases). NetworkX also allows you to specify additional properties for both nodes and edges.

Note the add_node method; additional keyword arguments are saved as a property. In this case, we set a TYPE property to determine whether the node is a comic book or a hero. NetworkX also allows the setting and retrieving of properties in bulk on nodes, using set_node_attributes (G, name, attributes) and get_node_attributes(G, name), which return a dictionary mapping the nodes to the attribute requested (or saving the attribute to the group of nodes).

Exploring subgraphs within a heroic network

The graph in the previous recipe is much too large for us to get a feel for what is happening at the individual level, although we'll soon look at analyses that tell us interesting things about populations and communities. However, in order for us to see something interesting immediately, let's extract a subgraph to play with. In particular, we'll collect a subgraph for a particular hero in our dataset. When a subgraph is generated with a single person or actor as a focal point, it is called an ego network, and, in fact, the degree of an ego network might be a measure of an individual's self-worth!

Getting ready

As long as you completed the previous recipe, you will be prepared for this one.

How to do it...

The following steps will lead you through extracting subgraphs from our large dataset and visualizing the ego networks:

1. Every social network has as many egos as nodes. The neighbors of an ego are called alters. The definition of the ego subgraph is bound by an n-step neighborhood, defining how many hops away from the ego to include in the subgraph. NetworkX provides a very simple mechanism to extract an ego graph, as shown in the following command:

   ```
   >>> ego = nx.ego_graph(graph, actor, 1)
   ```

   This function returns a subgraph of all the neighbors of the actor node, with a maximum path length as specified by the third argument.

2. To draw the graph of the ego network, we use the following function:

```python
def draw_ego_graph(graph, character, hops=1):
    """
    Expecting a graph_from_gdf
    """

    # Get the Ego Graph and Position
    ego = nx.ego_graph(graph, character, hops)
    pos = nx.spring_layout(ego)
    plt.figure(figsize=(12,12))
    plt.axis('off')

    # Coloration and Configuration
    ego.node[character]["TYPE"] = "center"
    valmap = { "comic": 0.25, "hero": 0.54, "center": 0.87 }
    types  = nx.get_node_attributes(ego, "TYPE")
    values = [valmap.get(types[node], 0.25) for node in
        ego.nodes()]

    # Draw
    nx.draw_networkx_edges(ego, pos, alpha=0.4)
    nx.draw_networkx_nodes(ego, pos,
                            node_size=80,
                            node_color=values,
                            cmap=plt.cm.hot, with_labels=False)

    plt.show()
```

3. Let's take a look at the ego networks for LONGBOW/AMELIA GREER, starting with a one-hop network:

```python
>>> graph = graph_from_gdf('comic-hero-network.gdf'))
>>> draw_ego_graph(graph, "LONGBOW/AMELIA GREER")
```

The preceding commands will give you the following graph:

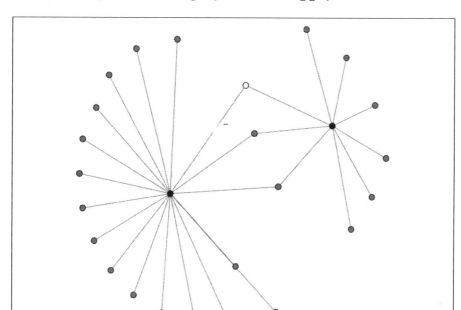

The preceding figure shows this one-hop ego network, which is derived from the expanded comic-to-hero social graph. Since there are two different types of nodes, we have visually colored them differently; orange nodes are characters and blue nodes are comic books. The ego node is white, LONGBOW/AMELIA GREER herself.

4. Let's create a two-hop ego network for the same character:

```
>>> draw_ego_graph(graph, "LONGBOW/AMELIA GREER", 2)
```

The preceding command will give you the following graph as output:

How it works...

Amelia Greer (also known as Longbow) is part of a mercenary special operations unit called the Harriers. She appears in two Marvel comics, particularly *The Uncanny X-Men Vol 1 #261* in May of 1990. Her ego network is very close knit (containing mostly members from the Harriers), as you can see in the preceding one-hop network figure.

The preceding two-hop network considerably expands the volume of the network. The black nodes represent the second hop to the next comic book community of characters. Clusters are readily apparent, even in this small ego network. Still, even one-hop network can say a lot about group membership and the importance of an actor. We will talk about how to build such graphs later on in this chapter.

There's more...

The ego can or cannot be a part of the network. In fact, membership testing on the ego is not important since the subgraph was generated based on the neighborhood of the ego! Instead, removal of the ego can show structural configurations of the network. Consider the social networks shown in the following figure:

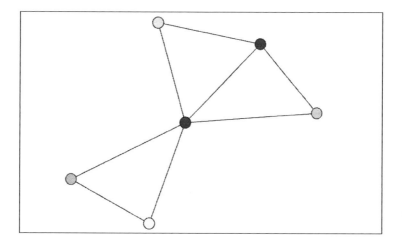

In the preceding figure, the ego is included as part of the graph; the structure of the network seems unified and cohesive.

As you can see, without the ego, isolations become important, as do obvious outliers. Aggregating these isolations across egos is how group membership and communities are discovered. We'll explore this more in the next sections.

Finding strong ties

Currently, our hero network simply measures whether two characters are connected. This computation is simple; do they appear in the same comic book together? We assume that in the small temporal space of a comic book, even cameos mean that the characters have interacted with each other. However, this does not tell us who the most important relations for a particular character are.

In order to determine the most important folks in an ego network (or to determine relative affinity between two actors), we need to determine edge weights. Since edges represent interaction, affiliation, or social relations, adding a weight determines the distance between two actors, relative to other actors with similar connections. Proxies for edge weights in social networks include:

- Frequency, for example, how often two actors communicate
- Reciprocity, for example, whether or not the relationship is reciprocal
- Type or attributes, for example, married actors have a stronger tie than college roommates
- Structure of the neighborhood, for example, the number of mutual friends

In our heroic social graph, we'll use the number of comic books in which a pair of characters appears together as a proxy for the strength of their tie. This seems to make sense; if one character is a villain that appears in the same comics as a hero, their relationship is that of a nemesis, it's not a simple protagonist/antagonist relationship! Another example is that of two heroes appearing together often. They might be part of a heroic team (for example, The Avengers) or share a sidekick relationship (for example, Bucky to Captain America).

Getting ready

If you completed the previous recipes, you should be ready to tackle this one.

How to do it...

The following steps will walk us through finding the strong ties in the network:

1. In order to compute the ties, we'll recreate the hero network graph from the comic hero network dataset. Since this represents an entire graph computation (for example, we will iterate through every node in the graph), we'll need to use a memory-safe iterator and save the intermediate data to disk. Here is the complete code; we'll go over it line by line, as follows:

```
def transform_to_weighted_heros(comics):
    # Create new graph to fill in
    heros = nx.Graph(name="Weighted Heroic Social Network")
```

```
# Iterate through all the nodes and their properties
for node, data in graph.nodes(data=True):
    # We don't care about comics, only heros
    if data['TYPE'] == 'comic': continue
    # Add the hero and their properties (this will also
      update data)
    heros.add_node(node, **data)

    # Find all the heros connected via the comic books
    for comic in graph[node]:
        for alter in graph[comic]:
            # Skip the hero that we're on
            if alter == node: continue

            # Setup the default edge
            if alter not in heros[node]:
                heros.add_edge(node, alter, weight=0.0,
                    label="knows")

            # The weight of the hero is the fraction of
              connections / 2
            heros[node][alter]["weight"] += 1.0 /
                (graph.degree(comic) *2)
    return heros
```

2. Let's see Longbow's social weighted graph now:

```
def draw_weighted_ego_graph(graph, character, hops=1):
    # Graph and Position
    ego = nx.ego_graph(graph, character, hops)
    pos = nx.spring_layout(ego)
    plt.figure(figsize=(12,12))
    plt.axis('off')

    # Coloration and Configuration
    ego.node[character]["TYPE"] = "center"
    valmap = { "hero": 0.0, "center": 1.0 }
    types  = nx.get_node_attributes(ego, "TYPE")
    values = [valmap.get(types[node], 0.25) for node in
      ego.nodes()]
```

```
char_edges = ego.edges(data=True, nbunch=[character,])
nonchar_edges = ego.edges(nbunch=[n for n in ego.nodes()
  if n != character])
elarge=[(u,v) for (u,v,d) in char_edges if d['weight'] >=0.12]
esmall=[(u,v) for (u,v,d) in char_edges if d['weight'] < 0.12]
print set([d['weight'] for (u,v,d) in char_edges])

# Draw
nx.draw_networkx_nodes(ego, pos,
                       node_size=200,
                       node_color=values,
                       cmap=plt.cm.Paired,
                         with_labels=False)

nx.draw_networkx_edges(ego,pos,edgelist=elarge,
                       width=1.5, edge_color='b')
nx.draw_networkx_edges(ego,pos,edgelist=esmall,
                       width=1,alpha=0.5,
                       edge_color='b',style='dashed')
nx.draw_networkx_edges(ego,pos,edgelist=nonchar_edges,
                       width=0.5,alpha=0.2,style='dashed')
plt.show()
```

The preceding commands will give you the following graph as output:

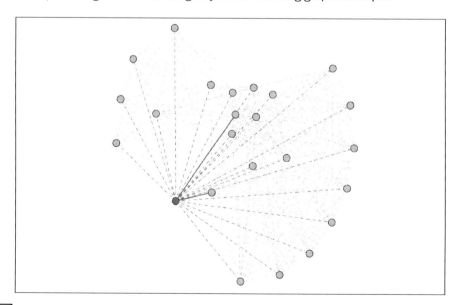

As you can see, Longbow shares two strong ties (represented by the heavy dark blue line), and this makes sense since she is in two comic books with only two other characters. The other characters she's directly related to have light blue dashed lines, representing her weaker ties to them.

Note that all characters are connected to the other characters with whom they share ties in the ego network (represented by light grey dashed lines). Already, we can start to see clustering, as the characters from different comic books have moved to either side of Longbow's red node. Characters that have affinities with characters from both comics are in the middle.

How it works...

The `transform_to_weighted_heros` function is key to this recipe, and we explain it line by line here. First, we create an empty graph in which to add our transformation. Note that in NetworkX, there are functions such as `create_empty_graph` and `Graph.subgraph`; however, the former won't transfer the data that we need and the latter will transfer too much data. We'll go over each node in the original graph, skipping over comic books. Note that we'll add heroes twice using the `heros.add_node` method because every time we add an edge, it creates the node, if it doesn't exist already. However, to ensure that we get all the data over, we call `add_node` for each hero, and it will simply update the node's properties if it is already in the graph.

Next, we'll connect the heroes together through their comic-book relationships. We'll gather all the heroes connected to the same comic books our current hero is in (skipping the current hero to prevent self-loops). If there is no edge, we'll create a default edge, before adding our weight computation. The weight we'll assign is related to the number of characters in a comic book. It stands to reason that if a comic book has more characters in it, they are more loosely connected. Therefore, we compute our weight as the inverse of the degree of the comic book, divided by two. The division by two is required since this is an undirected graph, otherwise we will double all the weights!

There's more...

Weighted edges are essential to be able to make predictions on a graph, partially because they allow ranking of paths, but mostly because they reflect the underlying semantic associations of the social network. Making predictions relies on relationships that create homophily—this is the tendency of people with similar interests to gather together, and it leads to the formation of homogenous groups called clusters. Homophilous ties can be strong or weak; for instance, folks who go to the same school together represent a stronger tie than people who live in the same city.

Transitivity is the property of edges that allow us to make predictions. Simply stated, it offers the ability to perform triadic closures. If nodes A and B are connected, and A and C are also connected, then it is likely that B and C are connected too. Transitivity is evidence of the existence of strong ties, but is not a necessary or sufficient condition, and it might not be applied equally to weak ties.

Bridges, on the other hand, are edges that connect nodes across groups. Bridges facilitate cluster communication, and are usually the product of weak ties or heterophilous relationships. Knowing and understanding these properties as they relate to your particular social graph are essential for unlocking key insights and being able to make future predictions about how the graph might change.

Finding key players

In the previous recipe, we began exploring ego networks and strong ties between individuals in our social network. We started to see that actors with strong ties with other actors created clusters that centered on themselves. This leads to the obvious question: who are the key figures in the graph, and what kind of pull do they have? We'll look at a couple of measures to determine how important a node is or its "centrality" to try to discover the degree centrality, betweenness centrality, closeness centrality, and eigenvector centrality.

Getting ready

If you completed the previous recipes, you will be ready to start this one.

How to do it...

The following steps will identify key players in this network of comic book characters:

1. To find the top ten nodes in the heroes network, we compute the nodes' degree and sort them:

```
import operator
>>> degrees = sorted(graph.degree().items(), key=operator.
itemgetter(1), reverse=True)
>>> for node in degrees: print node
```

2. Additionally, we compute the percent of nodes in the graph that a node is connected to; NetworkX provides a helpful function, `degree_centrality`, to do this for us. While we're at it, we might as well also set this as a property for our nodes for easy lookup:

```
>>> centrality = nx.degree_centrality(graph)
>>> nx.set_node_attributes(graph, 'centrality', centrality)
```

```
>>> degrees = sorted(centrality.items(), key=itemgetter(1),
reverse=True)
>>> for item in degrees[0:10]: print "%s: %0.3f" % item
```

The preceding commands give us our top ten key players in the dataset, and I think it's obvious that they are the most influential characters in the Marvel universe:

```
1.  CAPTAIN AMERICA:        0.297  (1908)
2.  SPIDER-MAN/PETER PAR:   0.270  (1737)
3.  IRON MAN/TONY STARK :   0.237  (1522)
4.  THING/BENJAMIN J. GR:   0.220  (1416)
5.  MR. FANTASTIC/REED R:   0.215  (1379)
6.  WOLVERINE/LOGAN :       0.213  (1371)
7.  HUMAN TORCH/JOHNNY S:   0.212  (1361)
8.  SCARLET WITCH/WANDA :   0.206  (1325)
9.  THOR/DR. DONALD BLAK:   0.201  (1289)
10. BEAST/HENRY &HANK& P:   0.197  (1267)
```

These characters are hugely influential with a high number of connections, considering the average degree is 52.045! While we're at it, we might as well create a histogram of the connectedness of the graph. A quick note before I show you the histogram: NetworkX does have a function, degree_histogram, which will return a list of the frequencies of degrees. However, in this case, the list's index is the degree value, and the bin width is 1; this means the length of the list can be very large (Order(len(edges))). Using graph.degree().values() is a bit more efficient, particularly for social network graphs, as we'll see next.

3. With the following little snippet, you should now be able to see just how far from normal our top characters are in terms of influence:

```
>>> import matplotlib.pyplot as plt
>>> plt.hist(graph.degree().values(), bins=500)
>>> plt.title("Connectedness of Marvel Characters")
>>> plt.xlabel("Degree")
>>> plt.ylabel("Frequency")
>>> plt.show()
```

The preceding snippet will give you the following graph as output:

4. In fact, you can filter out the number of characters whose node degree is greater than 500, that is the top 1 percent. This filter returns 98.8 percent of characters:

```
>>> filter(lambda v: v < 500, graph.degree().values())
```

If you do so, the curve becomes slightly more apparent:

```
>>> import matplotlib.pyplot as plt
>>> plt.hist(graph.degree().values(), bins=500)
>>> plt.title("Connectedness of Marvel Characters")
>>> plt.xlabel("Degree")
>>> plt.ylabel("Frequency")
```

The preceding commands will give you the following output:

5. To compute other centrality metrics, we will use NetworkX built-in functions. To compute betweenness centrality, use the following functions:

```
>>> centrality = nx.betweenness_centrality(graph)

>>> normalied  = nx.betweenness_centrality(graph, normalized=True)

>>> weighted   = nx.betweenness_centrality(graph, weight="weight")
```

The preceding function allows you to compute betweenness centrality, which will be discussed later, and can be normalized or weighted.

6. To compute the closeness centrality, we can use the following functions, which are similar to the betweenness centrality:

```
>>> centrality = nx.closeness_centrality(graph)

>>> normalied  = nx.closeness_centrality(graph,
normalized=True)

>>> weighted   = nx.closeness_centrality(graph,
distance="weight")
```

7. Finally, to compute the eigenvector centrality, you have two choices with NetworkX:

```
>>> centrality = nx.eigenvector_centality(graph)

>>> centrality = nx.eigenvector_centrality_numpy(graph)
```

8. In order to easily explore these centrality metrics on our graph, let's create a function that generically prints the top 10 nodes based on the centrality metric:

```python
def nbest_centrality(graph, metric, n=10,
attribute="centrality", **kwargs):

    centrality = metric(graph, **kwargs)

    nx.set_node_attributes(graph, attribute, centrality)

    degrees = sorted(centrality.items(), key=itemgetter(1),
      reverse=True)

    for idx, item in enumerate(degrees[0:n]):
        item = (idx+1,) + item
        print "%i. %s: %0.3f" % item
```

9. Now, we can simply use this function with our centrality metric to find the nbest (by default top 10) nodes according to their centrality. The usage is as follows:

```python
>>> nbest_centrality(graph, nx.degree_centrality)
>>> nbest_centrality(graph, nx.betweenness_centrality,
normalized=True)
>>> nbest_centrality(graph, nx.closeness_centrality)
>>> nbest_centrality(graph, nx.eigenvector_centrality_numpy)
```

How it works...

Clearly, there are far more minor characters in the Marvel Universe, and 100 or so major characters. Interestingly, this compares favorably with the real world! There are far more actors with few connections in real-world social graphs, and relatively few top echelon characters with a lot of ties. We know this intuitively, and we call the actors in the top 1 percent of connections celebrities.

In fact, celebrities are such extreme outliers who exert strong influence on their social graphs that we tend to call them "super nodes". Super nodes have the property that to a far enough hop distance, all traversals of the graph will inevitably find their shortest path through a super node. This can be very bad for computation; even the earlier Longbow graph experienced a huge computational lag, and we had a tough time drawing the graph because of the two super nodes Longbow was connected to: Wolverine and Jean Grey. While it's not only proof of Kevin Bacon's six degrees of separation, dealing with super nodes is also an important part of graph computation.

On the other end of the scale, we can calculate Dunbar's number for our social network. Dunbar identified and measured the correlation between neocortical volume and social group size not only for human communities, but also for primates. In order to calculate this number, we cannot simply compute the average degree across all nodes due to the strong left-hand skew in this dataset. Let's compare the mean, mode, and median as our corollary to Dunbar's number. Later, we'll look at using weighted relationships to further induce strong ties:

```
>>> import numpy as np
>>> import scipy.stats as st
>>> data = np.array(graph.degree().values())
>>> np.mean(data)
52.0445066916
>>> st.mode(data)
(array([ 11.]), array([ 254.]))
>>> np.median(data)
20.0
```

Dunbar's number for comic book heroes appears to be much lower than a typical social graph, but proportional to natural scale graphs (consider that your social graph in high school was probably smaller than your adult social graph). It seems that the heroic Dunbar's number is somewhere between 11 and 20 connections. Could this be because alien or mutant neocortical volume is less than a human's? Or, is it because our heroes are naturally isolated given their abilities that set them apart?

There's more...

The most common, and perhaps simplest, technique to find the key actors of a graph is to measure the degree of each vertex. Degree is a signal that determines how connected a node is, which can be a metaphor for influence or popularity. At the very least, the most connected nodes are the ones that spread information the fastest, or have the greatest effect on their community. Measures of degree tend to suffer from dilution, and benefit from statistical techniques to normalize datasets.

The betweenness centrality

A path is a sequence of nodes between a start node and an end node, where no node appears twice on the path and is measured by the number of edges included (also called hops). The most interesting path to compute for two given nodes is the shortest path, for example, the minimum number of edges required to reach another node, which is also called the node distance.

Note that paths can be of length 0, the distance from a node to itself. Consider the following graph as an example:

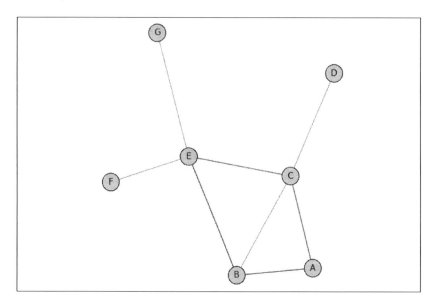

The shortest distance between **D** and **F** is the path {D, C, E, F}, which is a distance of three. On the other hand, the shortest paths from **A** to **E** are the two paths {A, C, E} and {A, B, E}, which share a path length of 2 (highlighted in purple and red).

Finding the shortest paths between two nodes brings up a question from the last section. If key nodes are often traversed to find the shortest path, is there a shortest path-based measure of centrality? The answer is yes. The betweenness centrality identifies the nodes that are more likely to be in the shortest path than others. This is extremely useful at discovering not only strong points in the social graph, but also weak points that will be cut off if a central node is removed.

The computation for the betweenness centrality for a given node is as follows. For a node, v, the betweenness centrality is defined as the sum of the fraction of all the pairs of shortest paths that pass through v. The betweenness centrality can also be normalized for the number of nodes in the graph, or weighted to accept edge weights:

```
>>> centrality = nx.betweeenness_centrality(graph)
>>> normalied  = nx.betweenness_centrality(graph, normalized=True)
>>> weighted   = nx.betweenness_centrality(graph, weight="weight")
```

The preceding commands will give you the following output:

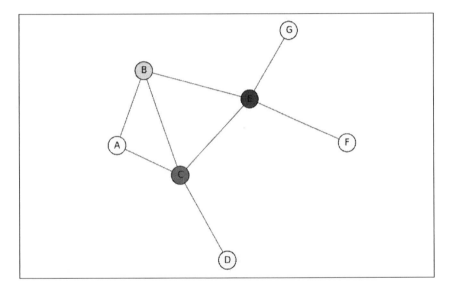

When the betweenness centrality is computed for our small example graph, **B** and **C** have good centrality scores (0.1 and 0.433, respectively). This is because they are in the middle of a large part of the network. **E**, however, has a centrality score of 0.6, which is because **E** connects two different sections of the network (there are no other paths to **G** and **F**).

As before, we can check the betweenness centrality for our heroic graph, and find the heroes that have the top betweenness centralities:

 Note that this computation is extremely expensive and could take a long time on your computer!

```
>>> nbest_centrality(graph, nx.betweenness_centrality, normalized=True)
```

The following is the output:

```
1.   SPIDER-MAN/PETER PAR: 0.074
2.   CAPTAIN AMERICA:      0.057
3.   IRON MAN/TONY STARK:  0.037
4.   WOLVERINE/LOGAN:      0.036
5.   HAVOK/ALEX SUMMERS:   0.036
6.   DR. STRANGE/STEPHEN:  0.029
7.   THING/BENJAMIN J. GR: 0.025
8.   HAWK:                 0.025
9.   HULK/DR. ROBERT BRUC: 0.024
10.  MR. FANTASTIC/REED R: 0.024
```

Compared to the degree centrality results, these numbers are very different. Spider-Man and Captain America have switched places at numbers one and two, but still share the top three spots with Iron Man. Wolverine has been promoted to number 4, and Mr. Fantastic and The Thing have been demoted. Truly interesting, however, are the new appearances of Hawk, The Hulk, Dr. Stange, and Havok to the list, replacing Beast, Thor, The Scarlet Witch, and The Human Torch, who, while popular, are not as able to link characters together!

The closeness centrality

Another centrality measure, closeness, takes a statistical look at the outgoing paths for a particular node, v. What is the average number of hops to reach any other node in the network from v? This is simply computed as the reciprocal of the mean distance to all other nodes in the graph, which can be normalized to *n-1 / size(G)-1*, where *n* is all nodes in the neighborhood, if all nodes in the graph are connected. The reciprocal ensures that nodes that are closer (for example, fewer hops) score better, for example closer to one as in other centrality scores:

```
>>> centrality = nx.closeness_centrality(graph)
>>> normalied  = nx.closeness_centrality(graph, normalized=True)
>>> weighted   = nx.closeness_centrality(graph, distance="weight")
```

Again, when we run this metric on our social network of heroes, you should find that it takes a while to run; however, if you use the normalized method, the process can be accelerated drastically:

```
>>> nbest_centrality(graph, nx.closeness_centrality)
1.   CAPTAIN AMERICA:      0.584
2.   SPIDER-MAN/PETER PAR: 0.574
3.   IRON MAN/TONY STARK : 0.561
4.   THING/BENJAMIN J. GR: 0.558
```

5. MR. FANTASTIC/REED R: 0.556

6. WOLVERINE/LOGAN :   0.555

7. HUMAN TORCH/JOHNNY S: 0.555

8. SCARLET WITCH/WANDA : 0.552

9. THOR/DR. DONALD BLAK: 0.551

10. BEAST/HENRY &HANK& P: 0.549

Once again, we return to our original list, obtained via the degree centrality. In this case, Kevin Bacon's rule applies. These very popular super node celebrities are going to have the most reach, that is, they have the ability to get to all other nodes in the fastest amount of time. Things have changed for our smaller graph, however:

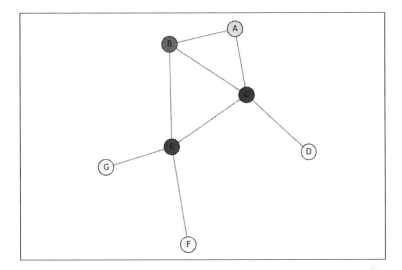

Here, we see that **C** and **E** are the most central nodes in terms of closeness; they can reach all other nodes equally. **B** is less close than **C** and **E**, but fares pretty well, and **A**, because it has two connections, does slightly better than **D**, **G**, or **F** at being able to reach all other nodes in the network.

The eigenvector centrality

The eigenvector centrality of a node, v, is proportional to the sum of the centrality scores of its neighbors. For example, the more important people you are connected to, the more important you are. This centrality measure is very interesting because an actor with a small number of hugely influential contacts might outrank ones with many more mediocre contacts. For our social network, it will hopefully allow us to get underneath the celebrity structure of heroic teams and see who actually is holding the social graph together.

To compute the eigenvector centrality, calculate the argmax of the eigendecomposition of the pairwise adjacency matrix of the graph. The ith element in the eigenvector gives the centrality of the ith node. If you're familiar with Google's PageRank, then this should sound familiar, and in fact, PageRank is a modified eigenvector centrality measure, where instead of computing against an adjacency matrix, Google uses probabilities and computes eigendecomposition across a stochastic matrix.

Adjacency matrices are two-dimensional matrices where each node's vector is a flag indicating if it and the other node share an edge. Undirected graphs always have symmetric adjacency matrices, while directed graphs can be more complex. For our simple graph example in this section, here is the adjacency matrix:

	A	B	C	D	E	F	G
A	–	1	1	0	0	0	0
B	1	–	1	0	1	0	0
C	1	1	–	1	1	0	0
D	0	0	1	–	0	0	0
E	0	1	1	0	–	1	1
F	0	0	0	0	1	–	0
G	0	0	0	0	1	0	–

However, we won't implement the algorithm to compute the eigenvector centrality, instead, we will rely on the many graph algorithms already built into NetworkX. In this case, we have two choices to compute the eigenvector centrality:

```
>>> centrality = nx.eigenvector_centality(graph)
>>> centrality = nx.eigenvector_centrality_numpy(graph)
```

The first choice uses the power method to find the eigenvector, and will only run up to the preset maximum number of iterations, offering no guarantee of convergence. The second choice will use the NumPy eigenvalue solver. You should use the second algorithm whenever possible to ensure a complete result. Why should you, you might ask? The NumPy version will continue to run until convergence, which means it has the possibility of getting stuck depending on the input data. The NumPy version can also be made to overfit the solution. However, the number one reason for which you'd use the power method is speed; very typically, the power method will solve the eigenvalue faster than the NumPy method does because of the fixed number of iterations. These properties of the solver, however, are all completely dependent on the size of the graph (the input data). For larger graphs, you might be forced to use the power method because anything else will become intractable.

Note that there are also corresponding `pagerank` and `pagerank_numpy` module functions to compute these scores. Let's see how our heroes did:

```
>>> nbest_centrality(graph, nx.eigenvector_centrality_numpy)
1.   CAPTAIN AMERICA:        0.117
2.   IRON MAN/TONY STARK:    0.103
3.   SCARLET WITCH/WANDA:    0.101
4.   THING/BENJAMIN J. GR:   0.101
5.   SPIDER-MAN/PETER PAR:   0.100
6.   MR. FANTASTIC/REED R:   0.100
7.   VISION:                 0.099
8.   HUMAN TORCH/JOHNNY S:   0.099
9.   WOLVERINE/LOGAN:        0.098
10.  BEAST/HENRY &HANK& P:   0.096
```

Once again, there is some upheaval in our top ten list! Captain America takes the top spot again, but Spider-Man loses more than just a place, dropping half way down the list. The Thing, Scarlet Witch, and Iron Man move up the list, and, as a surprise, a new actor, Vision, moves onto the list. Our smaller graph has now ranked our nodes a bit more strongly:

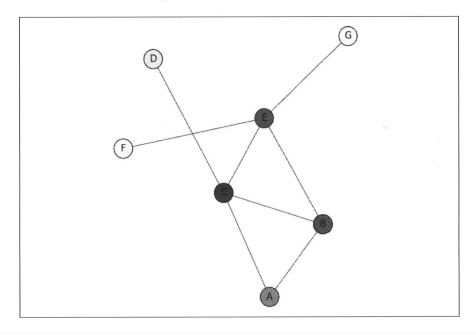

Now, **B** and **C** are the most strongly ranked nodes. **E** is also highly ranked, but it is not as central as before, and **A** is more central than it was. Additionally, **F**, **D**, and **G** have moved above zero for their centrality score, which can be important when determining thresholds.

Deciding on centrality algorithm

So, which measure of centrality should you use? Well, it depends on what you're looking for, as each centrality mechanism is designed to deal with different features of social networks. The following are a few measures of centrality:

-   **Degree**: This is a measure of popularity, and it is useful in determining nodes that can quickly spread information to a localized area, for example, the neighborhood. Think celebrities; these are nodes that can reach many people directly.

-   **Betweenness**: This shows which nodes are likely pathways of information, and can be used to determine where the graph will break apart if the node is removed. It is also used to show the direct path to other clusters or groups in the network.

-   **Closeness**: This is a measure of reach, that is, how fast information will spread to all other nodes from this particular node. Nodes with the most central closeness enjoy short durations during broadcast communication.

-   **Eigenvector**: This is a measure of related influence. Who is closest to the most important people in the graph? This can be used to show the power behind the scenes, or to show relative influence beyond popularity.

For many analyses, all measures of closeness can be used to achieve critical results for a single social network!

Exploring the characteristics of entire networks

In the next set of recipes, we will characterize our social network as a whole, rather than from the perspective of individual actors. This task is usually secondary to getting a feel of the most important nodes, but it is a chicken and an egg problem; determining the techniques to analyze and splitting the whole graph can be informed by key player analyses, and vice versa.

Getting ready

If you completed the previous recipes, you will be ready to proceed with this one.

How to do it...

The following steps will walk us through our first exploration of graph characteristics at the level of the whole graph:

1. Let's compute both the density of the entire network and that of the ego graphs:

    ```
    >>> nx.density(graph)
    0.00810031232554
    ```

```
>>> ego = nx.ego_graph(graph, "LONGBOW/AMELIA GREER")
>>> nx.density(ego)
0.721014492754
```

As you can see, our heroic social network is not very dense, it's not very cliquish as a whole. However, Longbow's social network is very dense and extremely cliquish. Typically speaking, density is used to compare subgraphs of the entire social network (like ego graphs), rather than as a model for how a particular graph will behave by itself.

2. Graphs can also be analyzed in terms of distance (the shortest path between two nodes). The longest distance in a graph is called the diameter of the social graph, and it represents the longest information flow along the graph. Typically, less dense (sparse) social networks will have a larger diameter than more dense networks. Additionally, the average distance is an interesting metric as it can give you information about how close nodes are to each other:

```
>>> for subgraph in nx.connected_component_subgraphs(graph):
...         print nx.diameter(subgraph)
...         print nx.average_shortest_path_length(subgraph)


diameter: 5
average distance: 2.638
```

Note that our heroic social graph is not completely connected, there are some isolated subgraphs, and therefore, we use the `nx.connected_component_subgraphs` generator to capture each subgraph. You can test if the social graph is connected with `nx.is_connected(G)` and determine the number of components via `nx.number_connected_components`. In the heroic social graph, there are four components, but only two have a significant number of nodes.

3. Finally, we can compute the reciprocity of the network, that is, the ratio of the number of relationships that are reciprocated (for example, if there is a bidirectional link) to the total number of relationships in the social network. Currently, there is no built-in NetworkX method to perform this computation. However, this methodology will work, using the `NetworkX.DiGraph` subclass of `Graph`:

```
>>> unigraph = digraph.to_undirected()
>>> return len(unigraph.edges()) / len(digraph.edges())
```

The reciprocal flag in the `to_undirected` method ensures that only edges that appear in both directions will be kept.

This method will only work for directed graphs. Unfortunately, our heroic network is completely reciprocal since we use the knows relationship, and it has a reciprocity of 1.00, as a result.

How it works...

In this recipe, we examined three different graph characteristics. The density of a network is the ratio of the number of edges in the network to the total number of possible edges in the network. The possible number of edges for a graph of *n* vertices is `n(n-1)/2` for an undirected graph (remove the division for a directed graph). Perfectly connected networks (every node shares an edge with every other node) have a density of 1, and are often called cliques.

Graphs can also be analyzed in terms of distance (the shortest path between two nodes). The longest distance in a graph is called the diameter of the social graph, and it represents the longest information flow along the graph. Typically, less dense (sparse) social networks will have a larger diameter than more dense networks. Additionally, the average distance is an interesting metric as it can give you information about how close nodes are to each other.

The last social network measure we'll discuss is reciprocity. This is the ratio of the number of relationships that are reciprocated (for example, there is a bidirectional link) to the total number of relationships in the social network. This only makes sense for directed graphs. For example, the Twitter social network is a directed graph; you can follow others, but this does not necessarily mean that they will also follow you. Since our social network of heroes is semantically undirected, we cannot perform this computation.

Clustering and community detection in social networks

Graphs exhibit clustering behavior, and identification of communities is an important task in social networks. A node's clustering coefficient is the number of triadic closures (closed triples) in the node's neighborhood. This is an expression of transitivity. Nodes with higher transitivity exhibit higher subdensity, and if completely closed, form cliques that can be identified as communities. In this recipe, we will look at clustering and community detection in social networks.

Getting ready

You will again need NetworkX and, for the first time in this chapter, the python-louvain library.

How to do it...

These steps will guide you through the detection of communities within social networks:

1. Let's actually get into some clustering. The python-louvain library uses NetworkX to perform community detection with the `louvain` method. Here is a simple example of cluster partitioning on a small, built-in social network:

```
G = nx.karate_club_graph()

#first compute the best partition
partition = community.best_partition(G)

#drawing
pos = nx.spring_layout(G)
plt.figure(figsize=(12,12))
plt.axis('off')

nx.draw_networkx_nodes(G, pos, node_size=200,
cmap=plt.cm.RdYlBu, node_color=partition.values())
nx.draw_networkx_edges(G,pos, alpha=0.5)
plt.savefig("figure/karate_communities.png")
```

The following is the resulting graph with shades of grey and/or colors representing different partitions:

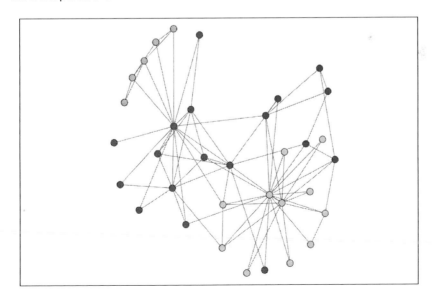

This is pretty neat! We can see there are yellow, light blue, and dark red cliques, but dark blue is pretty homogenous. We'll talk more about how to create graph visualizations with matplotlib later.

2. To partition our comic book characters, we'll add their partitions to each of their nodes; we'll then look at the relative sizes of each partition:

```
>>> graph = graph_from_csv(HERO_NETWORK)
>>> partition = community.best_partition(graph)
>>> print "%i partitions" % len(set(partition.values()))


25 partitions
>>> nx.set_node_attributes(graph, 'partition', partition)
```

As you can see, the `louvain` method has discovered 25 communities without our social graph.

3. To examine the relative size of each community, a histogram view may be helpful. To create the histogram, add the following function to your file:

```
import matplotlib.pyplot as plt


def communities_histogram(graph):
    graph, partition = detect_communities(graph)
    numbins = len(partition.values())

    plt.hist(partition.values(), bins=numbins),
    color="#0f6dbc")
    plt.title("Size of Marvel Communities")
    plt.xlabel("Community")
    plt.ylabel("Nodes")

    plt.show()
```

This should produce the following figure:

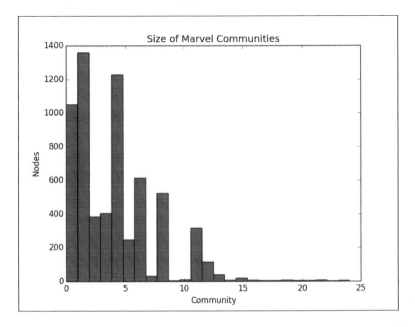

There are three major communities containing over a thousand nodes each. However, we also have eight medium-size communities around 400 actors strong. The other communities are much smaller, but it does appear that the Marvel social graph is indeed a real-world and small-world graph, much like the natural social networks observed in human culture!

4. An alternate, area-based approach to visualizing the size of the Marvel communities is to use a bubble chart. The area of each circle represents the size of each community. Graphs such as the following are often used to collapse large graphs into subgraphs based on community. To create this code, add the following function to your file:

```
def communities_bubblechart(graph):
    graph, partition = detect_communities(graph)

    parts = defaultdict(int)
    for part in partition.values():
        parts[part] += 1

    bubbles = nx.Graph()
    for part in parts.items():
        bubbles.add_node(part[0], size=part[1])
```

```
pos = nx.random_layout(bubbles)
plt.figure(figsize=(12,12))
plt.axis('off')

nx.draw_networkx_nodes(bubbles, pos,
    alpha=0.6, node_size=map(lambda x: x*6, parts.
    values()),
    node_color=[random.random() for x in parts.values()],
    cmap=plt.cm.RdYlBu)

plt.show()
```

When run, this code should produce the following figure for our Hero network:

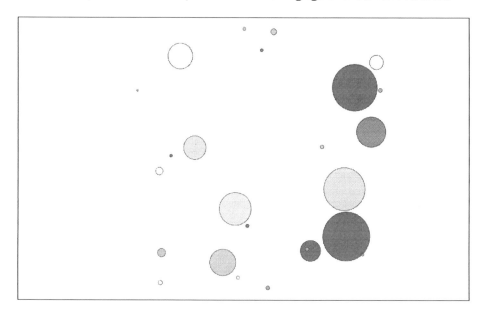

How it works...

NetworkX has several mechanisms to compute clusters:

```
>>> nx.transitivity(graph)
0.194539747093
>>> nx.average_clustering(graph)
0.774654121711
```

The `nx.transitivity` function uses the `nx.triangles` function to compute the ratio of the number of triangles to the number of possible triangles. The `nx.clustering` function computes the clustering coefficient for each node, and the `nx_average_clustering` function computes the average coefficient for the graph. Higher transitivity and clustering coefficients mean that the graph exhibits the small-world effect.

The small world is a network that appears random, but it has a high transitivity and a short average path length. This is a very common structure for social networks because the semantics of modern networks have strong ties and, therefore, strong transitivity. This essentially means that there are a series of large clusters with few bridge nodes. The heroes' social network exhibits both the small-world effect as well as a preferential attachment; the majority of new edges are to nodes with an already high degree, thus creating a long-tail, left-skewed distribution as we've seen in our graph.

There's more...

The Louvian method is a greedy optimization method that partitions the network, optimizing the modularity of each network partition. First, the method identifies small communities by attempting to optimize local modularity, then it aggregates the nodes belonging to the same community and performs the process again. In this way, a hierarchical data structure of communities is returned. The method is simple, efficient, and works against large networks of millions of nodes with billions of links.

The original method was developed by Etienne Lefebvre at UCL (Louvain-la-Neuve), then co-authored and improved along with Vincent Blondel, Jean-Loup Guillaume, and Renaud Lambiotte. It is the "Louvain method" because the method is devised when all the members of the team were at the Université catholique de Louvain. Together, the authors have created a Python method to compute these hierarchical communities, a method that depends on NetworkX. The basic detection algorithm is as follows:

```
import community
import networkx as nx
def detect_communities(graph):
```

```
partition = community.best_partition(graph)
nx.set_node_attributes(graph, 'partition', partition)
return graph, partition
```

This function expects an `nx.Graph` and uses the `community` module to compute the best root partition. The partition is hierarchical, so to get the subcommunities, we simply iterate over the parts in the partition and assign the nodes in our graph an attribute called `partition` which identifies a node with their community. The function then returns both the modified graph and the partition to use in visualization.

Visualizing graphs

Throughout this chapter, we have been visualizing social networks to help develop our understanding and intuition around graphs. In this recipe, we dig a little bit deeper into graph visualization.

Getting ready

Ensure that you have networkx and matplotlib installed.

How to do it...

Complete this list of steps to gain a better understanding of graph visualization in Python:

1. NetworkX wraps matplotlib or graphviz to draw simple graphs using the same charting library we saw in the previous chapter. This is effective for smaller-size graphs, but with larger graphs, memory can quickly be consumed. To draw a small graph, simply use the `networkx.draw` function, and then use `pyplot.show` to display it:

    ```
    >>> import networkx as nx
    >>> import matplotlib.pyplot as plt
    >>> nx.draw(graph)
    >>> plt.show()
    ```

2. There is, however, a rich drawing library underneath that lets you customize how the graph looks and is laid out with many different layout algorithms. Let's take a look at an example using one of the social graphs that comes with the NetworkX library, the Davis Southern Club Women graph:

    ```
    import networkx as nx
    import matplotlib.pyplot as plt
    ```

```
# Generate the Graph
G=nx.davis_southern_women_graph()
# Create a Spring Layout
pos=nx.spring_layout(G)

# Find the center Node
dmin=1
ncenter=0
for n in pos:
    x,y=pos[n]
    d=(x-0.5)**2+(y-0.5)**2
    if d<dmin:
        ncenter=n
        dmin=d
```

3. Next, we'll colorize the graph. First, we have to determine the center node, as we'll color this the darkest. Then, all nodes that are farther away will be colored lighter, until they become white. The spring layout has already determined the (x, y) coordinates for each node, so it's simple to compute the Euclidean distance of each node to the center of the graph (the point (0.5, 0.5), in this case), and find the node that has the lowest distance. Once determined, we compute the number of hops (for example, the path length) of every node to the center node. The nx.single_source_shortest_path_length function returns a dictionary of nodes and their distance to the node supplied as an argument. We will then use these distances to determine colors:

```
p=nx.single_source_shortest_path_length(G,ncenter)
```

4. Up next, it's time to draw the graph. We create a matplotlib figure, and then draw the edges using the NetworkX draw function. Then, we draw the nodes. This function uses a colormap (the cmap argument) to determine the range of colors to use, determined by the hop distance:

```
plt.figure(figsize=(8,8))
nx.draw_networkx_edges(G,pos,nodelist=[ncenter],alpha=0.4)
nx.draw_networkx_nodes(G,pos,nodelist=p.keys(),
                       node_size=90,
```

```
                              node_color=p.values(),

                              cmap=plt.cm.Reds_r)
```

```
plt.show()
```

Calling this function will result in a graph as shown in the following figure:

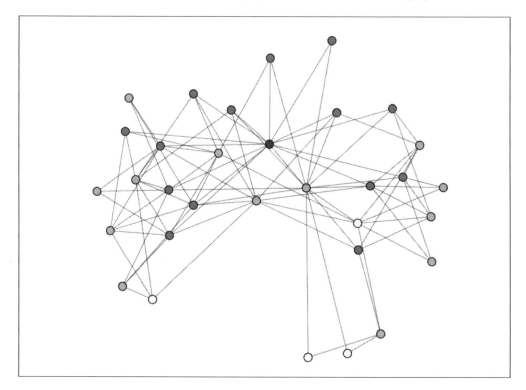

How it works...

In the preceding code, we create a graph, G, via the `davis_southern_women_graph` function, one of the many built-in graph generation functions that is included with NetworkX. We then find the position of every node in G using a layout. Layouts are algorithms that are designed to determine where nodes are placed on the graph to create an effective visualization. NetworkX comes with five positioning algorithms, by default. Circular layouts position nodes in a circle, and shell layouts position nodes in concentric circles. Random layouts uniformly distribute the nodes, and the spectral layout positions using the eigenvectors of the Laplacian graph.

The spring layout is perhaps the most common. Spring layouts are a force-directed layout, which means each node repulses other nodes around it, while edges hold them together. All the nodes are dropped onto the graph, and the repulsion/attraction is computed in a recursive manner. For each iteration, nodes will repulse and attract each other into a stable layout. There are several force-directed algorithms, but NetworkX uses the Fruchterman-Reingold algorithm.

9
Recommending Movies at Scale (Python)

In this chapter, we will cover the following recipes:

- ▶ Modeling preference expressions
- ▶ Understanding the data
- ▶ Ingesting the movie review data
- ▶ Finding the highest-scoring movies
- ▶ Improving the movie-rating system
- ▶ Measuring the distance between users in the preference space
- ▶ Computing the correlation between users
- ▶ Finding the best critic for a user
- ▶ Predicting movie ratings for users
- ▶ Collaboratively filtering item by item
- ▶ Building a nonnegative matrix factorization model
- ▶ Loading the entire dataset into the memory
- ▶ Dumping the SVD-based model to the disk
- ▶ Training the SVD-based model
- ▶ Testing the SVD-based model

Introduction

From books to movies to people to follow on Twitter, recommender systems carve the deluge of information on the Internet into a more personalized flow, thus improving the performance of e-commerce, web, and social applications. It is no great surprise, given the success of Amazon-monetizing recommendations and the Netflix Prize, that any discussion of personalization or data-theoretic prediction would involve a recommender. What is surprising is how simple recommenders are to implement yet how susceptible they are to vagaries of sparse data and overfitting.

Consider a non-algorithmic approach to eliciting recommendations; one of the easiest ways to garner a recommendation is to look at the preferences of someone we trust. We are implicitly comparing our preferences to theirs, and the more similarities you share, the more likely you are to discover novel, shared preferences. However, everyone is unique, and our preferences exist across a variety of categories and domains. What if you could leverage the preferences of a great number of people and not just those you trust? In the aggregate, you would be able to see patterns, not just of people like you, but also "anti-recommendations"— things to stay away from, cautioned by the people not like you. You would, hopefully, also see subtle delineations across the shared preference space of groups of people who share parts of your own unique experience.

It is this basic premise that a group of techniques called "collaborative filtering" use to make recommendations. Simply stated, this premise can be boiled down to the assumption that those who have similar past preferences will share the same preferences in the future. This is from a human perspective, of course, and a typical corollary to this assumption is from the perspective of the things being preferred—sets of items that are preferred by the same people will be more likely to preferred together in the future—and this is the basis for what is commonly described in the literature as user-centric collaborative filtering versus item-centric collaborative filtering.

The term collaborative filtering was coined by *David Goldberg* in a paper titled *Using collaborative filtering to weave an information tapestry, ACM,* where he proposed a system called Tapestry, which was designed at Xerox PARC in 1992, to annotate documents as interesting or uninteresting and to give document recommendations to people who are searching for good reads.

Collaborative filtering algorithms search large groupings of preference expressions to find similarities to some input preference or preferences. The output from these algorithms is a ranked list of suggestions that is a subset of all possible preferences, and hence, it's called "filtering". The "collaborative" comes from the use of many other peoples' preferences in order to find suggestions for themselves. This can be seen either as a search of the space of preferences (for brute-force techniques), a clustering problem (grouping similarly preferred items), or even some other predictive model. Many algorithmic attempts have been created in order to optimize or solve this problem across sparse or large datasets, and we will discuss a few of them in this chapter.

The goals of this chapter are:

- ▶ Understanding how to model preferences from a variety of sources
- ▶ Learning how to compute similarities using distance metrics
- ▶ Modeling recommendations using matrix factorization for star ratings

These two different models will be implemented in Python using readily available datasets on the Web. To demonstrate the techniques in this chapter, we will use the oft-cited MovieLens database from the University of Minnesota that contains star ratings of moviegoers for their preferred movies.

 Please note that this chapter is considered an advanced chapter and will most likely require significantly more time to complete than earlier chapters.

Modeling preference expressions

We have already pointed out that companies such as Amazon track purchases and page views to make recommendations, Goodreads and Yelp use 5 star ratings and text reviews, and sites such as Reddit or Stack Overflow use simple up/down voting. You can see that preference can be expressed in the data in different ways, from Boolean flags to voting to ratings. However, these preferences are expressed by attempting to find groups of similarities in preference expressions in which you are leveraging the core assumption of collaborative filtering.

More formally, we understand that two people, Bob and Alice, share a preference for a specific item or widget. If Alice too has a preference for a different item, say, sprocket, then Bob has a better than random chance of also sharing a preference for a sprocket. We believe that Bob and Alice's taste similarities can be expressed in an aggregate via a large number of preferences, and by leveraging the collaborative nature of groups, we can filter the world of products.

How to do it...

We will model preference expressions over the next few recipes, including:

- *Understanding the data*
- *Ingesting the movie review data*
- *Finding the highest rated movies*
- *Improving the movie rating system*

How it works...

A preference expression is an instance of a model of demonstrable relative selection. That is to say, preference expressions are data points that are used to show subjective ranking between a group of items for a person. Even more formally, we should say that preference expressions are not simply relative, but also temporal—for example, the statement of preference also has a fixed time relativity as well as item relativity.

 Preference expression is an instance of a model of demonstrable relative selection.

While it would be nice to think that we can subjectively and accurately express our preferences in a global context (for example, rate a movie as compared to all other movies), our tastes, in fact, change over time, and we can really only consider how we rank items relative to each other. Models of preference must take this into account and attempt to alleviate biases that are caused by it. The most common types of preference expression models simplify the problem of ranking by causing the expression to be numerically fuzzy, for example:

- Boolean expressions (yes or no)
- Up and down voting (such as abstain, dislike)
- Weighted signaling (the number of clicks or actions)
- Broad ranked classification (stars, hated or loved)

The idea is to create a preference model for an individual user—a numerical model of the set of preference expressions for a particular individual. Models build the individual preference expressions into a useful user-specific context that can be computed against. Further reasoning can be performed on the models in order to alleviate time-based biases or to perform ontological reasoning or other categorizations.

As the relationships between entities get more complex, you can express their relative preferences by assigning behavioral weights to each type of semantic connection. However, choosing the weight is difficult and requires research to decide relative weights, which is why fuzzy generalizations are preferred. As an example, the following table shows you some well-known ranking preference systems:

Reddit Voting		Online Shopping		Star Reviews	
Up Vote	1	Bought	2	Love	5
No Vote	0	Viewed	1	Liked	4
Down Vote	-1	No purchase	0	Neutral	3
				Dislike	2
				Hate	1

For the rest of this chapter, we will only consider a single, very common preference expression: star ratings on a scale of 1 to 5.

Understanding the data

Understanding your data is critical to all data-related work. In this recipe, we acquire and take a first look at the data that we will be using to build our recommendation engine.

Getting ready

To prepare for this recipe, and the rest of the chapter, download the MovieLens data from the GroupLens website of the University of Minnesota. You can find the data at `http://grouplens.org/datasets/movielens/`.

In this chapter, we will use the smaller MoveLens 100k dataset (4.7 MB in size) in order to load the entire model into the memory with ease.

How to do it...

Perform the following steps to better understand the data that we will be working with throughout this chapter:

1. Download the data from `http://grouplens.org/datasets/movielens/`. The 100K dataset is the one that you want (`ml-100k.zip`).

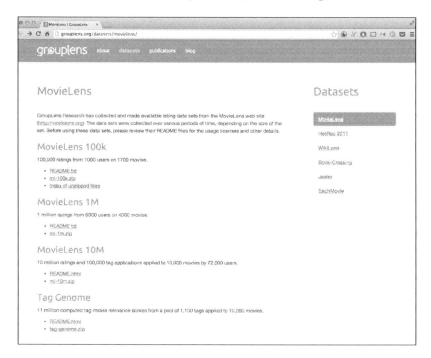

2. Unzip the downloaded data into the directory of your choice.

3. The two files that we are mainly concerned with are `u.data`, which contains the user movie ratings, and `u.item`, which contains movie information and details. To get a sense of each file, use the `head` command at the command prompt for Mac and Linux or the `more` command for Windows:

```
head -n 5 u.item
```

Note that if you are working on a computer running the Microsoft Windows operating system and not using a virtual machine (not recommended), you do not have access to the `head` command; instead, use the following command:

```
more u.item 2 n
```

The preceding command gives you the following output:

```
1|Toy Story (1995)|01-Jan-1995||http://us.imdb.com/M/title-
exact?Toy%20Story%20(1995)|0|0|0|1|1|1|0|0|0|0|0|0|0|0|0|0|0|0|0
|0

2|GoldenEye (1995)|01-Jan-1995||http://us.imdb.com/M/title-
exact?GoldenEye%20(1995)|0|1|1|0|0|0|0|0|0|0|0|0|0|0|0|0|0|1|0|0

3|Four Rooms (1995)|01-Jan-1995||http://us.imdb.com/M/title-
exact?Four%20Rooms%20(1995)|0|0|0|0|0|0|0|0|0|0|0|0|0|0|0|0|0|1|
0|0

4|Get Shorty (1995)|01-Jan-1995||http://us.imdb.com/M/title-
exact?Get%20Shorty%20(1995)|0|1|0|0|0|1|0|0|1|0|0|0|0|0|0|0|0|
0|0

5|Copycat (1995)|01-Jan-1995||http://us.imdb.com/M/title-
exact?Copycat%20(1995)|0|0|0|0|0|0|1|0|1|0|0|0|0|0|0|0|1|0|0
```

The following command will produce the given output:

```
head -n 5 u.data
```

For Windows, you can use the following command:

```
more u.item 2 n
196    242    3    881250949
186    302    3    891717742
22     377    1    878887116
244    51     2    880606923
166    346    1    886397596
```

How it works...

The two main files that we will be using are as follows:

- ▸ u.data: This contains the user moving ratings
- ▸ u.item: This contains the movie information and other details

Both are character-delimited files; u.data, which is the main file, is tab delimited, and u.item is pipe delimited.

For u.data, the first column is the user ID, the second column is the movie ID, the third is the star rating, and the last is the timestamp. The u.item file contains much more information, including the ID, title, release date, and even a URL to IMDB. Interestingly, this file also has a Boolean array indicating the genre(s) of each movie, including (in order) action, adventure, animation, children, comedy, crime, documentary, drama, fantasy, film-noir, horror, musical, mystery, romance, sci-fi, thriller, war, and western.

There's more...

Free, web-scale datasets that are appropriate for building recommendation engines are few and far between. As a result, the movie lens dataset is a very popular choice for such a task but there are others as well. The well-known Netflix Prize dataset has been pulled down by Netflix. However, there is a dump of all user-contributed content from the Stack Exchange network (including Stack Overflow) available via the Internet Archive (`https://archive.org/details/stackexchange`). Additionally, there is a book-crossing dataset that contains over a million ratings of about a quarter million different books (`http://www2.informatik.uni-freiburg.de/~cziegler/BX/`).

Ingesting the movie review data

Recommendation engines require large amounts of training data in order to do a good job, which is why they're often relegated to big data projects. However, to build a recommendation engine, we must first get the required data into memory and, due to the size of the data, must do so in a memory-safe and efficient way. Luckily, Python has all of the tools to get the job done, and this recipe shows you how.

Getting ready

You will need to have the appropriate movie lens dataset downloaded, as specified in the preceding recipe. If you skipped the setup in *Chapter 1, Preparing Your Data Science Environment*, you will need to go back and ensure that you have NumPy correctly installed.

How to do it...

The following steps guide you through the creation of the functions that we will need in order to load the datasets into the memory:

1. Open your favorite Python editor or IDE. There is a lot of code, so it should be far simpler to enter directly into a text file than **Read-Eval-Print Loop** (**REPL**).

2. We create a function to import the movie reviews:

```
import csv
import datetime


def load_reviews(path, **kwargs):
    """
    Loads MovieLens reviews
    """
    options = {
```

```
        'fieldnames': ('userid', 'movieid', 'rating',
    'timestamp'),
        'delimiter': '\t',
    }
    options.update(kwargs)


    parse_date = lambda r,k:
datetime.fromtimestamp(float(r[k]))
    parse_int  = lambda r,k: int(r[k])


    with open(path, 'rb') as reviews:
        reader = csv.DictReader(reviews, **options)
        for row in reader:
            row['userid']  = parse_int(row, 'userid')
            row['movieid'] = parse_int(row, 'movieid')
            row['rating']  = parse_int(row, 'rating')
            row['timestamp'] = parse_date(row, 'timestamp')
            yield row
```

We create a helper function to help import the data:

```
import os


def relative_path(path):
    """
    Returns a path relative from this code file
    """
    dirname = os.path.dirname(os.path.realpath('__file__'))
    path = os.path.join(dirname, path)
    return os.path.normpath(path)
```

3. We create another function to load the movie information:

```
def load_movies(path, **kwargs):
    """
    Loads MovieLens movies
    """

    options = {
```

```
            'fieldnames': ('movieid', 'title', 'release',
    'video', 'url'),'delimiter': '|','restkey': 'genre',
        }
        options.update(kwargs)


        parse_int  = lambda r,k: int(r[k])
        parse_date = lambda r,k: datetime.strptime(r[k], '%d-%b-
    %Y') if r[k] else None


        with open(path, 'rb') as movies:
            reader = csv.DictReader(movies, **options)
            for row in reader:
                row['movieid'] = parse_int(row, 'movieid')
                row['release'] = parse_date(row, 'release')
                row['video']   = parse_date(row, 'video')
                yield row
```

4. Finally, we start creating a `MovieLens` class that will be augmented in later recipes:

```
from collections import defaultdict


class MovieLens(object):
    """
    Data structure to build our recommender model on.
    """


    def __init__(self, udata, uitem):
        """
        Instantiate with a path to u.data and u.item
        """
        self.udata   = udata
        self.uitem   = uitem
        self.movies  = {}
        self.reviews = defaultdict(dict)
        self.load_dataset()


    def load_dataset(self):
        """
```

```
Loads the two datasets into memory, indexed on the ID.
"""

for movie in load_movies(self.uitem):
    self.movies[movie['movieid']] = movie


for review in load_reviews(self.udata):
    self.reviews[review['userid']][review['movieid']]
= review
```

5. Ensure that the functions have been imported into your REPL or the IPython workspace, and type the following, making sure that the path to the data files is appropriate for your system:

```
data  = relative_path('data/ml-100k/u.data')
item  = relative_path('data/ml-100k/u.item')
model = MovieLens(data, item)
```

How it works...

The methodology that we use for the two data-loading functions (`load_reviews` and `load_movies`) is simple, but it takes care of the details of parsing the data from the disk. We created a function that takes a path to our dataset and then any optional keywords. We know that we have specific ways in which we need to interact with the `csv` module, so we create default options, passing in the field names of the rows along with the delimiter, which is `\t`. The `options.update(kwargs)` line means that we'll accept whatever users pass to this function.

We then created internal parsing functions using a `lambda` function in Python. These simple parsers take a row and a key as input and return the converted input. This is an example of using `lambda` as internal, reusable code blocks and is a common technique in Python. Finally, we open our file and create a `csv.DictReader` function with our options. Iterating through the rows in the reader, we parse the fields that we want to be `int` and `datetime`, respectively, and then yield the row.

 Note that as we are unsure about the actual size of the input file, we are doing this in a memory-safe manner using Python generators. Using `yield` instead of `return` ensures that Python creates a generator under the hood and does not load the entire dataset into the memory.

We'll use each of these methodologies to load the datasets at various times through our computation that uses this dataset. We'll need to know where these files are at all times, which can be a pain, especially in larger code bases; in the *There's more...* section, we'll discuss a Python pro-tip to alleviate this concern.

Finally, we created a data structure, which is the `MovieLens` class, with which we can hold our reviews' data. This structure takes the `udata` and `uitem` paths, and then, it loads the movies and reviews into two Python dictionaries that are indexed by `movieid` and `userid`, respectively. To instantiate this object, you will execute something as follows:

```
data  = relative_path('../data/ml-100k/u.data')
item  = relative_path('../data/ml-100k/u.item')
model = MovieLens(data, item)
```

Note that the preceding commands assume that you have your data in a folder called `data`. We can now load the whole dataset into the memory, indexed on the various IDs specified in the dataset.

Did you notice the use of the `relative_path` function? When dealing with fixtures such as these to build models, the data is often included with the code. When you specify a path in Python, such as `data/ml-100k/u.data`, it looks it up relative to the current working directory where you ran the script. To help ease this trouble, you can specify the paths that are relative to the code itself:

```
import os


def relative_path(path):
    """
    Returns a path relative from this code file
    """
    dirname = os.path.dirname(os.path.realpath('__file__'))
    path = os.path.join(dirname, path)
    return os.path.normpath(path)
```

Keep in mind that this holds the entire data structure in memory; in the case of the 100k dataset, this will require 54.1 MB, which isn't too bad for modern machines. However, we should also keep in mind that we'll generally build recommenders using far more than just 100,000 reviews. This is why we have configured the data structure the way we have—very similar to a database. To grow the system, you will replace the `reviews` and `movies` properties with database access functions or properties, which will yield data types expected by our methods.

Finding the highest-scoring movies

If you're looking for a good movie, you'll often want to see the most popular or best rated movies overall. Initially, we'll take a naïve approach to compute a movie's aggregate rating by averaging the user reviews for each movie. This technique will also demonstrate how to access the data in our `MovieLens` class.

Getting ready

These recipes are sequential in nature. Thus, you should have completed the previous recipes in the chapter before starting with this one.

How to do it...

Follow these steps to output numeric scores for all movies in the dataset and compute a top-10 list:

1. Augment the `MovieLens` class with a new method to get all reviews for a particular movie:

```
class MovieLens(object):

    ...

    def reviews_for_movie(self, movieid):
        """
        Yields the reviews for a given movie
        """
        for review in self.reviews.values():
            if movieid in review:
                yield review[movieid]
```

2. Then, add an additional method to compute the top 10 movies reviewed by users:

```
import heapq
from operator import itemgetter

class MovieLens(object):

    ...

    def average_reviews(self):
        """
        Averages the star rating for all movies.
    Yields a tuple of movieid,
        the average rating, and the number of reviews.
        """
```

```
        for movieid in self.movies:
            reviews = list(r['rating'] for r in
self.reviews_for_movie(movieid))
            average = sum(reviews) / float(len(reviews))
            yield (movieid, average, len(reviews))


    def top_rated(self, n=10):
        """
        Yields the n top rated movies
        """
        return heapq.nlargest(n, self.average_reviews(),
key=itemgetter(1))
```

 Note that the ... notation just below `class MovieLens(object):` signifies that we will be appending the `average_reviews` method to the existing `MovieLens` class.

3. Now, let's print the top-rated results:

```
for mid, avg, num in model.top_rated(10):
    title = model.movies[mid]['title']
    print "[%0.3f average rating (%i reviews)] %s" % (avg,
num,title)
```

4. Executing the preceding commands in your REPL should produce the following output:

```
[5.000 average rating (1 reviews)] Entertaining Angels: The
Dorothy Day Story (1996)
    [5.000 average rating (2 reviews)] Santa with Muscles (1996)
    [5.000 average rating (1 reviews)] Great Day in Harlem, A (1994)
    [5.000 average rating (1 reviews)] They Made Me a Criminal (1939)
    [5.000 average rating (1 reviews)] Aiqing wansui (1994)
    [5.000 average rating (1 reviews)] Someone Else's America (1995)
    [5.000 average rating (2 reviews)] Saint of Fort Washington,
The (1993)
    [5.000 average rating (3 reviews)] Prefontaine (1997)
    [5.000 average rating (3 reviews)] Star Kid (1997)
    [5.000 average rating (1 reviews)] Marlene Dietrich: Shadow
and Light (1996)
```

How it works...

The new `reviews_for_movie()` method that is added to the `MovieLens` class iterates through our review dictionary values (which are indexed by the `userid` parameter), checks whether the `movieid` value has been reviewed by the user, and then presents that review dictionary. We will need such functionality for the next method.

With the `average_review()` method, we have created another generator function that goes through all of our movies and all of their reviews and presents the movie ID, the average rating, and the number of reviews. The `top_rated` function uses the `heapq` module to quickly sort the reviews based on the average.

The `heapq` data structure, also known as the priority queue algorithm, is the Python implementation of an abstract data structure with interesting and useful properties. Heaps are binary trees that are built so that every parent node has a value that is either less than or equal to any of its children nodes. Thus, the smallest element is the root of the tree, which can be accessed in constant time, which is a very desirable property. With `heapq`, Python developers have an efficient means to insert new values in an ordered data structure and also return sorted values.

There's more...

Here, we run into our first problem—some of the top-rated movies only have one review (and conversely, so do the worst-rated movies). How do you compare *Casablanca*, which has a 4.457 average rating (243 reviews), with *Santa with Muscles*, which has a 5.000 average rating (2 reviews)? We are sure that those two reviewers really liked *Santa with Muscles*, but the high rating for *Casablanca* is probably more meaningful because more people liked it. Most recommenders with star ratings will simply output the average rating along with the number of reviewers, allowing the user to determine their quality; however, as data scientists, we can do better in the next recipe.

See also

▶ The `heapq` documentation available at `https://docs.python.org/2/library/heapq.html`

Improving the movie-rating system

We don't want to build a recommendation engine with a system that considers the likely straight-to-DVD *Santa with Muscles* as generally superior to *Casablanca*. Thus, the naïve scoring approach used previously must be improved upon and is the focus of this recipe.

Getting ready

Make sure that you have completed the previous recipes in this chapter first.

How to do it...

The following steps implement and test a new movie-scoring algorithm:

1. Let's implement a new Bayesian movie-scoring algorithm as shown in the following function, adding it to the `MovieLens` class:

```
def bayesian_average(self, c=59, m=3):
    """
    Reports the Bayesian average with parameters c and m.
    """
    for movieid in self.movies:
        reviews = list(r['rating'] for r in self.reviews_for_
movie(movieid))
        average = ((c * m) + sum(reviews)) /
                float(c + len(reviews))
        yield (movieid, average, len(reviews))
```

2. Next, we will replace the `top_rated` method in the `MovieLens` class with the version in the following commands that uses the new `Bayesian_average` method from the preceding step:

```
def top_rated(self, n=10):
    """
    Yields the n top rated movies
    """
    return heapq.nlargest(n, self.bayesian_average(),
key=itemgetter(1))
```

3. Printing our new top-10 list looks a bit more familiar to us and `Casablanca` is now happily rated number 4:

```
[4.234 average rating (583 reviews)] Star Wars (1977)
[4.224 average rating (298 reviews)] Schindler's List (1993)
[4.196 average rating (283 reviews)] Shawshank Redemption,
The (1994)
[4.172 average rating (243 reviews)] Casablanca (1942)
[4.135 average rating (267 reviews)] Usual Suspects, The (1995)
```

```
[4.123 average rating (413 reviews)] Godfather, The (1972)

[4.120 average rating (390 reviews)] Silence of the Lambs,
The (1991)

[4.098 average rating (420 reviews)] Raiders of the Lost Ark
(1981)

[4.082 average rating (209 reviews)] Rear Window (1954)

[4.066 average rating (350 reviews)] Titanic (1997)
```

How it works...

Taking the average of movie reviews, as in shown the previous recipe, simply did not work because some movies did not have enough ratings to give a meaningful comparison to movies with more ratings. What we'd really like is to have every single movie critic rate every single movie. Given that this is impossible, we could derive an estimate for how the movie would be rated if an infinite number of people rated the movie; this is hard to infer from one data point, so we should say that we would like to estimate the movie rating if the same number of people gave it a rating on an average (for example, filtering our results based on the number of reviews).

This estimate can be computed with a Bayesian average, implemented in the `bayesian_average()` function, to infer these ratings based on the following equation:

$$rating = \frac{C \times m \times \sum stars}{C + n}$$

Here, m is our prior for the average of stars, and C is a confidence parameter that is equivalent to the number of observations in our posterior.

Determining priors can be a complicated and magical art. Rather than taking the complex path of fitting a Dirichlet distribution to our data, we can simply choose an m prior of 3 with our 5-star rating system, which means that our prior assumes that star ratings tend to be reviewed around the median value. In choosing C, you are expressing how many reviews are needed to get away from the prior; we can compute this by looking at the average number of reviews per movie:

```
print float(sum(num for mid, avg, num in model.average_reviews())) /
len(model.movies)
```

This gives us an average number of 59.4, which we use as the default value in our function definition.

There's more...

Play around with the C parameter. You should find that if you change the parameter so that C = 50, the top-10 list subtly shifts; in this case, *Schindler's List* and *Star Wars* are swapped in rankings, as are *Raiders of the Lost Ark* and *Rear Window*— note that both the swapped movies have far more reviews than the former, which means that the higher C parameter was balancing the fewer ratings of the other movie.

See also

▸   See how Yelp deals with this challenge at `http://venturebeat. com/2009/10/12/how-yelp-deals-with-everybody-getting-four- stars-on-average/`

Measuring the distance between users in the preference space

The two most recognizable types of collaborative filtering systems are user-based recommenders and item-based recommenders. If one were to imagine that the preference space is an N-dimensional feature space where either users or items are plotted, then we would say that similar users or items tend to cluster near each other in this preference space; hence, an alternative name for this type of collaborative filtering is nearest neighbor recommenders.

A crucial step in this process is to come up with a similarity or distance metric with which we can compare critics to each other or mutually preferred items. This metric is then used to perform pairwise comparisons of a particular user to all other users, or conversely, for an item to be compared to all other items. Normalized comparisons are then used to determine recommendations. Although the computational space can become exceedingly large, distance metrics themselves are not difficult to compute, and in this recipe, we will explore a few as well as implement our first recommender system.

In this recipe, we will measure the distance between users; in the recipe after this one, we will look at another similarity distance indicator.

Getting ready

We will continue to build on the `MovieLens` class from the section titled Modeling Preference. If you have not had the opportunity to review this section, please have the code for that class ready. Importantly, we will want to access the data structures, `MovieLens.movies` and `MovieLens.reviews`, that have been loaded from the CSV files on the disk.

How to do it...

The following set of steps provide instructions on how to compute the Euclidean distance between users:

1. Augment the MovieLens class with a new method, shared_preferences, to pull out movies that have been rated by two critics, A and B:

```python
class MovieLens(objects):

    ...

    def shared_preferences(self, criticA, criticB):
        """
        Returns the intersection of ratings for two critics
        """
        if criticA not in self.reviews:
            raise KeyError("Couldn't find critic '%s' in
data" % criticA)
        if criticB not in self.reviews:
            raise KeyError("Couldn't find critic '%s' in
data" % criticB)

        moviesA = set(self.reviews[criticA].keys())
        moviesB = set(self.reviews[criticB].keys())
        shared  = moviesA & moviesB # Intersection operator

        # Create a reviews dictionary to return
        reviews  = {}
        for movieid in shared:
            reviews[movieid] = (
                self.reviews[criticA][movieid]['rating'],
                self.reviews[criticB][movieid]['rating'],
            )
        return reviews
```

2. Then, implement a function that computes the Euclidean distance between two critics using their shared movie preferences as a vector for the computation. This method will also be part of the `MovieLens` class:

```python
from math import sqrt



    ...


        def euclidean_distance(self, criticA, criticB):
            """

            Reports the Euclidean distance of two critics, A&B by

            performing a J-dimensional Euclidean calculation of

        each of their preference vectors for the intersection

        of movies the critics have rated.
            """


            # Get the intersection of the rated titles in the
        data.
            preferences = self.shared_preferences(criticA,
        criticB)

            # If they have no rankings in common, return 0.
            if len(preferences) == 0: return 0

            # Sum the squares of the differences
            sum_of_squares = sum([pow(a-b, 2) for a, b in
        preferences.values()])

            # Return the inverse of the distance to give a higher
        score to
            # folks who are more similar (e.g. less distance) add
        1 to prevent
            # division by zero errors and normalize ranks in [0,
        1]
            return 1 / (1 + sqrt(sum_of_squares))
```

3. With the preceding code implemented, test it in REPL:

```
>>> data  = relative_path('data/ml-100k/u.data')
>>> item  = relative_path('data/ml-100k/u.item')
>>> model = MovieLens(data, item)
>>> print model.euclidean_distance(232, 532)
0.1023021629920016
```

How it works...

The new `shared_preferences()` method of the `MovieLens` class determines the shared preference space of two users. Critically, we can only compare users (the `criticA` and `criticB` input parameters) based on the things that they have both rated. This function uses Python sets to determine the list of movies that both A and B reviewed (the intersection of the movies A has rated and the movies B has rated). The function then iterates over this set, returning a dictionary whose keys are the movie IDs and the values are a tuple of ratings, for example, (`ratingA`, `ratingB`) for each movie that both users have rated. We can now use this dataset to compute similarity scores, which is done by the second function.

The `euclidean_distance()` function takes two critics as the input, A and B, and computes the distance between users in preference space. Here, we have chosen to implement the Euclidean distance metric (the two-dimensional variation is well known to those who remember the Pythagorean theorem), but we could have implemented other metrics as well. This function will return a real number from 0 to 1, where 0 is less similar (farther apart) critics and 1 is more similar (closer together) critics.

There's more...

The Manhattan distance is another very popular metric and a very simple one to understand. It can simply sum the absolute values of the pairwise differences between elements of each vector. Or, in code, it can be executed in this manner:

```
manhattan = sum([abs(a-b) for a, b in preferences.values()])
```

This metric is also called the city-block distance because, conceptually, it is as if you were counting the number of blocks north/south and east/west one would have to walk between two points in the city. Before implementing it for this recipe, you would also want to invert and normalize the value in some fashion to return a value in the [0, 1] range.

See also

- ▸ The distance overview from Wikipedia available at `http://en.wikipedia.org/wiki/Distance`
- ▸ The Taxicab geometry from Wikipedia available at `http://en.wikipedia.org/wiki/Taxicab_geometry`

Computing the correlation between users

In the previous recipe, we used one out of many possible distance measures to capture the distance between the movie reviews of users. This distance between two specific users is not changed even if there are five or five million other users.

In this recipe, we will compute the correlation between users in the preference space. Like distance metrics, there are many correlation metrics. The most popular of these are Pearson or Spearman correlations or Cosine distance. Unlike distance metrics, the correlation will change depending on the number of users and movies.

Getting ready

We will be continuing the efforts of the previous recipes again, so make sure you understand each one.

How to do it...

The following function implements the computation of the `pearson_correlation` function for two critics, which are `criticA` and `criticB`, and is added to the `MovieLens` class:

```python
def pearson_correlation(self, criticA, criticB):
    """
    Returns the Pearson Correlation of two critics, A and B by
    performing the PPMC calculation on the scatter plot of (a, b)
    ratings on the shared set of critiqued titles.
    """

    # Get the set of mutually rated items
    preferences = self.shared_preferences(criticA, criticB)

    # Store the length to save traversals of the len computation.
    # If they have no rankings in common, return 0.
```

```
length = len(preferences)
if length == 0: return 0


# Loop through the preferences of each critic once and
compute the
# various summations that are required for our final
calculation.
sumA = sumB = sumSquareA = sumSquareB = sumProducts = 0
for a, b in preferences.values():
    sumA += a
    sumB += b
    sumSquareA  += pow(a, 2)
    sumSquareB  += pow(b, 2)
    sumProducts += a*b


# Calculate Pearson Score
numerator   = (sumProducts*length) - (sumA*sumB)
denominator = sqrt(((sumSquareA*length) - pow(sumA, 2)) *
((sumSquareB*length) - pow(sumB, 2)))


# Prevent division by zero.
if denominator == 0: return 0


return abs(numerator / denominator)
```

How it works...

The Pearson correlation computes the "product moment", which is the mean of the product of mean adjusted random variables and is defined as the covariance of two variables (a and b, in our case) divided by the product of the standard deviation of a and the standard deviation of b. As a formula, this looks like the following:

$$Pearson\ Correlation = \frac{cov(A, B)}{\sigma_A \sigma_B}$$

For a finite sample, which is what we have, the detailed formula, which was implemented in the preceding function, is as follows:

$$Pearson\ Correlation = \frac{\sum_{i=1}^{n}(A_i - mean(A)) \times \sum_{i=1}^{n}(B_i - mean(B))}{\sqrt{\sum_{i=1}^{n}(A_i - mean(A))^2} \times \sqrt{\sum_{i=1}^{n}(B_i - mean(B))^2}}$$

Another way to think about the Pearson correlation is as a measure of the linear dependence between two variables. It returns a score of -1 to 1, where negative scores closer to -1 indicate a stronger negative correlation, and positive scores closer to 1 indicate a stronger, positive correlation. A score of 0 means that the two variables are not correlated.

In order for us to perform comparisons, we want to normalize our similarity metrics in the space of [0, 1] so that 0 means less similar and 1 means more similar, so we return the absolute value:

```
>>> print model.pearson_correlation(232, 532)
0.06025793538385047
```

There's more...

We have explored two distance metrics: the Euclidean distance and the Pearson correlation. There are many more, including the Spearman correlation, Tantimoto scores, Jaccard distance, Cosine similarity, and Manhattan distance, to name a few. Choosing the right distance metric for the dataset of your recommender along with the type of preference expression used is crucial to ensuring success in this style of recommender. It's up to the reader to explore this space further based on his or her interest and particular dataset.

Finding the best critic for a user

Now that we have two different ways to compute a similarity distance between users, we can determine the best critics for a particular user and see how similar they are to an individual's preferences.

Getting ready

Make sure that you have completed the previous recipes before tackling this one.

How to do it...

Implement a new method for the MovieLens class, similar_critics(), that locates the best match for a user:

```python
import heapq


...


    def similar_critics(self, user, metric='euclidean', n=None):
        """
        Finds, ranks similar critics for the user according to the
        specified distance metric. Returns the top n similar critics
        if n is specified.
        """

        # Metric jump table
        metrics  = {
            'euclidean': self.euclidean_distance,
            'pearson':   self.pearson_correlation,
        }

        distance = metrics.get(metric, None)

        # Handle problems that might occur
        if user not in self.reviews:
            raise KeyError("Unknown user, '%s'." % user)
        if not distance or not callable(distance):
            raise KeyError("Unknown or unprogrammed distance metric
'%s'." % metric)

        # Compute user to critic similarities for all critics
        critics = {}
        for critic in self.reviews:
            # Don't compare against yourself!
            if critic == user:
                continue
```

```
        critics[critic] = distance(user, critic)


    if n:
        return heapq.nlargest(n, critics.items(),
key=itemgetter(1))
        return critics
```

How it works...

The `similar_critics` method, added to the `MovieLens` class, serves as the heart of this recipe. It takes as parameters the targeted user and two optional parameters: the metric to be used, which defaults to `euclidean`, and the number of results to be returned, which defaults to `None`. As you can see, this flexible method uses a jump table to determine what algorithm is to be used (you can pass in `euclidean` or `pearson` to choose the distance metric). Every other critic is compared to the current user (except a comparison of the user against themselves). The results are then sorted using the flexible `heapq` module and the top n results are returned.

To test out our implementation, print out the results of the run for both similarity distances:

```
>>> for item in model.similar_critics(232, 'euclidean', n=10):
  print "%4i: %0.3f" % item
  688: 1.000
  914: 1.000
   47: 0.500
   78: 0.500
  170: 0.500
  335: 0.500
  341: 0.500
  101: 0.414
  155: 0.414
  309: 0.414

>>> for item in model.similar_critics(232, 'pearson', n=10):
  print "%4i: %0.3f" % item
   33: 1.000
   36: 1.000
  155: 1.000
  260: 1.000
```

```
289: 1.000
302: 1.000
309: 1.000
317: 1.000
511: 1.000
769: 1.000
```

These scores are clearly very different, and it appears that Pearson thinks that there are much more similar users than the Euclidean distance metric. The Euclidean distance metric tends to favor users who have rated fewer items exactly the same. Pearson correlation favors more scores that fit well linearly, and therefore, Pearson corrects grade inflation where two critics might rate movies very similarly, but one user rates them consistently one star higher than the other.

If you plot out how many shared rankings each critic has, you'll see that the data is very sparse. Here is the preceding data with the number of rankings appended:

```
Euclidean scores:
  688: 1.000 (1 shared rankings)
  914: 1.000 (2 shared rankings)
   47: 0.500 (5 shared rankings)
   78: 0.500 (3 shared rankings)
  170: 0.500 (1 shared rankings)


 Pearson scores:
   33: 1.000 (2 shared rankings)
   36: 1.000 (3 shared rankings)
  155: 1.000 (2 shared rankings)
  260: 1.000 (3 shared rankings)
  289: 1.000 (3 shared rankings)
```

Therefore, it is not enough to find similar critics and use their ratings to predict our users' scores; instead, we will have to aggregate the scores of all of the critics, regardless of similarity, and predict ratings for the movies we haven't rated.

Predicting movie ratings for users

To predict how we might rate a particular movie, we can compute a weighted average of critics who have also rated the same movies as the user. The weight will be the similarity of the critic to user—if a critic has not rated a movie, then their similarity will not contribute to the overall ranking of the movie.

Getting ready

Ensure that you have completed the previous recipes in this large, cumulative chapter.

How to do it...

The following steps walk you through the prediction of movie ratings for users:

1. First, add the `predict_ranking` function to the `MovieLens` class in order to predict the ranking a user might give a particular movie with similar critics:

```
    def predict_ranking(self, user, movie, metric='euclidean',
critics=None):
        """
        Predicts the ranking a user might give a movie based on
    the
        weighted average of the critics similar to the that user.
        """

        critics = critics or self.similar_critics(user,
metric=metric)
        total   = 0.0
        simsum  = 0.0

        for critic, similarity in critics.items():
            if movie in self.reviews[critic]:
                total  += similarity * self.reviews[critic]
[movie]['rating']
                simsum += similarity

        if simsum == 0.0: return 0.0
        return total / simsum
```

2. Next, add the `predict_all_rankings` method to the `MovieLens` class:

```
def predict_all_rankings(self, user, metric='euclidean',
n=None):
    """
    Predicts all rankings for all movies, if n is
specified returns
    the top n movies and their predicted ranking.
    """
    critics = self.similar_critics(user, metric=metric)
    movies = {
        movie: self.predict_ranking(user, movie, metric,
critics)
        for movie in self.movies
    }

    if n:
        return heapq.nlargest(n, movies.items(),
key=itemgetter(1))
    return movies
```

How it works...

The `predict_ranking` method takes a user and a movie along with a string specifying the distance metric and returns the predicted rating for that movie for that particular user. A fourth argument, `critics`, is meant to be an optimization for the `predict_all_rankings` method, which we'll discuss shortly. The prediction gathers all critics who are similar to the user and computes the weighted total rating of the critics, filtered by those who actually did rate the movie in question. The weights are simply their similarity to the user, computed by the distance metric. This total is then normalized by the sum of the similarities to move the rating back into the space of 1 to 5 stars:

```
>>> print model.predict_ranking(422, 50, 'euclidean')
4.35413151722
>>> print model.predict_ranking(422, 50, 'pearson')
4.3566797826
```

Here, we can see the predictions for *Star Wars* (ID 50 in our MovieLens dataset) for the user 422. The Euclidean and Pearson computations are very close to each other (which isn't necessarily to be expected), but the prediction is also very close to the user's actual rating, which is 4.

The `predict_all_rankings` method computes the ranking predictions for all movies for a particular user according to the passed-in metric. It optionally takes a value, n, to return the top n best matches. This function optimizes the similar critics' lookup by only executing it once and then passing those discovered critics to the `predict_ranking` function in order to improve the performance. However, this method must be run on every single movie in the dataset:

```
>>> for mid, rating in model.predict_all_rankings(578, 'pearson',
10):
...       print "%0.3f: %s" % (rating, model.movies[mid]['title'])
5.000: Prefontaine (1997)
5.000: Santa with Muscles (1996)
5.000: Marlene Dietrich: Shadow and Light (1996)
5.000: Star Kid (1997)
5.000: Aiqing wansui (1994)
5.000: Someone Else's America (1995)
5.000: Great Day in Harlem, A (1994)
5.000: Saint of Fort Washington, The (1993)
4.954: Anna (1996)
4.817: Innocents, The (1961)
```

As you can see, we have now computed what our recommender thinks the top movies for this particular user are, along with what we think the user will rate the movie! The top-10 list of average movie ratings plays a huge rule here and a potential improvement could be to use the Bayesian averaging in addition to the similarity weighting, but that is left for the reader to implement.

Collaboratively filtering item by item

So far, we have compared users to other users in order to make our predictions. However, the similarity space can be partitioned in two ways. User-centric collaborative filtering plots users in the preference space and discovers how similar users are to each other. These similarities are then used to predict rankings, aligning the user with similar critics. Item-centric collaborative filtering does just the opposite; it plots the items together in the preference space and makes recommendations according to how similar a group of items are to another group.

Item-based collaborative filtering is a common optimization as the similarity of items changes slowly. Once enough data has been gathered, reviewers adding reviews does not necessarily change the fact that *Toy Story* is more similar to *Babe* than *The Terminator*, and users who prefer *Toy Story* might prefer the former to the latter. Therefore, you can simply compute item similarities once in a single offline-process and use that as a static mapping for recommendations, updating the results on a semi-regular basis.

This recipe will walk you through item-by-item collaborative filtering.

Getting ready

This recipe requires the completion of the previous recipes in this chapter.

How to do it...

Construct the following function to perform item-by-item collaborative filtering:

```python
def shared_critics(self, movieA, movieB):
    """
    Returns the intersection of critics for two items, A and B
    """

    if movieA not in self.movies:
        raise KeyError("Couldn't find movie '%s' in data" %movieA)
    if movieB not in self.movies:
        raise KeyError("Couldn't find movie '%s' in data" %movieB)

    criticsA = set(critic for critic in self.reviews if movieA
in self.reviews[critic])
    criticsB = set(critic for critic in self.reviews if movieB
in self.reviews[critic])
    shared   = criticsA & criticsB # Intersection operator

    # Create the reviews dictionary to return
    reviews  = {}
    for critic in shared:
        reviews[critic] = (
            self.reviews[critic][movieA]['rating'],
            self.reviews[critic][movieB]['rating'],
        )
    return reviews

def similar_items(self, movie, metric='euclidean', n=None):
    # Metric jump table
```

```
metrics = {
    'euclidean': self.euclidean_distance,
    'pearson':  self.pearson_correlation,
}

distance = metrics.get(metric, None)

# Handle problems that might occur
if movie not in self.reviews:
    raise KeyError("Unknown movie, '%s'." % movie)
if not distance or not callable(distance):
    raise KeyError("Unknown or unprogrammed distance metric '%s'." % metric)

items = {}
for item in self.movies:
    if item == movie:
        continue

    items[item] = distance(item, movie, prefs='movies')

if n:
    return heapq.nlargest(n, items.items(),
key=itemgetter(1))
    return items
```

How it works...

To perform item-by-item collaborative filtering, the same distance metrics can be used but must be updated to use the preferences from `shared_critics` rather than `shared_preferences` (for example, item similarity versus user similarity). Update the functions to accept a `prefs` parameter that determines which preferences are to be used, but I'll leave that to the reader as it is only two lines of code (note that the answer is contained in the `sim.py` source file in the directory that contains the code for *Chapter 8, Working with Social Graphs (Python)*).

If you print out the list of similar items for a particular movie, you can see some interesting results. For example, review the similarity results for *The Crying Game* (1992), which has an ID of `631`:

```
for movie, similarity in model.similar_items(631, 'pearson').items():
    print "%0.3f: %s" % (similarity, model.movies[movie]['title'])
```

```
0.127: Toy Story (1995)
0.209: GoldenEye (1995)
0.069: Four Rooms (1995)
0.039: Get Shorty (1995)
0.340: Copycat (1995)
0.225: Shanghai Triad (Yao a yao yao dao waipo qiao) (1995)
0.232: Twelve Monkeys (1995)
...
```

This crime thriller is not very similar to *Toy Story*, which is a children's movie, but is more similar to *Copycat*, which is another crime thriller. Of course, critics who have rated many movies skew the results, and more movie reviews are needed before this normalizes into something more compelling.

It is presumed that the item similarity scores are run regularly but do not need to be computed in real time. Given a set of computed item similarities, computing recommendations are as follows:

```
    def predict_ranking(self, user, movie, metric='euclidean'):
        movies = self.similar_items(movie, metric=metric)
        total  = 0.0
        simsum = 0.0

        for relmovie, similarity in movies.items():
            # Ignore movies already reviewed by user
            if relmovie in self.reviews[user]:
                total  += similarity *
self.reviews[user][relmovie]['rating']
                simsum += similarity

        if simsum == 0.0: return 0.0
        return total / simsum
```

This method simply uses the inverted item-to-item similarity scores rather than the user-to-user similarity scores. Since similar items can be computed offline, the lookup for movies via the `self.similar_items` method should be a database lookup rather than a real-time computation.

```
>>> print model.predict_ranking(232, 52, 'pearson')
3.980443976
```

You can then compute a ranked list of all possible recommendations in a similar way as the user-to-user recommendations.

Building a nonnegative matrix factorization model

A general improvement on the basic cross-wise nearest-neighbor similarity scoring of collaborative filtering is a matrix factorization method, which is also known as **Singular Value Decomposition (SVD)**. Matrix factorization methods attempt to explain the ratings through the discovery of latent features that are not easily identifiable by analysts. For instance, this technique can expose possible features such as the amount of action, family friendliness, or fine-tuned genre discovery in our movies dataset.

What's especially interesting about these features is that they are continuous and not discrete values and can represent an individual's preference along a continuum. In this sense, the model can explore shades of characteristics, for example, perhaps a critic in the movie reviews' dataset, such as action flicks with a strong female lead that are set in European countries. A James Bond movie might represent a shade of that type of movie even though it only ticks the set in European countries and action genre boxes. Depending on how similarly reviewers rate the movie, the strength of the female counterpart to James Bond will determine how they might like the movie.

Also, extremely helpfully, the matrix factorization model does well on sparse data, that is data with few recommendation and movie pairs. Reviews' data is particularly sparse because not everyone has rated the same movies and there is a massive set of available movies. SVD can also be performed in parallel, making it a good choice for much larger datasets.

In the remaining recipes in this chapter, we will build a nonnegative matrix factorization model in order to improve our recommendation engine.

How to do it...

In the remaining recipes in this chapter, we will build a nonnegative matrix factorization model in order to improve our recommendation engine:

1. Loading the entire dataset into the memory.
2. Dumping the SVD-based model to the disk.
3. Training the SVD-based model.
4. Testing the SVD-based model.

How it works...

Matrix factorization, or SVD works, by finding two matrices such that when you take their dot product (also known as the inner product or scalar product), you will get a close approximation of the original matrix. We have expressed our training matrix as a sparse N x M matrix of users to movies where the values are the 5-star rating if it exists, otherwise, the value is blank or 0. By factoring the model with the values that we have and then taking the dot product of the two matrices produced by the factorization, we hope to fill in the blank spots in our original matrix with a prediction of how the user would have rated the movie in that column.

The intuition is that there should be some latent features that determine how users rate an item, and these latent features are expressed through the semantics of their previous ratings. If we can discover the latent features, we will be able to predict new ratings. Additionally, there should be fewer features than there are users and movies (otherwise, each movie or user would be a unique feature). This is why we compose our factored matrices by some feature length before taking their dot product.

Mathematically, this task is expressed as follows. If we have a set of U users and M movies, let R of size |U| x |M| be the matrix that contains the ratings of users. Assuming that we have K latent features, find two matrices, P and Q, where P is |U| x K and Q is |M| x K such that the dot product of P and Q transpose approximates R. P, which therefore represent the strength of the associations between users and features and Q represents the association of movies with features.

$$ R \approx P \times Q^{T} = \hat{R} $$

There are a few ways to go about factorization, but the choice we made was to perform gradient descent. Gradient descent initializes two random P and Q matrices, computes their dot product, and then minimizes the error compared to the original matrix by traveling down a slope of an error function (the gradient). This way, the algorithm hopes to find a local minimum where the error is within an acceptable threshold.

Our function computed the error as the squared difference between the predicted value and the actual value.

$$ e_{ij} = (r_{ij} - \hat{r}_{ij})^2 $$

To minimize the error, we modify the values `pik` and `qkj` by descending along the gradient of the current error slope, differentiating our error equation with respect to `p` yields:

$$ \frac{\partial}{\partial p_{ik}} e_{ij} = -2(r_{ij} - \hat{r}_{ij})(q_{kj}) = -2e_{ij}q_{kj} $$

We then differentiate our error equation with respect to the variable `q` yields in the following equation:

$$ \frac{\partial}{\partial q_{ik}} e_{ij} = -2(r_{ij} - \hat{r}_{ij})(p_{ik}) = -2e_{ij}p_{ik} $$

We can then derive our learning rule, which updates the values in P and Q by a constant learning rate, which is α. This learning rate, α, should not be too large because it determines how big of a step we take towards the minimum, and it is possible to step across to the other side of the error curve. It should also not be too small, otherwise it will take forever to converge.

$$ p'_{ik} = p_{ik} + \alpha \frac{\partial}{\partial p_{ik}} e_{ij} = p_{ik} + 2\alpha e_{ij}q_{kj} $$

$$ q'_{kj} = q_{kj} + \alpha \frac{\partial}{\partial q_{kj}} e_{ij} = q_{kj} + 2\alpha e_{ij}p_{ik} $$

We continue to update our P and Q matrices, minimizing the error until the sum of the error squared is below some threshold, `0.001` in our code, or until we have performed a maximum number of iterations.

Matrix factorization has become an important technique for recommender systems, particularly those that leverage Likert-scale-like preference expressions—notably, star ratings. The Netflix Prize challenge has shown us that matrix-factored approaches perform with a high degree of accuracy for ratings prediction tasks. Additionally, matrix factorization is a compact, memory-efficient representation of the parameter space for a model and can be trained in parallel, can support multiple feature vectors, and can be improved with confidence levels. Generally, they are used to solve cold-start problems with sparse reviews and in an ensemble with more complex hybrid-recommenders that also compute content-based recommenders.

See also

> ▶ Wikipedia's overview of the dot product available at `http://en.wikipedia.org/wiki/Dot_product`

Loading the entire dataset into the memory

The first step in building a nonnegative factorization model is to load the entire dataset in the memory. For this task, we will be leveraging NumPy highly.

Getting ready

In order to complete this recipe, you'll have to download the MovieLens database from the University of Minnesota GroupLens page at `http://grouplens.org/datasets/movielens/` and unzip it in a working directory where your code will be. We will also use NumPy in this code significantly, so please ensure that you have this numerical analysis package downloaded and ready. Additionally, we will use the `load_reviews` function from the previous recipes. If you have not had the opportunity to review the appropriate section, please have the code for that function ready.

How to do it...

To build our matrix factorization model, we'll need to create a wrapper for the predictor that loads the entire dataset into memory. We will perform the following steps:

1. We create the following `Recommender` class as shown. Please note that this class depends on the previously created and discussed `load_reviews` function:

```
import numpy as np
import csv


class Recommender(object):
    def __init__(self, udata):
```

```
        self.udata    = udata
        self.users    = None
        self.movies   = None
        self.reviews  = None
        self.load_dataset()


    def load_dataset(self):
        """

        Load an index of users & movies as a heap
and reviews table as a N x M array where N is
the number of users and M is the number of movies.
Note that order matters so that we can look up values
        outside of the matrix!
        """
        self.users  = set([])
        self.movies = set([])
        for review in load_reviews(self.udata):
            self.users.add(review['userid'])
            self.movies.add(review['movieid'])


        self.users  = sorted(self.users)
        self.movies = sorted(self.movies)


        self.reviews = np.zeros(shape=(len(self.users),
len(self.movies)))
        for review in load_reviews(self.udata):
            uid = self.users.index(review['userid'])
            mid = self.movies.index(review['movieid'])
            self.reviews[uid, mid] = review['rating']
```

2. With this defined, we can instantiate a model by typing the following command:

```
data_path = '../data/ml-100k/u.data'
model = Recommender(data_path)
```

How it works...

Let's go over this code line by line. The instantiation of our recommender requires a path to the `u.data` file; creates holders for our list of users, movies, and reviews; and then loads the dataset. We need to hold the entire dataset in memory for reasons that we will see later.

The basic data structure to perform our matrix factorization on is an N x M matrix where N is the number of users and M is the number of movies. To create this, we will first load all the movies and users into an ordered list so that we can look up the index of the user or movie by its ID. In the case of MovieLens, all of the IDs are contiguous from 1; however, this might not always be the case. It is good practice to have an index lookup table. Otherwise, you will be unable to fetch recommendations from our computation!

Once we have our index lookup lists, we create a NumPy array of all zeroes in the size of the length of our users' list by the length of our movies list. Keep in mind that the rows are users and the columns are movies! We then go through the ratings data a second time and then add the value of the rating at the `uid`, `mid` index location of our matrix. Note that if a user hasn't rated a movie, their rating is `0`. This is important! Print the array out by entering `model.reviews`, and you should see something as follows:

```
[[ 5.  3.  4. ...,  0.  0.  0.]
 [ 4.  0.  0. ...,  0.  0.  0.]
 [ 0.  0.  0. ...,  0.  0.  0.]
 ...,
 [ 5.  0.  0. ...,  0.  0.  0.]
 [ 0.  0.  0. ...,  0.  0.  0.]
 [ 0.  5.  0. ...,  0.  0.  0.]]
```

There's more...

Let's get a sense of how sparse or dense our dataset is by adding the following two methods to the `Recommender` class:

```python
def sparsity(self):
    """
    Report the percent of elements that are zero in the array
    """
    return 1 - self.density()


def density(self):
    """
    Return the percent of elements that are nonzero in the array
```

```
"""
    nonzero = float(np.count_nonzero(self.reviews))
    return nonzero / self.reviews.size
```

Adding these methods to our `Recommender` class will help us evaluate our recommender, and it will also help us identify recommenders in the future.

Print out the results:

```
print "%0.3f%% sparse" % model.sparsity()
print "%0.3f%% dense" % model.density()
```

You should see that the MovieLens 100k dataset is 0.937 percent sparse and 0.063 percent dense.

This is very important to keep note of along with the size of the reviews dataset. Sparsity, which is common to most recommender systems, means that we might be able to use sparse matrix algorithms and optimizations. Additionally, as we begin to save models, this will help us identify the models as we load them from serialized files on the disk.

Dumping the SVD-based model to the disk

Before we build our model, which will take a long time to train, we should create a mechanism for us to load and dump our model to the disk. If we have a way of saving the parameterization of the factored matrix, then we can reuse our model without having to train it every time we want to use it—this is a very big deal since this model will take hours to train! Luckily, Python has a built-in tool for serializing and deserializing Python objects—the `pickle` module.

How to do it...

Update the Recommender class as follows:

```
import pickle

class Recommender(object):

    @classmethod
    def load(klass, pickle_path):
        """
        Instantiates the class by deserializing the pickle.
        Note that the object returned may not be an exact match
        to the code in this class (if it was saved
    before updates).
```

```
        """
        with open(pickle_path, 'rb') as pkl:
            return pickle.load(pkl)


    def __init__(self, udata, description=None):
        self.udata    = udata
        self.users    = None
        self.movies   = None
        self.reviews  = None

        # Descriptive properties
        self.build_start  = None
        self.build_finish = None
        self.description   = None

        # Model properties
        self.model       = None
        self.features    = 2
        self.steps       = 5000
        self.alpha       = 0.0002
        self.beta        = 0.02

        self.load_dataset()


    def dump(self, pickle_path):
        """
        Dump the object into a serialized file using the pickle module.
        This will allow us to quickly reload our model in the future.
        """
        with open(pickle_path, 'wb') as pkl:
            pickle.dump(self, pkl)
```

How it works...

The `@classmethod` feature is a decorator in Python for declaring a class method instead of an instance method. The first argument that is passed in is the type instead of an instance (which we usually refer to as `self`). The `load` class method takes a path to a file on the disk that contains a serialized `pickle` object, which it then loads using the `pickle` module. Note that the class that is returned might not be an exact match with the `Recommender` class at the time you run the code—this is because the `pickle` module saves the class, including methods and properties, exactly as it was when you dumped it.

Speaking of dumping, the `dump` method provides the opposite functionality, allowing you to serialize the methods, properties, and data to disk in order to be loaded again in the future. To help us identify the objects that we're dumping and loading from disk, we've also added some descriptive properties including a description, some build parameters, and some timestamps to our `__init__` function.

Training the SVD-based model

We're now ready to write our functions that factor our training dataset and build our recommender model. You can see the required functions in this recipe.

How to do it...

We construct the following functions to train our model. Note that these functions are not part of the `Recommender` class:

```python
def initialize(R, K):
    """
    Returns initial matrices for an N X M matrix,
    R and K features.

    :param R: the matrix to be factorized
    :param K: the number of latent features

    :returns: P, Q initial matrices of N x K and M x K sizes
    """
    N, M = R.shape
    P = np.random.rand(N,K)
    Q = np.random.rand(M,K)
```

```
    return P, Q


def factor(R, P=None, Q=None, K=2, steps=5000, alpha=0.0002,
beta=0.02):
    """

    Performs matrix factorization on R with given parameters.

    :param R: A matrix to be factorized, dimension N x M
    :param P: an initial matrix of dimension N x K
    :param Q: an initial matrix of dimension M x K
    :param K: the number of latent features
    :param steps: the maximum number of iterations to optimize in
    :param alpha: the learning rate for gradient descent
    :param beta:  the regularization parameter

    :returns: final matrices P and Q
    """

    if not P or not Q:
        P, Q = initialize(R, K)
    Q = Q.T

    rows, cols = R.shape
    for step in xrange(steps):
        for i in xrange(rows):
            for j in xrange(cols):
                if R[i,j] > 0:
                    eij = R[i,j] - np.dot(P[i,:], Q[:,j])
                    for k in xrange(K):
                        P[i,k] = P[i,k] + alpha * (2 * eij * Q[k,j]
- beta * P[i,k])
                        Q[k,j] = Q[k,j] + alpha * (2 * eij * P[i,k]
- beta * Q[k,j])

        e = 0
        for i in xrange(rows):
            for j in xrange(cols):
```

```
                    if R[i,j] > 0:
                        e = e + pow(R[i,j] - np.dot(P[i,:], Q[:,j]), 2)
                        for k in xrange(K):
                            e = e + (beta/2) * (pow(P[i,k], 2) +
pow(Q[k,j], 2))
                if e < 0.001:
                    break


        return P, Q.T
```

How it works...

We discussed the theory and the mathematics of what we are doing in the previous recipe, *Building a nonnegative matrix factorization model*, so let's talk about the code. The `initialize` function creates two matrices, P and Q, that have a size related to the reviews matrix and the number of features, namely N x K and M x K, where N is the number of users and M is the number of movies. Their values are initialized to random numbers that are between 0.0 and 1.0. The `factor` function computes P and Q using gradient descent such that the dot product of P and Q is within a mean squared error of less than 0.001 or 5000 steps that have gone by, whichever comes first. Especially note that only values that are greater than 0 are computed. These are the values that we're trying to predict; therefore, we do not want to attempt to match them in our code (otherwise, the model will be trained on zero ratings)! This is also the reason that you can't use NumPy's built-in **Singular Value Decomposition (SVD)** function, which is `np.linalg.svd` or `np.linalg.solve`.

There's more...

Let's use these factorization functions to build our model and to save the model to disk once it has been built—this way, we can load the model at our convenience using the `dump` and `load` methods in the class. Add the following method to the `Recommender` class:

```python
def build(self, output=None):
    """
    Trains the model by employing matrix factorization on training
    data set, (sparse reviews matrix). The model is the dot product
    of the P and Q decomposed matrices from the factorization.
    """
    options = {
        'K':     self.features,
        'steps': self.steps,
```

```
        'alpha':  self.alpha,
        'beta':   self.beta,
    }


    self.build_start = time.time()
    self.P, self.Q = factor(self.reviews, **options)
    self.model = np.dot(self.P, self.Q.T)
    self.build_finish = time.time()


    if output:
        self.dump(output)
```

This helper function will allow us to quickly build our model. Note that we're also saving P and Q—the parameters of our latent features. This isn't necessary, as our predictive model is the dot product of the two factored matrices. Deciding whether or not to save this information in your model is a trade-off between re-training time (you can potentially start from the current P and Q parameters although you must beware of the overfit) and disk space, as `pickle` will be larger on the disk with these matrices saved. To build this model and dump the data to the disk, run the following code:

```
model = Recommender(relative_path('../data/ml-100k/u.data'))
model.build('reccod.pickle')
```

Warning! This will take a long time to build! On a 2013 MacBook Pro with a 2.8 GHz processor, this process took roughly 9 hours 15 minutes and required 23.1 MB of memory; this is not insignificant for most of the Python scripts you might be used to writing! It is not a bad idea to continue through the rest of the recipe before building your model. It is also probably not a bad idea to test your code on a smaller test set of 100 records before moving on to the entire process! Additionally, if you don't have the time to train the model, you can find the `pickle` module of our model in the errata of this book.

Testing the SVD-based model

This recipe brings this chapter on recommendation engines to a close. We use our new nonnegative matrix factorization-based model and take a look at some of the predicted reviews.

How to do it...

The final step in leveraging our model is to access the predicted reviews for a movie based on our model:

```
def predict_ranking(self, user, movie):
    uidx = self.users.index(user)
    midx = self.movies.index(movie)
    if self.reviews[uidx, midx] > 0:
        return None
    return self.model[uidx, midx]
```

How it works...

Computing the ranking is relatively easy; we simply need to look up the index of the user and the index of the movie and look up the predicted rating in our model. This is why it is so essential to save an ordered list of the users and movies in our `pickle` module; this way, if the data changes (we add users or movies) but the change isn't reflected in our model, an exception is raised. Because models are historical predictions and not sensitive to changes in time, we need to ensure that we continually retrain our model with new data. This method also returns `None` if we know the ranking of the user (for example, it's not a prediction); we'll leverage this in the next step.

There's more...

To predict the highest-ranked movies, we can leverage the previous function to order the highest predicted rankings for our user:

```
import heapq
from operator import itemgetter


def top_rated(self, user, n=12):
    movies = [(mid, self.predict_ranking(user, mid)) for
mid in self.movies]
    return heapq.nlargest(n, movies, key=itemgetter(1))
```

We can now print out the top-predicted movies that have not been rated by the user:

```
>>> rec = Recommender.load('reccod.pickle')
>>> for item in rec.top_rated(234):
...     print "%i: %0.3f" % item
 814: 4.437
1642: 4.362
1491: 4.361
1599: 4.343
1536: 4.324
1500: 4.323
1449: 4.281
1650: 4.147
1645: 4.135
1467: 4.133
1636: 4.133
1651: 4.132
```

It's then simply a matter of using the movie ID to look up the movie in our movies database.

10
Harvesting and Geolocating Twitter Data (Python)

In this chapter, we will cover the following recipes:

- ▸ Creating a Twitter application
- ▸ Understanding the Twitter API v1.1
- ▸ Determining your Twitter followers and friends
- ▸ Pulling Twitter user profiles
- ▸ Making requests without running afoul of Twitter's rate limits
- ▸ Storing JSON data to the disk
- ▸ Setting up MongoDB for storing the Twitter data
- ▸ Storing user profiles in MongoDB using PyMongo
- ▸ Exploring the geographic information available in profiles
- ▸ Plotting geospatial data in Python

Introduction

In this chapter, we are going to dive into the world of social media analysis through the use of RESTful web-service APIs. Twitter is a microblogging social network whose stream is invaluable for data mining, particularly text mining, and they have an excellent API that we will learn how to interact with via Python. We will use the API to fetch Twitter social connections and collect and store JSON data using both traditional file storage and the popular NoSQL database, `MongoDB[SK1]`. Our analysis will attempt to ascertain the geographic location of connections and produce a visualization from the data. Throughout the chapter, you should begin to notice patterns about how APIs are designed and their intended use. Interaction with APIs is an extremely important data science topic, and having a solid understanding of them will unlock a whole new world of data upon which you can perform a myriad of analyses.

API stands for Application Programming Interface, and in traditional computer science, it refers to methods that allow software applications to interact with each other. These days, most references to APIs refer to a web API—the use of the Internet to share data between your software application and a web application (such as Twitter). Data acquisition and management is an important part of the data science pipeline, and knowing how to use APIs is essential for getting actionable data sets off the Internet.

A special subset of APIs, called **RESTful APIs**, are actually the backbone of most web applications, and they are everywhere. Although we can avoid most of the technical jargon, we should point out that REST stands for Representational State Transfer, which is a fancy way of saying that documents or objects exist as representations, and modifications to their state should be transferred via the API. RESTful APIs are a direct extension of the **Hypertext Transfer Protocol** (**HTTP**) that the World Wide Web was built upon, which is why they are so popular as web APIs. HTTP allows for clients to connect to servers by making requests in the form of verbs: GET, POST, DELETE, and PUT. Traditionally, the response is an HTML document. Similarly, a RESTful API uses these verbs to make requests whose response is a JSON document. The former is for human consumption (such as when you visit a website such as `http://www.google.com`) and the latter is for application consumption.

For this chapter, we will only use HTTP GET requests and the occasional POST request. A GET request is just like it sounds; it asks the server to give you a particular resource. A POST request, on the other hand, means that a client is trying to provide data to the server (as in, submitting a form or uploading a file). An API provider, such as Twitter, allows us to make HTTP GET requests to a particular resource URL, which is often called an endpoint. For example, the endpoint to GET all the most recent tweets for a particular user is `https://api.twitter.com/1.1/statuses/user_timeline.json`. If we make the correctly authenticated HTTP GET request to this endpoint, Twitter will supply the data that composes the current user's timeline in the JSON format.

Creating a Twitter application

Twitter is the ubiquitous microblogging social media platform with 253 million active members as of 2014. Fortunately for us, Twitter makes the service's data more open and available to third parties than just about any other social media site of similar size and standing in the tech community. Additionally, Twitter offers a rich and user-friendly RESTful API that we will make use of extensively. This recipe will show you how to create a new Twitter application, which is a required step to access Twitter data programmatically.

Getting ready

Make sure that you have a web browser installed, and open up a new browser tab or window.

How to do it...

The following steps will walk you through the creation of a new Twitter application:

 Note that Twitter does like to update its **user interface** (**UI**) frequently and these steps, or the web-based forms, might change accordingly.

1. First, make sure that you have created a Twitter account. If you have not created one, go to `http://twitter.com` and sign up. If you have an account, simply log in to your Twitter account with your web browser.

2. Next, go to `https://dev.twitter.com/apps` and select the light blue button labeled **Create an Application** on the right-hand side of the screen.

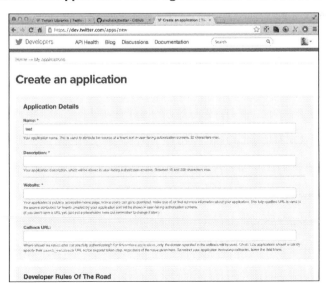

3. Here, it will prompt you to enter your application details in three mandatory fields and one optional one. Choose a name for your application that is no more than 32 characters.

4. Next, supply a brief description of your application between 10 and 200 characters.

5. You must supply a website for your application, although it is not applicable for our use case. Also, there is a specific format that is required for the form to be submitted successfully. Enter `http://127.0.0.1`.

6. Finally, you can ignore the **Callback URL** field, which is the last field on the form.

7. Go ahead and take some time to read the **Developer Rules of the Road** section, as this document details in plain and simple text what you should and should not do using your application.

8. Click on the **Create your Twitter Application**. After a few moments, you should be on the main settings page of your new application with a tabbed menu at the top of the screen. The current tab should be labeled **Details**.

9. Click on the **API Keys** tab and you should see the following screenshot:

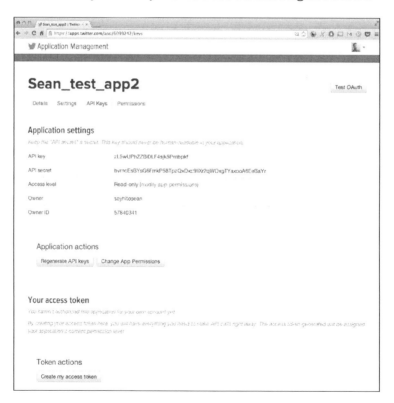

10. Now, click on **Create my access token** in the **Token actions** gray box at the bottom to authorize your application for your own account (you might have to click the button more than once). The result should look like the following screenshot:

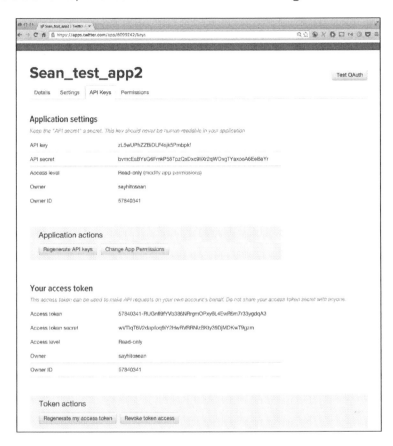

11. Record the API key, API secret, access token, and access token secret in a text file. These are important but must be protected like you would protect your e-mail password or ATM pin. You can take a screenshot to save the information, but it would be easier to copy and paste these values into a text file for now.

Now that you have MinGW and MSYS, there's no need to be jealous of those with a Linux installation anymore, since they implement in your system the most important parts of a Linux development environment.

How it works...

You might be asking yourself why we needed to create an application if all we want to do is to pull some simple data from Twitter. Early versions (1.0 and before) of the Twitter API allowed applications to make anonymous API requests, retrieving data from Twitter without Twitter knowing who was actually making the request. Since the deprecated Version 1.0 of the company's API was retired on June 11, 2013, all API requests to Twitter require authentication. This allows Twitter to keep track of who requests what information and how much information was requested.

In general, there are several signs in the industry that the halcyon days of social media data harvesting might be waning. Facebook's newest set of APIs, specifically Version 2.0 of Facebook Login, has strongly locked down what data can be obtained from the social graph. Further, Twitter acquired Gnip in April, 2014; Gnip is a reseller of Twitter data, and it allows its customers to buy large portions of Twitter data. This move suggests that Version 2.0 of the Twitter API might limit further access to Twitterverse.

See also

▸   The *Obtaining access tokens* article at `https://dev.twitter.com/docs/auth/obtaining-access-tokens`

▸   The *Tokens from dev.twitter.com* article at `https://dev.twitter.com/docs/auth/tokens-devtwittercom`

Understanding the Twitter API v1.1

APIs are both a blessing and a curse. Application Programming Interfaces make it much easier to gather data from services such as Twitter, Facebook, or LinkedIn and define exactly what data the company wants, and does not want, you to have. Unfortunately, companies set rate limits on accessing their APIs in order to control the frequency (and therefore, the amount) of data that can be harvested. They have also been known to radically alter their APIs from one version to the next, thus resulting in a great deal of code rewrites for all efforts dependent on the original API. Twitter's large API change from Version 1.0 to Version 1.1 offers a cautionary tale.

Twitter offers three main APIs: the search API, the REST API, and the streaming API. The search API gives us a programmatic method that makes queries to Twitter in order to retrieve historical content, namely tweets. The REST API offers access to Twitter's core features, including timelines, status updates, and user information. Finally, the streaming API is the real-time API designed for "low latency access to Twitter's global stream of Tweet data".

With the streaming API, one must keep a persistent HTTP connection open to Twitter. For our data mining and analysis purposes, this is an overkill, as we will only be periodically requesting data from Twitter. Thus, we will be focusing on the first two APIs and don't have to concern ourselves with the streaming API.

Getting ready

Once you have created your application in the preceding recipe and copied your keys, you are ready to proceed.

How to do it...

Perform the following steps in order to access the Twitter API programmatically using Python:

1. First, install the `Twython` library. Open a new command prompt and type the following:

   ```
   (sudo) pip install twython
   ```

   The `sudo` command is needed if your current user account does not have sufficient privileges.

2. Next, open a new terminal and start the default Python REPL or IPython. If you want to go the extra mile, you can also use IPython Notebook.

3. Enter and execute the following Python code, filling in the needed application keys:

   ```python
   from twython import Twython

   API_KEY = 'INSERT HERE'
   API_SECRET = 'INSERT HERE'
   ACCESS_TOKEN = 'INSERT HERE'
   ACCESS_TOKEN_SECRET = 'INSERT HERE'


   twitter = Twython(API_KEY, API_SECRET,
           ACCESS_TOKEN, ACCESS_TOKEN_SECRET)
   ```

> Note that Twitter updates its developer interface frequently and the `API_KEY` used to be called `CONSUMER_KEY`. Also, note that the keys given in the code snippet need to be replaced with the values collected during the previous recipe.

4. If you are using IPython, type the following at the REPL and then hit the *Tab* key:

    ```
    In [12]: twitter.
    ```

    This will bring up the impressive list of API calls that are now available to you.

```
In [7]: twitter.
twitter.access_token                          twitter.get_favorites                          twitter.lookup_friendships
twitter.access_token_url                       twitter.get_followers_ids                      twitter.lookup_user
twitter.add_list_member                        twitter.get_followers_list                     twitter.oauth_token
twitter.api_url                                twitter.get_friends_ids                        twitter.oauth_token_secret
twitter.api_version                            twitter.get_friends_list                       twitter.oauth_version
twitter.app_key                                twitter.get_geo_info                           twitter.obtain_access_token
twitter.app_secret                             twitter.get_home_timeline                      twitter.post
twitter.authenticate_url                       twitter.get_incoming_friendship_ids            twitter.remove_profile_banner
twitter.client                                 twitter.get_lastfunction_header                twitter.report_spam
twitter.client_args                            twitter.get_list_members                       twitter.request
twitter.construct_api_url                      twitter.get_list_memberships                   twitter.request_token_url
twitter.create_block                           twitter.get_list_statuses                      twitter.retweet
twitter.create_favorite                        twitter.get_list_subscribers                   twitter.retweeted_of_me
twitter.create_friendship                      twitter.get_list_subscriptions                 twitter.reverse_geocode
twitter.create_list                            twitter.get_mentions_timeline                  twitter.search
twitter.create_list_members                    twitter.get_oembed_tweet                       twitter.search_gen
twitter.create_place                           twitter.get_outgoing_friendship_ids            twitter.search_geo
twitter.create_saved_search                    twitter.get_place_trends                       twitter.search_users
twitter.cursor                                 twitter.get_privacy_policy                     twitter.send_direct_message
twitter.delete_list                            twitter.get_profile_banner_sizes               twitter.show_friendship
twitter.delete_list_member                     twitter.get_retweeters_ids                     twitter.show_lists
twitter.delete_list_members                    twitter.get_retweets                           twitter.show_owned_lists
twitter.destroy_block                          twitter.get_saved_searches                     twitter.show_saved_search
twitter.destroy_direct_message                 twitter.get_sent_messages                      twitter.show_status
twitter.destroy_favorite                       twitter.get_similar_places                     twitter.show_user
twitter.destroy_friendship                     twitter.get_specific_list                      twitter.subscribe_to_list
twitter.destroy_saved_search                   twitter.get_supported_languages                twitter.unicode2utf8
twitter.destroy_status                         twitter.get_tos                                twitter.unsubscribe_from_list
twitter.encode                                 twitter.get_twitter_configuration              twitter.update_account_settings
twitter.get                                    twitter.get_user_ids_of_blocked_retweets       twitter.update_delivery_service
twitter.get_account_settings                   twitter.get_user_suggestions                   twitter.update_friendship
twitter.get_application_rate_limit_status      twitter.get_user_suggestions_by_slug           twitter.update_list
twitter.get_authentication_tokens              twitter.get_user_suggestions_statuses_by_slug  twitter.update_profile
twitter.get_authorized_tokens                  twitter.get_user_timeline                      twitter.update_profile_background_image
twitter.get_available_trends                   twitter.html_for_tweet                         twitter.update_profile_banner_image
twitter.get_closest_trends                     twitter.invalidate_token                       twitter.update_profile_colors
twitter.get_contributees                       twitter.is_list_member                         twitter.update_profile_image
twitter.get_contributors                       twitter.is_list_subscriber                     twitter.update_status
twitter.get_direct_message                     twitter.list_block_ids                         twitter.update_status_with_media
twitter.get_direct_messages                    twitter.list_blocks                            twitter.verify_credentials

In [7]: twitter.
```

5. As a test, we can enter the following at the Python prompt:

    ```
    In [14]: temp = twitter.get_user_timeline()
    ```

    This command will fetch the last 20 status updates from your timeline as a 20-element list of Python dictionaries.

6. Further, Twython gives us access to the response headers received from Twitter:

    ```
    In [15]: twitter.get_lastfunction_header('x-rate-limit-
    remaining')
    Out[15]: '179'
    ```

How it works...

With the preceding code, we are setting up our API keys and access tokens that we pass in order to instantiate an instance of the `Twython` class. This new object serves as our main interface to the Twitter API and defaults to using OAuth v1 for authentication purposes. As this is a pretty common requirement, we can wrap this functionality in its own function as shown in the following snippet. Before using the following function code, make sure that you enter the needed application keys:

```
def  twitter_oauth_login():
  API_KEY = 'INSERT HERE'
  API_SECRET = 'INSERT HERE'

  ACCESS_TOKEN = 'INSERT HERE'
  ACCESS_TOKEN_SECRET = 'INSERT HERE'

  twitter = Twython(API_KEY, API_SECRET, ACCESS_TOKEN,
  ACCESS_TOKEN_SECRET)
  return(twitter)
```

If you are checking your code into GitHub or another cloud-based version control solution (such as Bitbucket), please check whether that repository is public or private. All free repositories on GitHub are public. If your repository is public, the world will have access to your *secret* Twitter API keys. We strongly advise that you only use private repositories for such matters and note that `bitbucket.org` provides private repositories for free.

OAuth, which stands for the Open Authentication protocol, allows a user to give permission to a third-party application to access an aspect of the user's account (in this case, his or her Twitter account) without giving up the user's login and password. Diving into the details of how OAuth works is outside the scope of this recipe. However, it is important to discuss the two different types of resource authentication for Twitter applications. The most common authentication is the application-user authentication, which we will not use. In this mode, your application makes a request on behalf of a user who has granted the needed permissions to your application. For our project, we care about the application-only authentication, where our application makes API requests not for a user but for itself. Note that some API calls do not support application-only requests and that the rate limits for such requests are typically different.

There's more...

The Twython library is not the only Python library available to simplify access to Twitter's API. The following are three popular choices, including the popular **Python Twitter Tools**, and you are free to explore or choose whichever you see fit:

> ▸ **Python Twitter Tools** (`https://github.com/sixohsix/twitter`): This is a minimalist Python API for Twitter that includes a command-line tool in order to get friends' tweets and send your own announcements.

> ▸ **Twython 3.1.2** (`https://github.com/ryanmcgrath/twython`): This is a pure Python wrapper that supports both search and streaming APIs, which are actively maintained. This is the library that we will be using.

> ▸ **python-twitter** (`https://github.com/bear/python-twitter`): This is a pure Python interface for the current v1.1 Twitter API.

Twitter maintains a list of alternatives across programming languages at `https://dev.twitter.com/docs/twitter-libraries`. Please note that the code from this chapter uses Twython exclusively but it could be a useful exercise for the reader to rewrite examples using the other Python libraries.

See also

> ▸ The Twython documentation at
>   `http://twython.readthedocs.org/en/latest/`

> ▸ *Detailed OAuth 1.0 Guide* at `http://hueniverse.com/oauth/guide/`

> ▸ The Twitter's OAuth implementation at
>   `https://dev.twitter.com/docs/auth/oauth`

> ▸ Twitter's *OAuth FAQ* web page
>   `https://dev.twitter.com/docs/auth/oauth/faq`

> ▸ The OAuth home page at `http://oauth.net/`

> ▸ Additional Twitter libraries at
>   `https://dev.twitter.com/docs/twitter-libraries`

Determining your Twitter followers and friends

In the Twitter social network, users are labeled either as followers or friends relative to a particular user. Your friends are the people that you follow and your followers are the people that follow you. In this recipe, we determine who your friends are, who your followers are, and how much overlap there is in each group.

Getting ready

For this recipe, we will be using the results of the previous two recipes and the `twitter_oauth_login()` function. Also, we will be working in IPython or the default Python REPL, if you prefer that instead. Feel free to use an editor in order to start capturing and modifying the code as it grows in complexity.

How to do it...

The following steps will allow you to determine all of your Twitter friends and followers:

1. In IPython or your favorite REPL, enter the following:

   ```
   twitter = twitter_oauth_login()

   friends_ids = twitter.get_friends_ids(count=5000)
   friends_ids = friends_ids['ids']

   followers_ids = twitter.get_followers_ids(count=5000)
   followers_ids = followers_ids['ids']
   ```

2. With all of your followers' and friends' Twitter IDs collected, let's see how many you have:

   ```
   In [26]: len(friends_ids), len(followers_ids)
   Out[26]: (352, 554)
   ```

3. We will use Python sets, which are based on the sets that you might have encountered in math class, to examine some properties of our friends and followers:

   ```
   friends_set = set(friends_ids)
   followers_set = set(followers_ids)

   print('Number of Twitter users who either are our friend or
   follow you (union):')
   ```

```
print(len(friends_set.union(followers_set)))


print('Number of Twitter users who follow you and are your
friend (intersection):')
print(len(friends_set & followers_set))


print("Number of Twitter users you follow that don't follow
you (set difference):")
print(len(friends_set - followers_set))


print("Number of Twitter users who follow you that you don't
follow (set difference):")
print(len(followers_set - friends_set))
```

The preceding snippet should result in the following output:

```
Number of Twitter users who either are our friend or follow you (union):
980
Number of Twitter users who follow you and are your friend (intersection):
205
Number of Twitter users you follow that don't follow you (set difference):
354
Number of Twitter users who follow you that you don't follow (set difference):
421
```

 The numbers shown in the preceding screenshot will most likely be different based on the number of friends and followers you have.

How it works...

This recipe demonstrates just how useful the Twython package is and how easy it makes certain tasks. After we logged in using the `twitter_oauth_login` function, we make two basic calls using the `twitter` object, one to get friends' IDs and one to get followers' IDs. Note that we set the count parameter to 5000, which is the maximum value allowed by the Twitter API. The `twitter` object returns a dictionary from which we extract the actual IDs.

One of the nice things about the Twython interface is how closely it mirrors the Twitter API. If you ever have a question about a particular function, just check the Twitter documents.

Once we have collected our list of friends' and followers' IDs, we turn to the Python set type for some quick navel gazing. The Python `set` type, which has been built into Python since Version 2.4, is an unordered collection of unique objects. The key word for us is the word **unique**. If we create a set from a list with duplicates, we will get a set with only unique elements; `set([1, 2, 2, 3, 3, 3])` will return $\{1, 2, 3\}$.

We unite the set of friends' IDs with the followers' IDs to determine the total set of unique IDs of Twitter users that either follow or are followed by us. In the preceding code, we use the union method of the `set` type, but there are several other ways in which we could have done this:

```
(friends_set | followers_set)

(set(friends_ids + followers_ids))
```

There's more...

While Twython's beautiful abstraction hides some of the complexity of using the API, this simplicity or magic can be problematic if we don't have an understanding of what is actually happening behind the scenes. When we call the `twitter.get_friends_ids(count=5000)` method, we are sending an HTTP GET request to a particular URL. In the case of `twitter.get_friends_ids()`, the URL is `https://api.twitter.com/1.1/friends/ids.json`.

The `count=5000` input parameter to the function call shows up as field-value pairs in the URL and as such, the URL becomes `https://api.twitter.com/1.1/friends/ids.json?count=5000`.

Now, the actual API endpoint requires some default parameter values that Twython fills in for us, as shown in the following URL for clarity:

```
https://api.twitter.com/1.1/friends/ids.json?cursor=-
1&screen_name=sayhitosean&count=5000
```

The Twitter v1.1 API requires all requests to be authenticated using OAuth. The required information is actually embedded in the header of the GET request, and the process of constructing the appropriate header is extensive (for more information, go to `https://dev.twitter.com/docs/auth/authorizing-request`). Thus, Twython not only forms the proper URL for making the request, but also handles the relatively painful Open Authorization so that we don't have to. If you are interested, you can go down a level lower and construct your own GET requests using the excellent request library or an alternative of your choosing. We leave this for the reader to explore.

 Note that different Twitter API endpoints have different rate limits. In the case of GET friends/IDs, we are only allowed 15 calls over a 15 minute period for Version 1.1 of the API as of May 2014. Other endpoints are less stingy with their data.

See also

▸ The *GET friends/ids* article at `https://dev.twitter.com/docs/api/1.1/get/friends/ids`

▸ The *GET followers/ids* article at `https://dev.twitter.com/docs/api/1.1/get/followers/ids`

▸ The *Requests: HTTP for Humans* article at `http://docs.python-requests.org/en/latest/`

Pulling Twitter user profiles

For this recipe, we are going to use the Twitter API to pull JSON data about Twitter users. Each Twitter user, identified by either a screen name (such as SayHiToSean) or a unique integer, has a profile containing a rich set of information about someone.

Getting ready

You will need the list of followers' and friends' IDs from the previous recipe.

How to do it...

The following steps guide you through retrieving a set of Twitter users' profiles:

1. First, we create a function that will manage pulling twitter profiles:

```python
def pull_users_profiles(ids):
    users = []
    for i in range(0, len(ids), 100):
        batch = ids[i:i + 100]
        users += twitter.lookup_user(user_id=batch)
        print(twitter.get_lastfunction_header('x-rate-limit-
        remaining'))
    return (users)
```

2. We put this function to use, pulling profiles of both friends and followers:

```python
friends_profiles = pull_users_profiles(friends_ids)
followers_profiles = pull_users_profiles(followers_ids)
```

3. To check whether everything works, we use a list comprehension to extract all of the friends' screen names from the profiles:

```
friends_screen_names = [p['screen_name'] for p in
friends_profiles]
```

4. Using the following command, you should be greeted by a list of your friends' screen names:

```
print(friends_screen_names)
```

How it works...

The first step in this recipe was the creation of a function that manages the `twitter.lookup_user` method call. The Twitter users/lookup endpoint accepts 100 user IDs at a time. Thus, we need to loop over our list of friends' or followers' IDs and batch them into groups of 100 for the requests. Twitter returns a JSON object that Twython converts into a list of Python dictionaries, ready for use.

There is an alternative way of retrieving profiles. Instead of pulling friends' and followers' IDs and then using those to request user profiles, we could have queried the friends/list endpoint with simply the current user's screen name (in this case, mine, which is @SayHiToSean) or user ID. Twitter would then return up to 200 user profiles per request. If you work out the API limits, either path works out to the same number of user profiles pulled in the 15 minute default time window that Twitter uses for rate-limiting purposes.

There's more...

The `pull_users_profiles` function that we created has an extra feature in the last line of the loop:

```
print(twitter.get_lastfunction_header('x-rate-limit-remaining'))
```

We retrieve the header of the response from the last API call and check the `x-rate-limit-remaining` value. This value tells us exactly how many API calls we have left in a given 15 minute window. Although we print this value out with each loop, we do absolutely nothing to prevent us from slamming up against Twitter's rate limit, which varies by the endpoint.

Further, the list comprehension that we used in step 3 can fail if, for some reason, one of the Twitter user profiles that were received did not have a `screen_name` key. Thus, it would be better to add a condition to the comprehension:

```
friends_screen_names = [p['screen_name'] for p in friends_profiles if
'screen_name' in p]
```

Or, as an alternative and potentially, a more Pythonic way, we could use the GET method of the dictionary:

```
friends_screen_names = [p.get('screen_name') for p in friends_profiles]
```

In this case, profiles that do not have a `screen_name` key are not skipped but are replaced with `None`, instead.

See also

▶ The description of the Twitter user profile JSON at `https://dev.twitter.com/docs/platform-objects/users`

▶ The *GET users/lookup* documentation at `https://dev.twitter.com/docs/api/1.1/get/users/lookup`

▶ The *GET friends/list* documentation at `https://dev.twitter.com/docs/api/1.1/get/friends/list`

Making requests without running afoul of Twitter's rate limits

For this recipe, we are going to modify the function created in the previous recipe in order to avoid hitting the dreaded Twitter API rate limits.

Getting ready

You will again need the list of followers' and friends' IDs from the previous recipe as well as the authenticated Twython object.

How to do it...

The following function demonstrates how you can retrieve a set of Twitter users' profiles in a rate-limit-aware fashion:

```
import time
import math


def pull_users_profiles_limit_aware(ids):
    users = []
    start_time = time.time()
    # Must look up users in
```

```
for i in range(0, len(ids), 10):

    batch = ids[i:i + 10]

    users += twitter.lookup_user(user_id=batch)

    calls_left = float(twitter.get_lastfunction_header('x-rate-
    limit-remaining'))

    time_remaining_in_window = rate_limit_window - (time.time()-
    start_time)

    sleep_duration =
    math.ceil(time_remaining_in_window/calls_left)

    print('Sleeping for: ' + str(sleep_duration) + ' seconds; ' +
    str(calls_left) + ' API calls remaining')

    time.sleep(sleep_duration)


    return (users)
```

How it works...

This function is a modified version of the previous recipe's function that pulls users' profiles so that we do not run afoul of Twitter's ubiquitous rate limit. We insert a dynamic pause into each iteration of the loop with the length determined by the number of API calls remaining in the time window. Before the loop starts, we capture the current system time in the start_time variable. After each API call made by the twitter object, we grab the header of the response and check the number of API calls remaining in the 15-minute time window. We compute the time that has elapsed since start_time and subtract this from 900 seconds, yielding the time left in the 15-minute window. Finally, we compute the number of seconds needed per remaining API calls and sleep for the required period. We use the math.ceil function to round up and make sure that we always give just a little bit of extra time so as to not hit the rate limit.

You might ask why one would care about hitting the Twitter API rate limit. Why not just keep hitting the API even after the limit has been reached? The simple answer is that Twitter can and will block applications that abuse the prescribed rate limits too often. Thus, it is in your best interest to play by the rules. Further, you can't pull any additional information if you try once the rate limit has been exceeded, so why bother?

Storing JSON data to the disk

Calls to the API can be expensive in terms of bandwidth and the rate limits that service providers place on their API. While Twitter is quite generous about these limits, other services are not. Regardless, it is good practice to save the retrieved JSON structures to the disk for later use.

Getting ready

For this recipe, you will need previously retrieved data, preferably from the previous recipes.

How to do it...

The following steps walk us through saving the JSON data to the disk and then loading it back into the Python interpreter's memory:

1. First, we must import the `json` package and create two helper functions:

```
import json


def save_json(filename, data):
    with open(filename, 'wb') as outfile:
        json.dump(data, outfile)


def load_json(filename):
    with open(filename) as infile:
        data = json.load(infile)
    return data
```

2. At the Python prompt, let's test our functions by saving our friends' JSON-based Twitter profiles to the disk:

```
fname  = "test_friends_profiles.json"
save_json(fname, friends_profiles)
```

3. Check to make sure that the file was created. If you are using IPython, simply type `ls` or open up a terminal shell, change to the current directory, and type `ls`. You should see `test_friends_profiles.json` in the current directory.

4. Now, let's load the file back into our Python workspace:

```
test_reload = load_json(fname)
print(test_reload[0])
```

How it works...

The `json` library, which is part of the Python standard library, provides a simple but effective JSON encoder and decoder. When writing a file via the `save_json` function, we use the `json.dump` method to serialize the data object (in this case, a Python dictionary) as a JSON-formatted stream with a default UTF-8 encoding and send it to the outfile. Conversely, the `load_json` function uses `json.load`, which deserializes the infile to a Python object.

Setting up MongoDB for storing Twitter data

The default response format for the REST API is JSON, and thus, it is easiest to store this data as JSON in order to avoid extra data wrangling. While there are a number of different databases and data stores that can handle JSON data, we want to choose one that is relatively easy to set up, handles JSON data natively, is free to use, and is relatively popular. Thus, we will go with MongoDB.

Getting ready

For this recipe, you will need to download MongoDB on your local machine, so make sure that you have a broadband connection to the Internet.

How to do it...

The following steps will walk you through setting up MongoDB and using it through the command shell:

1. The first step for this stage is to install MongoDB. The easiest way to do this is to download the latest binary distribution (currently, 2.6) from the `http://www.mongodb.org/downloads`. 64-bit binary distributions that are available for Windows, Linux, Mac OS X, and Solaris.

2. Once downloaded, follow the pertinent installation guide at `http://docs.mongodb.org/manual/installation/`

3. Next, we need to start MongoDB by typing in `mongod` at the command prompt.

4. With the DB running, we need to connect to it via the included mongo shell. For this, open another terminal window or command line and type the following:

   `mongo`

5. This command assumes that MongoDB is running on port 27017 and at localhost. If this is not the case, start the mongo shell as shown, with the correct address of host and port number specified:

   `mongo address_of_host:port_number`

6. Now that we are running the mongo shell, we can get to work. Let's create a database named `test`, so type in the following:

   `use test`

7. Once the `test` database has been created, we need to create the tweets collection that will actually store all of the tweets that we are going to harvest. For this, use the following:

   `db.createCollection('user_profiles')`

8. We want to check whether the collection was created, so we must first switch to the current database by using the following command:

    ```
    use test
    ```

9. Ask the mongo shell to show all collections in this database, and you will receive a simple list of collections in the local database:

    ```
    show collections
    ```

How it works...

In this straightforward recipe, we have laid the foundation on how to use the popular MongoDB. We have installed and run MongoDB and have connected to it using the mongo shell. Further, we have named a new database, which is `test` , and created a document collection called `user_profiles`. Collections in MongoDB are groupings of MongoDB documents that are somewhat similar to a table in a relational database, such as `Postgres`. These documents are usually similar in structure and purpose but, unlike relational databases, do not have to be completely uniform and can evolve easily over time. For our purposes, the group of Twitter users' profiles make a great collection.

Personally, we don't like to run the mongod process either in the background or upon login, so we start MongoDB from the command line. This way, when we're not using MongoDB, it is not running in the background, consuming CPU cycles, or draining the battery.

There's more...

MongoDB is not the only NOSQL document store that is well suited for JSON data and many alternatives exist, including CouchDB (`http://couchdb.apache.org/`). Most key/value stores such as Amazon's Dynamo or Riak from Basho are great for storing JSON data with relatively minimal setup and configuration as well. With Amazon's Dynamo, you also get the added benefit of it being a fully cloud-based, pay-as-you-go solution that can scale almost infinitely. Finally, some relational databases, including Postgres, natively support a JSON datatype and perform error checking on the data in order to make sure that the stored data is valid JSON. However, the setup and configuration of Postgres tends to be a bit more challenging than MongoDB.

An additional advantage with MongoDB, although not an exclusive advantage, is that free, hosted platform-as-a-service options exist. In other words, you can provision a completely configured MongoDB database running in the cloud without doing anything more than walking through a fairly straightforward, web-based interface to log in and create your database. The best part is that both MongoLab and MongoHQ offer a free service tier, which means that you set up and use your own MongoDB database in the cloud without paying any money!

Since this section was first written, authors have had the opportunity to test and use RethinkDB (`http://rethinkdb.com/`), which is a relatively new open-sourced distributed database that easily handles JSON datatypes yet offers joins across tables of documents much like a relational database. If we were to rewrite this chapter, we would do so using RethinkDB.

See also

▶ *The MongoDB v2.4 Manual* at `http://docs.mongodb.org/v2.4/`

▶ The *Getting Started with MongoDB* guide at `http://docs.mongodb.org/manual/tutorial/getting-started/`

▶ CRUD in MongoDB at `http://docs.mongodb.org/manual/crud/`

▶ The CouchDB home page at `http://couchdb.apache.org/`

▶ The MongoLab home page `https://mongolab.com/welcome/`

▶ The MongoHQ home page at `http://www.mongohq.com/`

Storing user profiles in MongoDB using PyMongo

With user profile data retrieved and MongoDB installed and ready for action, we need to store the user profile JSON into the appropriate collection, and we want to do so from within our Python scripts and not using the mongo shell. For this, we are going to use PyMongo, which is the recommended way to work with MongoDB from Python, as per the MongoDB people themselves. As of January 2014, PyMongo was sitting at Version 2.6.3 (`http://api.mongodb.org/python/current/`).

Getting ready

You must already have MongoDB installed and have some sample user profile data to be ready pulled for this recipe.

How to do it...

The following steps will guide you through saving Python dictionaries as JSON documents within MongoDB:

1. To get started, we must install PyMongo on our systems. On a command-line prompt, type the following:

    ```
    pip install pymongo
    ```

2. Depending on your current user privileges, you might have to use `sudo` with these commands:

    ```
    sudo pip install pymongo
    ```

3. If the preceding installations do not work and report errors, please see the more detailed instructions online at `http://api.mongodb.org/python/current/installation.html`, as there are some potential C dependencies that might have to be compiled separately, depending on your system.

4. With PyMongo installed, drop in to a Python, IPython, or IPython Notebook session and enter the following:

    ```python
    import pymongo


    host_string = "mongodb://localhost"
    port = 27017
    mongo_client = pymongo.MongoClient(host_string, port)


    # get a reference to the mongodb database 'test'
    mongo_db = mongo_client['test']


    # get a reference to the 'user profiles' collection in the 'test'
    database
    user_profiles_collection = mongo_db['user_profiles']


    user_profiles_collection.insert(friends_profiles)
    user_profiles_collection.insert(followers_profiles)
    ```

How it works...

After we installed `pymongo`, there weren't many steps required to get us connected to and then storing JSON, in our local MongoDB database.

We first created a MongoClient that is connected to the mongod specified in the host string and port. We then use dictionary-style access to access the needed `mongo_db` database (in this case, `test`) and the particular collection (in this case, `user_profiles`). We call the `insert` method of the collection and pass it the JSON data to save. For this effort, we receive either one ObjectID or a list of ObjectIDs for the newly stored objects.

There are a number of things to be noted here. We choose to use the dictionary-style access (`mongo_client['test']`) just in case the database name contains characters such as - that would prevent the attribute style access to the database (`client.test`). Also, please note that MongoDB does nothing until a document is actually stored in the collection.

Alternatively, we can wrap the preceding commands in a function for easier reuse later. In the following command, `save_json_data_to_mongo` takes either a single JSON document or an iterable list of JSON documents and the specifications required in order to access the particular database and collection in MongoDB. The `host_string` parameter defaults to `localhost` and the port defaults to 27017:

```
def save_json_data_to_mongo(data, mongo_db,
                            mongo_db_collection,
                            host_string = "localhost",
                            port = 27017):
    mongo_client = pymongo.MongoClient(host_string, port)
    mongo_db = mongo_client[mongo_db]
    collection = mongo_db[mongo_db_collection]
    inserted_object_ids = collection.insert(data)
    return(inserted_object_ids)
```

We can improve this function by performing a check to see whether the number of JSON documents matches the number of ObjectIDs returned, but we will leave this exercise to the reader.

Exploring the geographic information available in profiles

The Twitter users' profiles contain two different, potential sources of geographic information: the profile itself and the most recently tweeted status update. We will utilize both options in this recipe with an eye toward usability in constructing a geographic visualization of our friends.

Getting ready

You will need the harvested friends' and/or followers' profiles from Twitter, as directed in the previous recipes.

How to do it...

Perform the following steps to extract the geographic data that we need to visualize the approximate locations of our connections:

1. We start this exercise in IPython or your favorite Python REPL. Load your friends' profiles from the file:

   ```
   In[1]: fname = 'test_friends_profiles.json'
   In[2]: load_json(fname)
   ```

2. Next, we build lists from all of the values of the geo_enabled field in the user profiles' data structures for our friends. Then, we use the count method to find the number of user profiles that have the geo_enabled flag set to true:

   ```
   In[3]: geo_enabled = [p['geo_enabled'] for p in
   friends_profiles]
   In[4]: geo_enabled.count(1)
   Out[4]: 127
   ```

3. We repeat a very similar process to the one used in the second step to count how many friends' user profiles have a blank location field:

   ```
   In[5]: location = [p['location'] for p in friends_profiles]
   In [6]: location.count('')
   Out[6]: 79
   ```

4. To get a quick ID of the data contained in the `location` field of user profiles, we print out a unique list and note the "messiness" of the data. It would appear that `location` is a free text field, which is very disappointing:

```
In[7]: print(set(location))


Out[7]:

...

u'Washington D.C.',

u'Washington DC',

u'iPhone: 50.122643,8.670158',

u'london',

u'new world of work',

u'san francisco',

u'seattle, wa',

u'usually in Connecticut',

u'washington, dc',

...
```

5. Now, we turn our attention to the `time_zone` field:

```
In[8]: time_zone = [p['time_zone'] for p in friends_profiles]
In[9]: time_zone.count(None)
Out[9]: 62
In[10]: print(set(time_zone))
Out[10]:
{None,
u'Alaska',
u'Amsterdam',
u'Arizona',
u'Atlantic Time (Canada)',
u'Berlin',
...
```

6. Finally, as each user profile contains that user's most recent status update (or tweet), we want to check how many of these tweets were geotagged by the user. Note the logical and conditional portion of the list comprehension. We only want `p['status']['geo']` if these keys are present in the data structure:

```
In[11]: status_geo = [p['status']['geo'] for p in
friends_profiles if ('status' in p and p['status']['geo'] is
not None)]

In [12]: if status_geo: print status_geo[0]

Out[12]: {u'coordinates': [38.91431189, -77.0211878], u'type':
u'Point'}

In[13]: len(status_geo)

Out[13]: 13
```

How it works...

In this recipe, we are using list comprehensions to extract potentially useful geographic information contained in the user profiles of friends. With each data element, we are asking two questions:

▸ What percentage of profiles contain this information, as coverage is important?

▸ What form and, therefore, how useful is the information that is available in the profiles?

We find that about 80 percent of profiles have a location set in their profile (very promising) and an even higher percentage have a time zone set (an even coarser grained geographic indicator). Of the last status update that is captured in the user profile data, more than 90 percent is not geocoded even though a third of user profiles (127/352) have `geo_enabled` set to `True`, which means that users might sometimes opt to geocode a tweet. Thus, if we harvested historical tweets for our friends, we should be able to get locations for about a third of them, at best.

With the coverage established, we look back at the actual data available, which paints a more complicated picture of the problem. The location characteristic of the user profile is available in most profiles, but it is a jumble of content. Some locations are a latitude and longitude value (highly useful), some are a recognizable address as a text string, some are a city and state, and some are not quite a traditional address format or even a location. The time zone data appears to be less obviously problematic, but we would still have to ensure that the time zone names captured by Twitter cleanly and unambiguously map to *real* times zones.

There's more...

If we want to plot our friends on Twitter, we can do so using a few approaches, listed as follows:

- ▶ If we use the coordinates of geotagged tweets, we can immediately jump to plotting. The only concern here is the sparsity of the data. To ameliorate this situation, we should pull tweets for each friend in an attempt to uncover more geotagged tweets. Doing this, we would expect to uncover geographic data for as much as a third of our friends.

- ▶ Although the location characteristic is quite messy, we can run the results through a geocoding service such as Google Maps or Bing and see what happens. Given the creativity of some of the locations in user profiles, this might not be the most productive path possible. Alternatively, we could attempt to pull out state abbreviations or ZIP codes using regular expressions, but this too would be a bit messy and time consuming.

- ▶ Graphing the count of friends in different time zones can be really interesting, and it would appear that this data might be easy to extract. The one question that becomes relevant is how hard will it be to graph time zones?

See also

- ▶ The *Users* Twitter documentation at `https://dev.twitter.com/docs/platform-objects/users`

Plotting geospatial data in Python

One of Python's greatest strengths is the number and diversity of available packages that make many complex tasks as simple as someone else has already written most of the code. As a result, we sometimes encounter the paradox of choice where too many options confuse the issue and we just want one good option. In this recipe, we will plot a set of latitude and longitude coordinates using an excellent Python package—folium—that wraps a JavaScript library, which is leaflet.js. You will learn more about folium further along in the recipe.

Getting ready

You will need the geographic data extracted in the previous recipes (a set of longitude and latitude coordinates). Also, we need to install the folium package, which is shown in the following section, so you will need an Internet connection.

How to do it...

The following steps will help you convert the latitude and longitude data you have to plot on a map:

1. Open your terminal. We need to install the Python package folium:

    ```
    (sudo) pip install folium
    ```

2. Change to your source directory and start up IPython or your favorite Python REPL. We first need to create two lists that will contain the geographic data and the associated screen names that we will use for labels. The following code is very similar to the last list comprehension in the previous recipe but is represented as a loop:

    ```
    status_geo = []
    status_geo_screen_names = []
    for fp in friends_profiles:
        if ('status' in fp and fp['status']['geo'] is not None and
          'screen_name' in fp):
            status_geo.append(fp['status']['geo'])
            status_geo_screen_names.append(fp['screen_name'])
    ```

3. We now import the two libraries that we will need:

    ```
    import folium
    from itertools import izip
    ```

4. We instantiate the `Map` object, setting the desired initial view location and level of zoom, add markers and labels to the map in a loop, and finally, render the map to HTML:

    ```
    map = folium.Map(location=[48, -102], zoom_start=3)

    for sg, sn in izip(status_geo,status_geo_screen_names):
        map.simple_marker(sg['coordinates'], popup=str(sn))

    map.create_map(path='us_states.html')
    ```

5. Now, there should be an HTML file in your working directory. Double-click on it and you should see something similar to what is shown in the following screenshot:

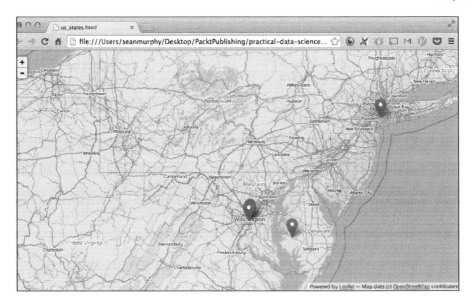

How it works...

It is impressive that we went from less than a dozen lines of code to a fully interactive map, complete with geographic markers denoting the location of some of the users that follow us on Twitter. For this, we leveraged the power of the folium Python package, which in turn, is a Pythonic wrapper for the Leaflet.js JavaScript library. Folium allows us to bind data from Python to a map for choropleth visualizations or render markers at specific map locations, as we did in the fourth step.

Folium uses the Jinja2 template package to create an HTML file containing a very simple HTML page with a single div container that holds the map and the customized JavaScript code in order to use the leaflet.js library. It is the leaflet.js library that handles the actual map generation:

```
<!DOCTYPE html>
<head>
    <link rel="stylesheet" href="http://cdn.leafletjs.com/leaflet-
    0.5/leaflet.css" />
    <script src="http://cdn.leafletjs.com/leaflet-
    0.5/leaflet.js"></script>

<style>
#map {
  position:absolute;
  top:0;
  bottom:0;
  right:0;
  left:0;
}
```

```
    </style>
    </head>
    <body>
        <div id="map" style="width: 960px; height: 500px"></div>
    <script>
    var map = L.map('map').setView([48, -102], 4);

    L.tileLayer('http://{s}.tile.openstreetmap.org/{z}/{x}/{y}.png', {
        maxZoom: 18,
        attribution: 'Map data (c) <a
        href="http://openstreetmap.org">OpenStreetMap</a>
        contributors'
    }).addTo(map);

    var marker_1 = L.marker([38.56127809, -76.04610616]);
    marker_1.bindPopup("Pop Text");
    map.addLayer(marker_1)

    </script>
    </body>
```

We highly recommend that you take a closer look at both the additional features of folium (and leaflet.js) and the underlying source code of this library.

There's more...

Visualizing geographic data is complex. Not only do you need the ability to render one or more complex coordinate systems, but you also need the original map data that defines countries, roads, rivers, and anything else you might want on display, in addition to your own data. We are fortunate that Python provides so many options when tackling this problem.

These packages tend to fall into two broad categories. The first class of geospatial visualization packages arose out of scientific and research needs that have existed for decades. For this software, the renderer and the required geographic data reside on the user's local machine. This typically necessitates the compilation and installation of several additional layers of the software in order to get the Python package working.

The very powerful Matplotlib Basemap Toolkit is an excellent example of this. Browsing the instructions, we see numerous dependencies. While we have already handled matplotlib and NumPy, two additional requirements—GEOS and Proj4 map library—stand out as potentially problematic. The C++ source code for the **Geometry Engine - Open Source** (**GEOS**) is actually included with the basemap but must be compiled and built separately. This need to compile software in another language is a giant red flag. For Python packages, this often leads one down a rabbit hole of compile errors and technical issues (missing header files, slightly nonstandard directory structures, wrong compiler, and so on) that can take hours or days to resolve. If you are on Mac OS X, especially Mavericks, you are in for even more fun, as Apple has a tendency to make slight alterations with each release, which break previously functional makefiles. As a result, we chose a mapping library from category two, which is described as follows.

The second class of the package provides a Pythonic way of interacting with a JavaScript library that actually handles the rendering of maps and data. This often requires us to output our results as HTML, which is more often than not fine. These JavaScript libraries themselves fall into two categories. First, there are more "pure" mapping libraries such as Google Maps and Leaflet.js that were built to render maps online but can be repurposed for more specialized geospatial data visualization needs. Second, there is D3.js, the all-purpose library for manipulating documents based on data that is capable of some beautiful geographic visualizations. We chose folium due to its simplicity and elegance; when software works, it makes our lives and analyses easier.

See also

- ▶ The GEOS home page at `http://trac.osgeo.org/geos/`
- ▶ The Cartopy home page at `http://scitools.org.uk/cartopy/`
- ▶ The Shapely home page at `http://toblerity.org/shapely/`
- ▶ The Kartograph home page at `http://kartograph.org/`
- ▶ The Leaflet.js home page at `http://leafletjs.com/`

11
Optimizing Numerical Code with NumPy and SciPy (Python)

In this chapter, we will cover the following recipes:

- ▸ Understanding the optimization process
- ▸ Identifying common performance bottlenecks in code
- ▸ Reading through the code
- ▸ Profiling Python code with the Unix time function
- ▸ Profiling Python code using built-in Python functions
- ▸ Profiling Python code using IPython's %timeit function
- ▸ Profiling Python code using line_profiler
- ▸ Plucking the low-hanging (optimization) fruit
- ▸ Testing the performance benefits of NumPy
- ▸ Rewriting simple functions with NumPy
- ▸ Optimizing the innermost loop with NumPy

Introduction

Optimizing code to decrease the execution time can be a very rewarding task. Unfortunately, in most situations, optimization is almost always the last step in writing software and is only performed if absolutely necessary. If your code executes in an acceptable amount of time, optimization is not required.

Given this, why bother with code optimization? As data scientists, we often face ever-larger datasets where the code that executes on a single data element might be executed billions of times to generate results. If this code is written poorly, the analysis could literally take days to run. Further, in many scientific and numeric applications, software is computationally bound and not limited to bandwidth. As the models employed by data practitioners grow in complexity, every drop of performance matters. Why else do we optimize code? The reasons are as follows:

- **Time is money**: If you are running software in the cloud, time is money. Each extra minute of processing is going to cost you, especially if it is spread across a thousand machines. Also remember that Amazon EC2 still charges by the hour and not by the minute, like Google Compute Engine does; 61 minutes of EC2 time are twice as expensive as 59 minutes.

- **Number of iterations**: Cycle time, or the number of iterations you can achieve before a fixed deadline, is another critical issue. If your entire analytics process requires a week to run and generate results, you cannot learn from this iteration, tweak the process, and regenerate updated results nearly as fast as you can if that process only consumed 24 hours. Trust us, it is virtually impossible to get an exploratory analysis perfect the first time or even the third time. Iterations matter.

- **Deployment to production**: A production environment can introduce new execution time requirements on your code. Does your code need to run in real time? Must your calculation complete to return a result to a user who is otherwise left waiting? Or, does your code run in the batch mode overnight and have a window of time in which to complete? As you transition your code from prototype to production, the execution time can become a critical issue.

- **Power savings**: Code that performs the same task with fewer instructions, less memory, and fewer CPU cycles results in power savings. Thus, if you must worry about the power consumption for your mobile device or the thermal performance of your server, optimized code is better.

▶ **Preparing for the coming transition from big data to big computation**: In the world of big data (potentially, more relevant to the average data scientist), once people get bored of counting clicks and computing simple statistics at scale, practitioners will move on to performing much more interesting calculations. All of a sudden, we will transition from big data to big computation with CPU cycles being the scarce commodity as opposed to the storage bandwidth. At this point, the code optimization will become critically important, and much of the work done in the **High Performance Computing** (**HPC**) world will transition from fringe to mainstream.

▶ **Fun, enjoyment, and personal development**: Coercing better performance out of the code is a fantastic puzzle that requires one to understand the target programming language at a much deeper level (often, understanding key design decisions made by the authors of the language) and, in more extreme cases, the constraints and capabilities of the underlying hardware. Plus, in today's world of high-level languages, prebuilt libraries, and frameworks that handle almost anything for you, many people do not have this type of programming depth.

Understanding the optimization process

In this abstract recipe, we will talk about the steps required to optimize software.

How to do it...

Perform the following steps to learn about the optimization process that we will be employing:

1. Establish the baseline performance of your existing code in terms of the relevant parameters (execution time, memory consumed, peak I/O bandwidth, and so on).

2. Determine the performance targets or system constraints. One of the seven habits of highly effective people was to always start with the end in mind, and optimization is no different. How quickly must the code get executed? What is the longest acceptable time to complete the processes? What is the maximum amount of memory that can be consumed by your software? How accurate must the computed results be? Don't forget about the fidelity of the results.

3. Set up a development and measurement environment that allows you to easily and rapidly measure and record the relevant performance characteristics. The easier it is for you to measure the performance of your code line by line, the faster you will optimize your code. If it is painful or difficult or requires you to remember commands that you keep forgetting, the optimization will be painful and slow.

4. Capture and record all test parameters and a snapshot of the current state of the code.

5. Identify the bottlenecks in the code using the profiler.

6. Attempt to address the bottlenecks, starting with the largest bottleneck first. Depending on the code complexity, it is often safest to address a single issue with each testing cycle.

7. Rerun the code with the implemented change(s) using the profiler. Check whether the computed results or output remain unchanged!

8. Jump to step 4 and repeat as many times as necessary.

How it works...

Just like when painting a room, you set yourself up for success by preparing properly. Before the paintbrush touches the wall, you must move all of the furniture away from the walls and cover each piece with a sheet or cloth. The floor must be protected, often with a drop cloth, and pictures, shelves, and other items hanging on the walls must be taken down and nails removed. The walls need to be wiped down with a wet cloth in order to remove dust and dirt and then address any areas that need repair. Finally, you should tape the areas where you don't want the paint to go, such as the trim, windows, and electrical sockets. With all of this done, the actual application of the paint to walls takes very little time. Optimization is similar in that you must create an environment where optimization is a simple extension of what you are doing. Thus, the setup of your development and measurement environment—the third step—is crucial.

When optimizing code, you will be constantly tweaking and testing small (and sometimes, large) changes to your source code. Some changes will break the code, some changes won't. Some changes will enhance the performance, some changes won't. As you continue to tweak and test, it becomes increasingly important that you can recover that change you tried five or six attempts back that worked best. It is equally important to keep a record of the performance impact of each tweak so that when you are testing an array of possible changes, you know which one(s) to keep. Git, Mercurial, or whatever source code versioning tool you prefer, is your best friend.

In the sixth step, the order in which we address bottlenecks is usually a function of the ease by which the bottleneck can be eliminated. Smaller performance bottlenecks that can be easily fixed by a new line of code, or similarly, a quick change should be considered if the main bottleneck requires a much larger rewrite of the code to the address.

There's more...

Every change in code that might increase performance can also create a bug. Thus, whenever optimizing code, never do more than you have to in order to achieve the desired gain in performance. That last brilliant update might introduce a particularly difficult-to-find bug or, worse yet, a numerical discrepancy. Also, be aware that as you optimize the code, you risk making it more difficult to read both for yourself and the next person who will use it.

Identifying common performance bottlenecks in code

When optimizing a data science project, it is crucial to look at the entire analytics pipeline and understand the time and effort spent at each stage and their interdependencies.

Let's simplify the problem to decrease the execution time of the software implemented in a particular language. We won't worry about shuffling around large blocks of data, say, from a production database to the analytics data store.

At its most abstract level, the execution time of your code is a function of the code itself and the hardware used to run it. If you want to decrease the time required to run your code, you can upgrade the hardware, modify the software, or do both.

For optimization purposes, we want to start with the end in mind: what type of optimization must be achieved or how much faster must the software run. Decreasing the execution time by a factor of two often mandates a very different course of action than an order of magnitude decrease that might require more radical code changes.

How to do it...

While a profiler (software that provides information about the execution behavior of other software) will help highlight your slowest lines or blocks of code, there are certain types of code / patterns / problem areas, that you can learn to spot, that are often ripe for speed improvements:

1. Highlight any and all loops, especially nested loops: the higher the level of nesting, the slower they often are.

2. Locate slow mathematical operations such as square roots, trigonometric functions, and so on, or anything that is not an addition or subtraction.

3. Shrink the size of key data structures.

4. Determine the precision (float, double, int, uint8, and so on) of often used variables.

5. Avoid unnecessary calculations when possible.

6. Attempt to simplify mathematical equations.

How it works...

For step 1, loops indicate areas of code that are executed multiple times, with nested loops often indicating a much larger number of repetitions. Most of the code that is repeatedly executed represents a prime area for optimization, as the loop will magnify even a small gain in the performance. Further, there are some languages, especially domain specific languages such as R and MATLAB, where loops perform poorly due to properties of the language itself. In these cases, loops can often be replaced by a different programmatic construct (a functional approach in the case of R or a vectorized method in MATLAB).

For step 2, locating slow mathematical operations is often another opportunity to radically speed up the execution of computationally intense code. A surprisingly large number of natural phenomena are described by equations using the square root, including the simple Euclidean distance measure between two points in n-dimensional space. Unfortunately, the square root calculation itself is quite slow compared to basic multiplication, division, addition, subtraction, and logical comparisons. Even then, multiplications and divisions are usually significantly slower than your basic addition, subtraction, and logical comparisons.

Basically, all of those extra buttons on your TI-85 graphing calculator or, dare I say, your HP 48G for all of those engineers out there (long live the reverse Polish notation!) represent mathematical functions that are significantly slower than the basic four operations. This means stay on the look out for:

- cos: cosine
- sin: sine
- tan: tangent
- acos: arc cosine
- asin: arc sine
- atan: arc tangent
- exp: exponentiation
- pow: log—base 10 logarithm
- ln: natural (or base e) logarithm
- cosh: hyperbolic cos
- sinh: hyperbolic sin
- tanh: hyperbolic tan
- acosh: inverse hyperbolic cos
- asinh: inverse hyperbolic sin
- atan: inverse hyperbolic tangent

We see this a lot in numeric code where a conditional is dependent on a distance calculation. For example, take a look at the following command:

```
if distance_between(point1, point2) > 1.0 ...
```

Or, take a look at this even more explicitly written command:

```
if square_root( (x1-x2)^2 + (y1-y2)^2 ) > 1.0 ...
```

Both signify an opportunity. If one squares both sides, the computationally expensive square root can be eliminated. The only thing to be concerned about is the behavior of the square root and squares at 1, -1, and 0. Negative numbers become positive when squared and fractional values get closer to zero when squared. When dealing with distances and other physical quantities, negative values aren't often an issue.

As a general rule, the smaller the data structure, the faster your computation. Smaller data structures fit in faster levels of the hierarchy of the memory available to your CPU. Ideally, all calculations would be done on values that are already stored in registers on the CPU with no need to access L1, L2 or slower levels of cache memory, let alone the massive performance hit that going into the system memory incurs. Object-oriented languages can be especially problematic, as there might be many unused methods attached to your large data structures that need to be moved around with each loop iteration.

Technically, step 4 could fall into the shrinking your data size step discussed previously but is worth a separate mention. Some languages default to 64-bit integers and 64-bit floats. The problem with these data types is that they are 64-bits in size. For integers, many numbers are simply not that large and do not require 64-bits of space. In fact, often, an 8-bit integer will do, and sometimes an unsigned integer, which is incapable of expressing a negative value, is even better.

Many calculations with floating point numbers simply do not require this level of precision. Will a 16-bit float do? How about a 32-bit float? You can literally reduce your data size by a factor of two to four, resulting in large performance gains.

For step 5, look for calculations that were performed right before any type of branching code, especially calculations involving expensive mathematical operators. If an infrequently executed code path requires an expensive operation or function call, only perform the calculation when that branch is taken.

When writing computationally complex code, most code is written as simply and as clearly as possible so that the author gets it correct the first time. Often, this means that slow, complicated calculations are done unnecessarily, especially when situated near conditional statements. If you are using a compiled language, the compiler might be smart enough to reorder the sequence of calculations, but it is safer to assume it is not (and in dynamic languages or languages that run within the JVM, it is often difficult to know exactly what will happen).

For step 6, most equations were written to express a particular mathematical point for humans and were not written in a form that was optimized for modern software and hardware. It often pays to simplify the equation by canceling terms or to express it in a slightly different form that transforms a multiplication into an addition or even a division into a multiplication. For equations that get repeated millions or billions of times, these simple steps can save large numbers of calculations and an impressive amount of time. Additions and subtractions are faster than multiplications that are usually faster than division operations.

Reading through the code

The Python code to be optimized calculates the **Accessible Surface Area (ASA)** of a molecule. The ASA quantifies the surface area of a molecule that is open or available to a solvent and has many uses in biology and biochemistry. For the purposes of this recipe, a deeper background into the ASA is unnecessary. However, for those curious, I highly recommend that you read Bosco K. Ho's excellent post about both this code and the ASA. He is the author of the original code that was written for clarity and accuracy but not speed.

For the purpose of optimization, this code was going to be integrated into a web application that would compute the ASA for a molecule upon an upload by the user. As all calculations were computed synchronously, the longer the code takes, the longer the user waits for a result.

In this recipe, we are going to read through the critical portions of the code, which are contained primarily in the asa.py source file, in order to gain an understanding of what the code does and identify potential performance bottlenecks.

Getting ready

Open the asa.py file in your text editor or IDE. This file is included in the code from the book's repository.

How to do it...

The following steps will have you look through the code that we will be optimizing in more detail. The *How it works...* section will thoroughly explain how the code works.

1. Scroll through the asa.py file in your text editor. Take note of the packages being imported, the functions defined in the beginning, and read through the comments left in the code.

2. Move to the main() function and note the sequence of function calls that occurs. What is the role of main() in asa.py?

3. Next, read through each function in depth, starting with the workhorse function, which is calculate_asa.

How it works...

The `main()` function of `asa.py` handles the required command-line arguments including the filename of the molecule to be analyzed. Once it has successfully imported the molecule's structure using methods from `molecule.py`, it calls the `calculate_asa` function that handles all calculations.

Jumping to the top of the file, we encounter the first function, `generate_sphere_points()`, which computes the number of equidistance points on a sphere of a given radius and returns the points as a list of three elements.

This function uses the golden section spiral algorithm, which is one of the several different methods that generate equidistant points on a sphere (check the *See also* section for additional alternatives). The single input parameter to the function increases or decreases the number of points that were used to represent a sphere—a higher or lower fidelity or resolution sphere. If we increased this value to infinity, we would eventually get a perfect sphere.

In terms of performance optimization, let's start with some details. The list points are initialized to empty and are appended with each iteration of the loop. Growing data structures are often a cardinal sin when trying to write fast code.

Second, `range(int(n))` generates a list of `int(n)` elements from 0 to `int(n)-1`. For this, the memory needs to be allocated for the entire n-element list, which is a process that can be time consuming for large n. It would be better to use a generator, and replacing the `range` function with `xrange()`. `xrange` only allocates memory for the `xrange` object and provides numbers on demand and as required. Also, `xrange()` is implemented in pure C.

 This only applies to Python versions up to before 3.0 as `range` now provides an iterator.

Finally, and most importantly, Python `for` loops are often ripe for performance improvements. The underlying idea is that we want to get the loop out of the interpreter and into the compiled C code.

The `find_neighbor_indices` function accepts three variables as inputs:

- `atoms`: This is a list of the atoms in the molecule as type atoms
- `probe`: This is the probe distance, which is usually set to `1.4`
- `k`: This is the atom for which we are finding neighbors

It then returns a list of the indices of the atoms that are within the specified distance (probe) from the atom of interest.

We see a loop over the number of indices, a `neighbor_indices` list that is growing with each iteration, and a call to the `pos_distance` function defined in `vector3d.py`. Looking at this function, we see that it computes the squared distance between points `p1` and `p2` and then takes the square root via nested function calls shown in the following commands:

```
def pos_distance(p1, p2):
  return math.sqrt(pos_distance_sq(p2, p1))

def pos_distance_sq(p1, p2):
  x = p1.x - p2.x
  y = p1.y - p2.y
  z = p1.z - p2.z
  return x*x + y*y + z*z;
```

Note the call to the `math.sqrt` function, as this can be computationally expensive.

The `calculate_asa(atoms, probe, n_sphere_point=960)` function is the main workhorse function that handles and orchestrates the required calculations. It takes three variables as inputs:

▸   `atoms`: This is a list of atoms in the molecule

▸   `probe`: This is the probe distance (usually, `1.4`)

▸   `n_sphere_point`: This is the number of equidistant points that we will use to approximate a sphere (more points is better but takes longer)

The most important input here is the list of atoms for which the ASA is to be computed. Each atom will have an x, y, z coordinate plus an associated radius. `Atom` is a class that is defined in the `molecule.py` file.

The function starts out by generating a set of spherical points via the `generate_sphere_points` function and initializing an empty list. We then see a triple-nested set of `for` loops. The outermost loop walks across all atoms in the list of atoms. For a typical molecule, this will be hundreds or thousands of atoms. For each atom, it generates a list of the closest neighboring atoms using `find_neighbor_indices`, which involves a `for` loop.

We then hit the second `for` loop where we loop over every point in `sphere_points`. If we use the default 960 points, this loop will have 960 iterations. For each point in our set of equidistant spherical points, we add the center coordinate of the current atom.

We then hit the innermost loop where we loop over all neighboring atoms. For each neighbor, we compare the distance of the `test_point` variable to the center of the neighbor atom. If the two points are within a particular distance of each other, we say that that particular `test_point` variable is not accessible to a solvent molecule.

Explained another way, the inner two loops take the pregenerated sphere of equidistant points and translate it to the atom being tested. For each of these points, it checks to see whether at least one neighboring atom is within a specified distance. If so, the point on the sphere is considered not accessible.

We then compute the accessible area for an atom as the fraction of a sphere surrounding the atom that is not blocked by neighboring atoms.

Three nested loops and a lot of calculations suggest that most likely, there is a lot of room to improve the code's performance.

See also

▸ The *Calculating the Solvent Accessible Surface-Area* article available at `http://boscoh.com/protein/calculating-the-solvent-accessible-surface-area-asa.html`.

▸ The original paper on calculating the accessible surface area—*Environment and exposure to solvent of protein atoms. Lysozyme and insulin, A. Shrake, J.A. Rupley.* J Mol Biol 79 (2): 351–71. doi:10.1016/0022-2836(73)90011-9.

Profiling Python code with the Unix time function

There are a large number of tools that one can use to profile the performance of code in Python. The simplest option for most is the Unix `time` command, which measures the amount of time or resources that executing a particular command requires. This recipe demonstrates the usage of this command.

Getting ready

Fortunately, the Unix `time` command is available on virtually every Linux distribution and on OS X at the command line. The `time` command is even available in Cygwin on Windows machines. Thus, you should be ready for this recipe.

How to do it...

Perform the following simple steps to conduct your first Python benchmark:

1. Open a new terminal window.
2. Change the directory to the location of `asa.py`.

3. At the command prompt, type the following:

```
time python asa.py 1R0R.pdb
```

4. After about a minute—depending on your machine—the `time` command will report back two to three pieces of information—depending on your operating system—that describe the length of time consumed by executing your code:

```
12078.1 angstrom squared.
python asa.py 1R0R.pdb  49.60s user 0.15s system 97% cpu
51.194 total
```

> The `asa.py` script required `51.194` seconds to complete while running on a Mac Book Air with a 1.8 GHz Intel Core I5 processor, 8 GB 1600 MHz DDR3, and OSX 10.9.2. Also note that we are using the default setting of 960 sphere points in the script.

How it works...

There isn't much complexity to the `time` command, and it is a great tool to get a quick idea of how long a program or script takes to execute. As per the main page (enter `man time` at the command line to access), the time utility has output-formatting options that allow you to see various metrics that describe the memory and input/output usage. Also, the output is a little bit cryptic. In this case, `51.194 total` is the elapsed actual time that the command took to complete with a `97%` CPU utilization. The user and sys time values can be ignored.

See also

▸ http://unixhelp.ed.ac.uk/CGI/man-cgi?time

Profiling Python code using built-in Python functions

Python comes with two profiling options, `profile` and `cProfile`, which share the same interface but differ in their impact on the profiled program's performance. The `profile` module is pure Python but adds significant overhead to the software being profiled and, therefore, isn't well suited for long running programs. The `cProfile` profiling option is a C extension and has much lower overhead, thus impacting program execution times to a lesser degree. As a result, we will use `cProfile`.

Getting ready

Part of the beauty of Python is its batteries included nature. The `cProfile` and `profile` profiling options both come built in to the Python distribution that you are using.

How to do it...

Perform the following steps to benchmark the code using `cProfile`:

1. To benchmark the preceding `asa` code, we need to be at the command line in the directory of the source code.

2. Type the following into the command line:

```
python -m cProfile asa.py '1R0R.pdb'
```

3. You should see output similar to the following screenshot. Note that the screenshot is truncated and your output should be longer.

How it works...

We see that benchmarking the original `asa.py` script consumed 65 seconds, which is slightly more than the amount used by the Unix `time` command, probably due to the overhead of `cProfile`.

The output from `cProfile` consists of plain text organized into five columns as follows:

- ► `ncalls`: This shows you how many times the function is called
- ► `tottime`: This shows you the time spent on the function, excluding the time spent on calling other functions
- ► `percall`: This shows you the total time, divided by `ncalls`
- ► `cumtime`: This shows you the time spent on the function, including calls to other functions
- ► `percall`: This shows you the `cumtime` value divided by `tottime`

The last column identifies the relevant filename, function, and line number.

The `cProfile` profiling option sheds some light on which functions are consuming the bulk of our execution time and suggests some possible issues. We see over 5 million calls to the `math.sqrt` function, over 2 million calls to the `extend` method of list, and over 4 million calls to the `range` function.

See also

- ► The Python profilers at `http://docs.python.org/2/library/profile.html`

Profiling Python code using IPython's %timeit function

Often, when we are working in the Python REPL, we would like to be able to quickly and easily benchmark a line of code or a function. IPython makes this possible through a magic function called `timeit`.

How to do it...

Perform the following set of steps to try out `%timeit` to profile the code:

1. Open up a new terminal and change to the direction of the `asa.py` source code.

2. Fire up IPython by typing the following:

   ```
   ipython
   ```

3. Let's see how fast or slow the built-in square root function is, as follows:

   ```
   In [1]: import math
   In [2]: %timeit math.sqrt(10000)
   ```

4. This should produce output similar to the following:

   ```
   10000000 loops, best of 3: 166 ns per loop
   ```

5. We see that `%timeit`, due to the rapid execution of the `math.sqrt()` method, tested the function execution 10,000,000 times to get a more accurate measurement.

6. Next, we will use `%timeit` to test the main loop of the `asa` code calculation. For this, we must first import the relevant functions:

   ```
   In [2]: from asa import *
   In [3]: import math
   In [4]: from vector3d import pos_distance, Vector3d,
   pos_distance_sq
   In [5]: import molecule
   ```

7. We then create the variables that are required to call the `calculate_asa` function:

   ```
   In [13]: mol = molecule.Molecule('1R0R.pdb')
   In [14]: atoms = mol.atoms()
   In [15]: molecule.add_radii(atoms)
   In [16]: n_sphere = 960
   ```

8. We then use the magic `%timeit` command to profile the function in question:

   ```
   In [18]: %timeit asas = calculate_asa(atoms, 1.4, n_sphere)
   ```

9. This produces the output that agrees relatively well with the simple Unix `time` command:

   ```
   1 loops, best of 3: 52.5 s per loop
   ```

Notice that there appears to be a bit of an overhead added to the execution time using `%timeit`.

How it works...

The %timeit magic function is a bit smarter than the previously mentioned profiling tools in that it will run the specified code multiple times to get a better estimate of the code's true execution time. If the code takes longer to run, it will reduce the number of repetitions performed for benchmarking.

Profiling Python code using line_profiler

Only cProfile gave us comprehensive information about the performance of all functions in the asa.py file. However, what happens if you want to drill down further and understand the performance of each line in the Python code? Robert Kern's line_profiler module is a Python module that enables you to do just this, and this is exactly the level of detail that you want for this chapter.

Getting ready

The installation and setup of the line profiler is a little bit more complicated than usual, so we will discuss this in the next recipe.

How to do it...

The steps that are listed will introduce you to profiling with the line_profiler module:

1. To use the line_profiler module, we must first install it using the pip command:

   ```
   (sudo) pip install line_profiler
   ```

2. Next, we want to grab the kernprof.py Python script from the website (http://pythonhosted.org/line_profiler/) and place it in the directory where we are running asa.py.

3. Open the asa.py script in your favorite editor, and we will decorate the function that we wish to profile line by line. Note that you can profile multiple functions if you so desire. In this case, we decorate the main workhorse function, which is calculate_asa, as follows:

   ```
   @profile
   def calculate_asa(atoms, probe, n_sphere_point=960):
   ```

4. From the command line and not the Python interpreter, we run the following:

   ```
   python kernprof.py -l asa.py "1R0R.pdb"
   ```

5. Once complete, we see a new file, which is the asa.py.lprof output file, in the current directory.

6. To view the results, type the following:

```
python -m line_profiler asa.py.lprof
```

7. The `line_profiler` module provides the treasure trove of information displayed in the following screenshot:

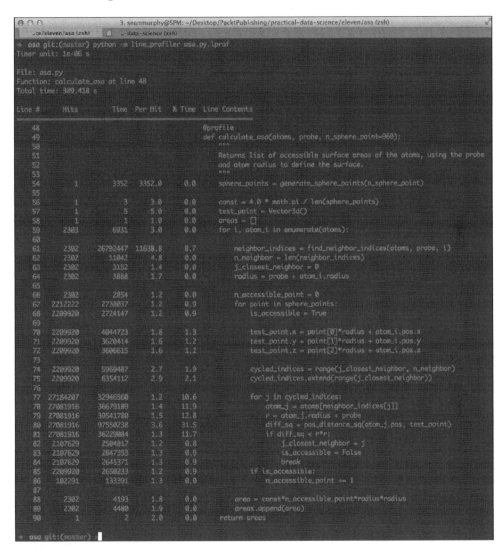

Note that the `line_profiler` module is reporting back detailed information for each of the lines, referenced by line number, in each profiled function (in this case, `calculate_asa`), including the all-important percentage of total time (`% Time`).

From this output, we see that the lines of code in the innermost loop (78-81) of the `calculate_asa` function are eating up over half of the execution time, and it is here that we should focus our optimization effort. Also, notice that there are a lot of variable assignments, lines 70-72 that are chewing up time as well.

There's more...

Also, notice that the total execution time is a whopping 309.418 seconds. Profiling line by line adds a great deal of overhead to the execution and slows it down by a factor of five. Since optimizing is highly iterative, we do not want to wait 5 minutes for each run to complete. Thus, we want to find some way of decreasing the execution time so that each instrumented profiling run gets completed much faster.

Given the nature of this code, the easiest fix would be to decrease the number of "sphere points" that the code loops over. The default value is 960, and if we lower the value, we should expect much lower execution times. Changing this value to 60 and rerunning the `time` Unix command, we see that the code executes in 11 seconds.

See also

- ▸ More details about the `line_profiler` module at `http://pythonhosted.org/line_profiler/`
- ▸ A great post on optimization at `http://www.huyng.com/posts/python-performance-analysis/`

Plucking the low-hanging (optimization) fruit

When optimizing, always perform just enough to get the job done so as to not introduce new bugs. In this recipe, we introduce some simple optimizations that require minimal modification to the source code and test how effective they are at decreasing the execution time.

Getting ready

To prepare, change the directory to the source directory and open `asa.py` in an editor.

How to do it...

The following steps walk you through establishing a new performance baseline for the code and implementing several small optimizations:

1. In the `main` function, edit the line that sets the number of sphere points, changing it from `960` to `60`:

    ```
    n_sphere = 60
    ```

2. At the command line, use the Unix `time` command to benchmark the new code configuration and compute the new result:

    ```
    time python asa.py 1ROR.pdb
    12114.7 angstrom squared.
    python asa.py 1ROR.pdb   11.05s user 0.04s system 97% cpu
    11.334 total
    ```

3. Let's copy `asa.py` into a new file as a local code-versioning system. You can also just use Git if you are comfortable using it to roll back to previous versions of the code. At the command line, enter the following command:

    ```
    cp asa.py asa_v1.py
    ```

4. Next, we will make several small code changes to test simple optimizations. In the `calculate_asa` function, change the original version:

    ```
    for point in sphere_points:
    is_accessible = True
    test_point.x = point[0]*radius + atom_i.pos.x
    test_point.y = point[1]*radius + atom_i.pos.y
    test_point.z = point[2]*radius + atom_i.pos.z
    ```

    To:

    ```
    atom_i_pos_x = atom_i.pos.x
    atom_i_pos_y = atom_i.pos.y
    atom_i_pos_z = atom_i.pos.z
    n_accessible_point = 0
    for point in sphere_points:
    is_accessible = True
    test_point.x = point[0]*radius + atom_i_pos_x
    test_point.y = point[1]*radius + atom_i_pos_y
    test_point.z = point[2]*radius + atom_i_pos_z
    ```

5. Next, we eliminate one of the `math.sqrt` functions in the `find_neighbor_indices` function, transforming the original code:

```
dist = pos_distance(atom_k.pos, atom_i.pos)
if dist < radius + atom_i.radius:
```

Into:

```
dist = pos_distance_sq(atom_k.pos, atom_i.pos)
if dist < (radius + atom_i.radius)**2:
```

6. Now, let's use the Unix `time` command again to see the end result:

```
time python asa_v1.py 1R0R.pdb

12114.7 angstrom squared.

python asa_v1.py 1R0R.pdb  9.42s user 0.03s system 99% cpu
9.500 total
```

7. Check whether the output returned in the optimized code, `12114.7`, is the same value that was computed previously (which it is).

How it works...

With this first optimization effort, we tried to make only very small tweaks to the code and not introduce any new libraries or radical restructuring.

The first trick was to use local variables inside the loops to remove unneeded dereferencing. In the original code, , we must locate the `pos` attribute of the `atom_i` object for each point in `sphere_points` and then access the `x` attribute of the `vector3d.Vector3d` object:

```
for point in sphere_points:
...
test_point.x = point[0]*radius + atom_i.pos.x
```

We perform this same lookup for each iteration of this loop despite the fact that `atom_i` has not changed. The simple solution is to pull this lookup to just before the loop and cache the value in a local variable used inside the loop. This is shown in the new version of the code as follows:

```
atom_i_pos_x = atom_i.pos.x
...
for point in sphere_points:
...
test_point.x = point[0]*radius + atom_i_pos_x
```

The second optimization we used was to remove an unnecessary call to the square root. Remember, square roots are painfully expensive in comparison to other mathematical operations that can be tested:

```
In [1]: %timeit sqrt(29111)
10000000 loops, best of 3: 116 ns per loop
In [2]: %timeit 29111 + 372.1
10000000 loops, best of 3: 30.9 ns per loop
```

This factor of approximately 4x differential is actually on the low side and we have seen square root calculations require ten times the time of additions and multiplications.

In the original code, a square root was concealed in the `pos_distance` function call. We then test the result against the sum of `radius` and `atom_i.radius`:

```
dist = pos_distance(atom_k.pos, atom_i.pos)
if dist < radius + atom_i.radius:
```

Assuming that the smallest possible `dist` value is greater than 1, we can square both sides of the inequality and remove the need for the original square root:

```
dist = pos_distance_sq(atom_k.pos, atom_i.pos)
if dist < (radius + atom_i.radius)**2:
```

The two simple changes in the preceding code resulted in an approximately 15 percent decrease in the execution time of the code. We can take these two ideas and roll them out to all other locations in `asa.py`. We can also implement a number of other simple changes such as preallocating lists that could offer additional performance increases. However, our target is to get the code execution time down from 60 seconds to 1 second, and it is unlikely that these little changes will yield the improvement we need.

Testing the performance benefits of NumPy

Minor changes to the original code did not get the job done, so we must consider more drastic approaches. Luckily, with Python, we have the `NumPy` library. `NumPy` provides a very fast n-dimensional array (called `ndarray`) data structure for Python and offers a number of operations on this data type that have been implemented in C and are highly optimized.

Before we make any major changes to `asa.py`, we use this recipe to try a few toy examples to see how much faster the `NumPy` library's faster yet less flexible `ndarray` arrays are versus naïve Python lists.

Getting ready

For this recipe, we only need to fire up the Python REPL or, even better, start up IPython. Also, this recipe assumes that you have NumPy installed.

How to do it...

Perform the following steps to test out the performance differential between Python and NumPy:

1. We must import both the NumPy, random, and math libraries:

   ```
   import numpy as np
   import math, random
   ```

   Note that it is standard practice to import NumPy as np.

2. Next, we create two different input variables, one a Python list and the other a NumPy ndarray:

   ```
   s = 100000
   x_py = [random.random() for i in xrange(s)]
   x_np = np.random.rand(1,s)
   ```

   Both variables contain the same number of elements.

3. We define two test functions, one using pure Python and the other using NumPy functions:

   ```
   def slow(x):
   output = [0] * len(x)
   for i,num in enumerate(x):
   output[i] = num * 5.2 + num*num + math.cos(num)
   return(output)

   def fast(x):
   return(5.2 * x + x*x + np.cos(x))
   ```

4. We then use IPython's magic %timeit function to measure the performance differential:

   ```
   %timeit slow(x_py)
   10 loops, best of 3: 51.2 ms per loop
   %timeit fast(x_np)
   10000 loops, best of 3: 184 µs per loop
   ```

How it works...

What we did in this recipe was create a `slow` function and a `fast` function that take in a list or `ndarray` of random values and perform some simple mathematics, returning an output list or array. The `slow` function uses a `for` loop and the `fast` function uses the `NumPy` library's ability to operate over an entire array. In the function named `slow`, we made sure that we preallocated the output array to ensure a more equitable test as `NumPy` handles that for us by default:

```
output = [0] * len(x)
```

We then tested the performance of each function using a `100000` element test vector, and the results are incredible. The NumPy-based version is over two orders of magnitude faster.

One of the keys to NumPy's performance is that each element of the array must be of the same data type. This homogeneity allows for very efficient memory packing and locality of reference. This is in stark contrast to Python lists, which can contain objects of varied data types and occupy different amounts of memory. In a Python list, each element is simply a memory address that points to the actual element in the list (an object, string, integer, and so on). Thus, to access the first element of a Python list, you retrieve the first pointer that then redirects you to the memory location of the item that you are looking for. When accessing the first element of `ndarray`, you simply grab the first element of the array without the additional level of indirection. This locality of reference provided by NumPy's `ndarray` offers over two orders of magnitude speed improvements! This is simply incredible.

Also, notice that the computation in the NumPy-based function does not contain a single loop, yet NumPy is smart enough to know that the specified calculations should be performed on each element in `ndarray`. This is a very simple case of array broadcasting, where NumPy intelligently handles calculations between arrays (and scalars) with different shapes and vectorizes the operations, thus pushing the looping into the C code instead of Python (the loop still happens but in highly optimized C code in the `NumPy` library).

There's more...

Hopefully, you are impressed by the incredible performance gain that NumPy can offer. However, this performance gain comes at a cost of several trade-offs. NumPy is practically a separate language with its own data types and opinions about how the world should work. Thus, there is an added cognitive burden for the developer. Second, NumPy has numerous C dependencies and can be difficult to install on some machines and in some environments. This can be a cause for concern when working with code that must run on a specific platform-as-a-service, such as Heroku or Google App Engine. Many times, it can be difficult or simply not possible to use NumPy in these environments. Finally, NumPy allows one to construct very complex mathematical expressions over multidimensional data structures in very terse syntax that can be challenging to understand.

See also

▶ Broadcasting in NumPy at `http://docs.scipy.org/doc/numpy/user/basics.broadcasting.html`

Rewriting simple functions with NumPy

With the impressive test results from the previous recipe, this recipe will focus on rewriting some of the smaller functions in `asa.py` using NumPy. We will start with the smaller, more manageable `find_neighbor_indices` function as a prototype for changes to the `main` function.

Getting ready

To prepare for this recipe, we will create a copy of `asa.py` and call it `asa_np_v1.py`.

How to do it...

The following steps will walk you through this recipe:

1. First, add the `@profile` decorator to the `find_neighbor_indices` function in `asa.py`:

   ```
   @profile
   def find_neighbor_indices(points, radii, probe, k):
   ```

2. We will use `line_profile` to benchmark the original `find_neighbor_indices` function:

   ```
   python kernprof.py -l asa_np_v1.py "1ROR.pdb"
   ```

3. The results are shown in the following command-line output, and the computed result matches the reference value:

   ```
   12114.7 angstrom squared.
   Wrote profile results to asa_np_v1.py.lprof
   ```

4. We use `line_profiler` again to visualize the results:

   ```
   python -m line_profiler asa_np_v1.py.lprof
   ```

You can refer to the following screenshot:

5. Inspecting the results, we see that the `pos_distance` function call takes up over 50 percent of the total execution time for this function.

6. The `atoms` data structure is somewhat problematic, as it packages the spatial coordinates and the radius together. At the top of the `calculate_asa` function, we decompose the list of atoms into two separate data structures:

```
points = np.array([ [a.pos.x, a.pos.y, a.pos.z] for a in
atoms ])
radii = np.array([a.radius for a in atoms])
```

7. We then rewrite the `find_neighbor_indices` function using NumPy:

```
def find_neighbor_indices(points, radii, probe, k):
"""
Returns list of atom indices in probe dist to atom k
"""
radius = radii[k] + probe + probe
test_radii = (radius + radii) ** 2
dist_sq = np.sum(((points - points[k,:])** 2), axis=1)
neighbor_indices = (dist_sq < test_radii)

#Must remove self distance
neighbor_indices[k] = False

#Need to return an array of ints not Booleans
return (np.where(neighbor_indices)[0])
```

8. Make sure that we update the `calculate_asa` function with the correct function call just inside the first loop:

   ```
   neighbor_indices = find_neighbor_indices(points, radii, probe, i)
   ```

9. We now profile the newest function using `line_profiler`:

   ```
   python kernprof.py -l asa_np_v1.py "1ROR.pdb"
   ```

10. Take a look at the results:

    ```
    python -m line_profiler asa_np_v1.py.lprof
    ```

    You will see the following screenshot:

```
→ asa git:(master) ✗ python kernprof.py -l asa_np_v1.py "1ROR.pdb"
12114.7 angstrom squared.
Wrote profile results to asa_np_v1.py.lprof
→ asa git:(master) ✗ python -m line_profiler asa_np_v1.py.lprof
Timer unit: 1e-06 s

File: asa_np_v1.py
Function: find_neighbor_indices at line 18
Total time: 0.346843 s

Line #      Hits         Time  Per Hit   % Time  Line Contents
==============================================================
    18                                           @profile
    19                                           def find_neighbor_indices(points, radii, probe, k):
    20                                               """
    21                                               Returns list of indices of atoms within probe distance to atom k.
    22                                               """
    23      2302        12455      5.4      3.6        radius = radii[k] + probe + probe
    24      2302        36325     15.8     10.5        test_radii = (radius + radii) ** 2
    25
    26      2302       234933    102.1     67.7        dist_sq = np.sum(((points - points[k,:])** 2), axis=1)
    27
    28      2302        19970      8.7      5.8        neighbor_indices = (dist_sq < test_radii)
    29
    30                                               #Must remove self distance
    31      2302         3478      1.5      1.0        neighbor_indices[k] = False
    32
    33                                               #Need to return a list/array of integers not a boolean array
    34      2302        39682     17.2     11.4        return (np.where(neighbor_indices)[0])
```

Note that this result matches the correct area for the test calculation, which is `12114.7 angstrom squared`.

11. Finally, we use the Unix `time` command to benchmark the run after commenting out the `@profile` decorator above the `find_neighbor_indices` function:

    ```
    time python asa_np_v1.py '1ROR.pdb'
    ```

    ```
    12114.7 angstrom squared.
    ```

    ```
    python asa_np_v1.py '1ROR.pdb'  3.32s user 0.05s system 99%
    cpu 3.397 total
    ```

How it works...

First, let's discuss the results and end product. We completely removed the original loop using NumPy and achieved an incredible increase in speed, with the total time dropping from 11 seconds to less than 3.5 seconds.

The first step and one of the keys is that the largest data structure in the code is the list of atoms of the `Atom` class. Each object of the `Atom` class has an x, y, z coordinate, a radius attribute, and a number of other attributes. Using the Python `sys.getsizeof` method for a single `Atom` object reveals that each atom consumes 72 bytes of memory. For the ASA calculation, only the x, y, z coordinates and the radii are needed. Thus, the first thing we did was to create an `ndarray` for the atoms' coordinates and an `ndarray` for the radii using list comprehensions:

```
points = np.array([ [a.pos.x, a.pos.y, a.pos.z] for a in atoms ])
radii = np.array([a.radius for a in atoms])
```

We can perform this step either within the `find_neighbor_indices` function or in the main calling function, which is `calculate_asa`. If we had created the points and radii arrays in the `find_neighbor_indices` function, this variable creation and memory allocation would be performed each time the function is called. Thus, it is far better to do this once, in the main `calculate_asa` function, and simply pass in slightly different parameters to the `find_neighbor_indices` function.

Now, let's examine the new version of the `find_neighbor_indices` function that returns a list of atom indices within a certain distance to atom k. The first line of the function remains unchanged:

```
radius = radii[k] + probe + probe
```

We then encounter the heart of this function— a single line of code that computes the distance between the atom k and every other atom in the molecule:

```
dist_sq = np.dot(((points - points[k,:]) ** 2), np.ones(3))
```

Let's unpack this code. The innermost set of parentheses is:

```
(points - points[k,:])
```

This uses NumPy to compute the coordinate-wise differences between atom k and every other atom in the molecule. This results in an array with length equal to the number of atoms and width equal to three:

```
((points - points[k,:]) ** 2)
```

We square each value in this array, yielding an array of length equal to the number of atoms and width equal to three, which is the number of coordinates:

```
np.sum(((points - points[k,:]) ** 2), axis=1)
```

Finally, we sum the squared coordinate-wise differences together to yield the squared distance:

```
test_radii = (radius + radii) ** 2
```

We then create a `test_radii` NumPy array that contains the square of the sum of the radius and every other atom in the molecule:

```
neighbor_indices = (dist_sq < test_radii)
```

In a single line of code, we compare the `dist_sq` array to the `test_radii` array, creating a Boolean array of the same size. A `true` value in the array indicates that the corresponding atom is a neighbor to atom `k`:

```
#Must remove self distance
neighbor_indices[k] = False
```

We don't want to return the `k` atom's own index, so we set this value to `False` (k can't be a neighbor of itself). We use the `np.where` function in the following line of code:

```
return (np.where(neighbor_indices)[0])
```

As we need to return integer indexes and not a Boolean array, we use the `np.where` function to find the indices of all `True` values of the array.

Optimizing the innermost loop with NumPy

In this recipe, we are going to rewrite the `calculate_asa` function, replacing a double-nested loop with NumPy and SciPy functions that have been heavily optimized for performance.

Getting ready

Take a moment and review the original `calculate_asa` function in the `asa.py` source file. Note the three levels of `for` loops present. Copy the `asa_np_v1.py` file to a new file named `asa_np_v2.py`, and open this in your editor of choice. Again, if you are proficient with the code-versioning tool of your choice, feel free to use it to handle the versioning for you.

How to do it...

The following steps complete this chapter:

1. First, we heavily modify the `calculate_asa` function as shown in the following code:

```
def calculate_asa(atoms, probe, n_sphere_point=960):
"""
Returns accessible surface areas for atoms, using the probe
and atom radius to define the surface.
"""
sphere_points =
np.array(generate_sphere_points(n_sphere_point))
points = np.array([ [a.pos.x, a.pos.y, a.pos.z] for a in
atoms ])

radii = np.array([a.radius for a in atoms])
radii_plus_probe = radii + probe
radii_plus_probe_sq = (radii_plus_probe)**2

const = 4.0 * math.pi / float(n_sphere_point)

num_atoms = len(atoms)
areas = np.zeros(num_atoms)

for i in xrange(0, num_atoms):
    neighbor_indices = find_neighbor_indices(points,
radii,
                                          probe, i)
    test_sphere_points =
sphere_points*radii_plus_probe[i] + points[i, :]
    neighbor_radii_sq =
radii_plus_probe_sq[neighbor_indices]
    diff_sq = cdist(test_sphere_points,
                    points[neighbor_indices, :],
                    'sqeuclidean')
    dist_test = (diff_sq < neighbor_radii_sq)
    inaccessible_points = np.any(dist_test,1)
    areas[i] = np.sum(inaccessible_points)

areas = (n_sphere_point-areas)*const*radii_plus_probe_sq
return areas
```

2. This new `calculate_asa` function depends on a key function from SciPy that must be imported:

```
from scipy.spatial.distance import cdist
```

3. As we are now using Boolean indexing, we want `find_neighbor_indices` to return a Boolean array and not a list of integers. We therefore modify the `return` statement of the `find_neighbor_indices` function, thus eliminating the expensive `np.where` function call:

```
#return (np.where(neighbor_indices)[0])
return(neighbor_indices)
```

How it works...

The first thing that you should notice is that this version is much shorter compared to the original. There is now a single loop over all atoms in place of the triple-nested original. Let's explain what happened, starting with the simpler changes that occur before the main loop.

First, the outermost `for` loop has moved on from walking along a list of `Atom` objects:

```
for i, atom_i in enumerate(atoms):
```

It has moved to iterating from zero to the number of atoms:

```
for i in xrange(0, num_atoms):
```

We no longer use the `Atom` object anywhere in the `calculate_asa` function except to extract the three-dimensional coordinates and radii of the atoms. In the original code, we initialized an empty list of areas to capture the accessible surface area of each atom. Now, we use the NumPy `zeros` function to allocate the memory for the entire array upfront:

```
areas = np.zeros(num_atoms)
```

Finally, and potentially most confusing at this point, we precompute several arrays that we will need in the main loop including the probe distance added to the radius of each atom and this squared value:

```
radii_plus_probe = radii + probe
radii_plus_probe_sq = (radii_plus_probe)**2
```

To help explain the new main loop of `calculate_asa`, it will help us walk through the original loop and explain what is happening conceptually. For each atom k, we find all neighboring atoms within a particular probe distance. We then test to see whether any of these neighboring atoms are within a probe range of a shell of points surrounding our current atom k. If there are no atoms near that point on the surrounding sphere, we consider that area of the sphere around atom k to be accessible. We perform this test for all 960 points that compose our test sphere and sum the accessible areas. We perform this entire process for each atom in the molecule, one by one.

In the new version of the `calculate_asa` function, we still iterate over each atom in the molecule. For each atom, we perform the following steps. First, we find the atoms that are neighbors to the current atom of interest:

```
neighbor_indices = find_neighbor_indices(points, radii, probe, i)
```

We scale and translate the entire sphere of test points to the center of the current atom of interest at the same time, which is a bit clearer intuitively. Thanks to NumPy's broadcasting abilities, we execute this in a single line of code:

```
test_sphere_points = sphere_points*radii_plus_probe[i] + points[i, :]
```

We select only the squared radii values of the neighboring atoms:

```
neighbor_radii_sq = radii_plus_probe_sq[neighbor_indices]
```

Luckily for us, the `SciPy` Python library contains a very useful function, `scipy.spatial.distance.cdist`, that takes two arrays of points as inputs and computes the pairwise distance between each. While we used to compute the distance between the neighboring atoms and a single test point one by one, we now use `cdist` to compute the pairwise distance between the neighboring atoms and the entire sphere of test points:

```
diff_sq = cdist(test_sphere_points, points[neighbor_indices, :],
'sqeuclidean')
```

We compare these distances to the squared radii plus the probe distance of all the neighbors and determine which test points are not accessible using the `np.any` function:

```
dist_test = (diff_sq < neighbor_radii_sq)
inaccessible_points = np.any(dist_test,1)
```

We finish up the calculations for a single atom by totaling the number of inaccessible points on the test sphere:

```
areas[i] = np.sum(inaccessible_points)
```

When moving loops into array operations, it is always good to check the dimensions of the arrays to see whether they are what we expect. For the first atom in the molecule, we see that there are 19 neighboring atoms and the `neighbor_radii_sq` array is (19, 3). The array of squared distances between the sphere of test points and the neighboring atoms is (60, 19). Comparing this array of distances to the neighbor's radii yields a (60, 19) array. Summing up the number of accessible points yields a (60,) vector, which is what we would expect, given that there are 60 test sphere points.

Performance-wise, we have used NumPy and SciPy to push arithmetically intense calculations and loops out of the Python code and into native, highly optimized C-code. Further, we have changed our basic data structures from Python objects to NumPy arrays in order to exploit the performance gains possible when leveraging the locality of reference.

There's more...

We see that the function now runs in a blazing fast 0.78 seconds compared to the original function time of 21 seconds. We set `n_sphere` back to the original value of `960` and rerun the code. The entire script now gets executed in just under 2 seconds compared to 50 plus seconds before we started optimizing.

Can we do better? If we use the `line_profiler` module, we see that 30 percent of the execution time is spent computing which atoms are neighbors and 40 percent of the time is spent computing the distance between neighboring atoms and the sphere of test points. To try to milk additional performance gains from the code, we would most likely have to drastically rethink how this calculation is performed. Thus, we will stop here, satisfied with a 25x speed increase.

Index

data.table object 152
data.table package 152
datatypes, R
    URL 38
ddply function 43, 209
degree 239
degree centrality 246
delta function 172
directed graphs 219
Discretize function 136
disk
    JSON data, storing to 323, 324
    SVD-based model, dumping to 298-300
displ variable 206
distance overview
    URL 280
domain-specific language (DSL) 13
dot product
    URL 295
dplyr package
    about 120, 135
    arrange function 135
    filter function 135
    group_by function 135
    mutate function 135
    select function 135
    URL 136
dplyr reference
    URL 121

E

ego networks
    about 225
    visualizing 225-229
eigenvector centrality 243-246
employment data
    exploring 123-125
    importing, into R 121-123
Enthought Canopy Express web page
    URL 20
entire dataset
    loading, into memory 295-298
entire networks, characteristics
    exploring 246-248
Environment object 180

euclidean_distance() function 279
eval statement 128

F

Federal Information Processing Standards
        (FIPS) 129
figure function 164
filter function 135, 159
filtering 261
find_neighbor_indices function
    about 347, 365
    atoms 347
    k 347
    probe 347
first project
    R, preparing for 34
football data
    acquiring 61-64
    analyzing 65-74
    cleaning 61-64
fread function 122
fuel efficiency data
    about 199-202
    exploring 199-202
fuel efficiency performance metrics
    URL 187
functions
    rewriting, with NumPy 362-366

G

generate_sphere_points() function 347
genfromtext function 161
geographical information
    adding 129-132
geographic data
    extracting 330-333
GEOS
    about 337
    URL 337
geospatial data
    plotting, in Python 333-337
geospatial data visualization
    creating 136-139
geospatial time series
    maps, animating for 143-146

Y

Yelp website
  URL 276

Z

ZeroMQ
  URL 195
zeros function 368

Thank you for buying
Practical Data Science Cookbook

About Packt Publishing

Packt, pronounced 'packed', published its first book "*Mastering phpMyAdmin for Effective MySQL Management*" in April 2004 and subsequently continued to specialize in publishing highly focused books on specific technologies and solutions.

Our books and publications share the experiences of your fellow IT professionals in adapting and customizing today's systems, applications, and frameworks. Our solution based books give you the knowledge and power to customize the software and technologies you're using to get the job done. Packt books are more specific and less general than the IT books you have seen in the past. Our unique business model allows us to bring you more focused information, giving you more of what you need to know, and less of what you don't.

Packt is a modern, yet unique publishing company, which focuses on producing quality, cutting-edge books for communities of developers, administrators, and newbies alike. For more information, please visit our website: www.packtpub.com.

About Packt Open Source

In 2010, Packt launched two new brands, Packt Open Source and Packt Enterprise, in order to continue its focus on specialization. This book is part of the Packt Open Source brand, home to books published on software built around Open Source licenses, and offering information to anybody from advanced developers to budding web designers. The Open Source brand also runs Packt's Open Source Royalty Scheme, by which Packt gives a royalty to each Open Source project about whose software a book is sold.

Writing for Packt

We welcome all inquiries from people who are interested in authoring. Book proposals should be sent to author@packtpub.com. If your book idea is still at an early stage and you would like to discuss it first before writing a formal book proposal, contact us; one of our commissioning editors will get in touch with you.

We're not just looking for published authors; if you have strong technical skills but no writing experience, our experienced editors can help you develop a writing career, or simply get some additional reward for your expertise.

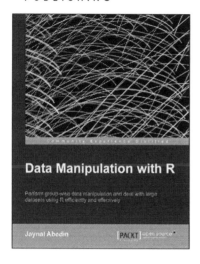

Data Manipulation with R

ISBN: 978-1-78328-109-1   Paperback: 102 pages

Perform group-wise data manipulation and deal with large datasets using R efficiently and effectively

1. Perform factor manipulation and string processing.

2. Learn group-wise data manipulation using plyr.

3. Handle large datasets, interact with database software, and manipulate data using sqldf.

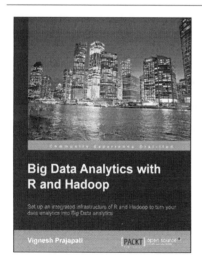

Big Data Analytics with R and Hadoop

ISBN: 978-1-78216-328-2   Paperback: 238 pages

Set up an integrated infrastructure of R and Hadoop to turn your data analytics into Big Data analytics

1. Write Hadoop MapReduce within R.

2. Learn data analytics with R and the Hadoop platform.

3. Handle HDFS data within R.

4. Understand Hadoop streaming with R.

5. Encode and enrich datasets into R.

Please check **www.PacktPub.com** for information on our titles

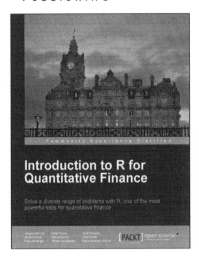

Introduction to R for
Quantitative Finance

Solve a diverse range of problems with R, one of the most
powerful tools for quantitative finance

Introduction to R for Quantitative Finance

ISBN: 978-1-78328-093-3   Paperback: 164 pages

Solve a diverse range of problems with R, one of the
most powerful tools for quantitative finance

1. Use time series analysis to model and forecast
   house prices.

2. Estimate the term structure of interest rates using
   prices of government bonds.

3. Detect systemically important financial institutions
   by employing financial network analysis.

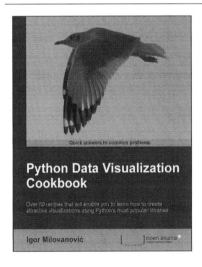

Python Data Visualization
Cookbook

Over 60 recipes that will enable you to learn how to create
attractive visualizations using Python's most popular libraries

Igor Milovanovic

Python Data Visualization Cookbook

ISBN: 978-1-78216-336-7   Paperback: 280 pages

Over 60 recipes that will enable you to learn how to
create attractive visualizations using Python's most
popular libraries

1. Learn how to set up an optimal Python
   environment for data visualization.

2. Understand the topics such as importing data for
   visualization and formatting data for visualization.

3. Understand the underlying data and how to use
   the right visualizations.

Made in the USA
Lexington, KY
22 November 2014